Faith in the Familiar

Numen Book Series

Studies in the History of Religions

Series Editors

Steven Engler (Mount Royal University, Calgary, Canada)
Richard King (University of Kent, UK)
Kocku von Stuckrad (University of Groningen,
The Netherlands)
Gerard Wiegers (University of Amsterdam,
The Netherlands)

VOLUME 143

The titles published in this series are listed at brill.com/nus

Faith in the Familiar

Religion, Spirituality and Place in the South of the Netherlands

By

Kim Esther Knibbe

BRILL

LEIDEN • BOSTON
2013

Library of Congress Cataloging-in-Publication Data

Knibbe, Kim E.
  Faith in the familiar : religion, spirituality, and place in the south of the Netherlands / by Kim
Esther Knibbe.
    pages cm. — (Numen book series ; VOLUME 143)
  Includes bibliographical references and index.
  ISBN 978-90-04-25052-9 (alk. paper) — ISBN 978-90-04-21493-4 (e-book) 1. Limburg
(Netherlands)—Religion—20th century. 2. Limburg (Netherlands)—Religion—21st century.
3. Catholic Church—Netherlands—Limburg—History—20th century. 4. Catholic Church—
Netherlands—Limburg—History—21st century. 5. Secularization—Netherlands—Limburg—
History—20th century. 6. Secularization—Netherlands—Limburg—History—21st century. I. Title.

  BL980.N5K56 2013
  306.609492'48—dc23

                                                                                       2013011333

This publication has been typeset in the multilingual "Brill" typeface. With over 5,100 characters
covering Latin, IPA, Greek, and Cyrillic, this typeface is especially suitable for use in the
humanities. For more information, please see www.brill.com/brill-typeface.

ISSN 0169-8834
ISBN 978-90-04-25052-9 (hardback)
ISBN 978-90-04-21493-4 (e-book)

For my grandmother, my mother and my daughter

CONTENTS

ACKNOWLEDGMENTS

This book is the outcome of a very long process; the research, the writing and dealing with the effects of this writing has been a part of my life since 2001. In the meantime, I have had countless discussions with colleagues, with friends and partners, with family, with journalists and the public.

In the first place I should thank those people who helped me during my research in Limburg, who made me feel at home, or not, but in any case consented to be the subject of the research in some way and contributed to it. I should also thank VU University and the supervisor of my research, professor emiritus André Droogers. He guided by giving trust, for which I cannot thank him enough. At the VU, I was part of a vibrant community of researchers, first as a PhD student and later as a post-doc. Science was never a lonely adventure for me, I always felt surrounded by supportive colleagues with whom to share the joys and hardships of research. Since 2010 I am part of the Faculty of Theology and Religious Studies at Groningen University, where I have again found interesting and stimulating colleagues. I feel privileged to be a part of this group. Kocku von Stuckrad, editor of this series and head of our department, I should thank for his interest in seeing this book published, his patience, and for the ways in which he facilitated me in finding time to complete it.

If not for my family, especially on my mother's side, I would never have felt compelled to do this research and write this book. Finally, I should thank my husband, Andrei Angnged, and my daughter, Ariadne, for the joy they give me and the daily reminders that life is not only to be researched, but also to be lived.

CHAPTER ONE

SITUATING THE RESEARCH

1. Introduction

In the minds of the Dutch, the province of Limburg, in the south of the Netherlands, is distinctive for one major reason: it has hills. Also in other ways, this region is considered 'different': until now, it is considered to be almost homogenously Catholic, in a nation historically dominated by Protestantism (although Protestants were never a real majority). In this ethnography I will describe and analyze the changing location of religion in people's daily life since the 1950s in the south of the Netherlands. In many ways, this ethnography goes against current trends in social research: it focuses on a rural area rather than on an urban area; on locality, rather than on globalization; on what happens to 'old' religion, rather than on the many new trends available in the religious landscape, and on popular forms of 'spirituality' rather than highbrow and avant garde spirituality. This chapter will explain the reasons for this contrary focus.

Like the rest of the Netherlands, Limburg has experienced an emptying of the church pews. The decline of religion in this province and the rest of the Netherlands is catalogued in a series of studies.[1] In the space of fifty years, the Netherlands as a society has moved from a situation where everything was organized around a particular denomination or worldview, to a detraditionalized, secularized and pluralistic society.

Meanwhile, it has become obvious that the classical secularization theories, which posited religion as incompatible with modernity, cannot adequately account for the persistence of religion: outside the walls of the traditional institutions, religious repertoires are flourishing. Worldwide, religion is becoming more important as a marker for identity, creating

---

[1] E.g. J.W. Becker and J.S.J. de Wit, *Secularisatie in De Jaren Negentig. Kerklidmaatschap, Veranderingen in Opvattingen en Een Prognose.* (Den Haag: Sociaal en Cultureel planbureau, 2000); Gerard Dekker, *God in Nederland, 1966–1996* (Amsterdam: Anthos, 1997); Ton Bernts, Gerard Dekker, and Joep de Hart, *God in Nederland, 1996–2006* (Ten Have, 2007); Manfred te Grootenhuis and Peer Schepers, "Churches in Dutch: Causes of Religious Disaffiliation in The Netherlands 1937–1995," *Journal for the Scientific Study of Religion* 40, no. 4 (2001): 591–606.

transnational social fields and generating its own forms of globalization.[2] Only a small minority of Dutch people describe themselves as atheists, while belief in an afterlife and other 'religious' concepts is rising again and people seem to attach more importance to 'faith' and 'spirituality'.[3] These developments are not confined to the Netherlands, but can also be observed in other Western European countries.[4]

'New' theories on the role and place of religion in western societies often refer to the conditions of (post) modernity or high modernity that are thought to produce the need for religion, often based in subjective life. The description of these conditions might lead us to assume that authority is dispersed and highly unstable. However, departing from a particular understanding of socio-cultural realities, authority, or to phrase it differently, discursive power, cannot disappear, it can only transform. Distinguishing between sense and nonsense has not ceased because post-modern philosophers have proclaimed the end of the 'grand narratives'. Although churches can no longer monopolize peoples' worldview option, this does not mean that people do not relate to religious authority and knowledge at all. And although in theory, individualization has crowned us all as kings of our own universe, the individualism that this requires is nevertheless a social and cultural phenomenon, and can be analysed as such.[5]

On the level of daily life, questions concerning what is considered knowledge and fact, who has the authority to proclaim this and in what context, who is supposed to be 'in control', and what this means for how one should act will always remain. Proximity and the need for social

---

[2] E.g. Peter Beyer and Lori G. Beaman, *Religion, Globalization and Culture* (BRILL, 2007).

[3] J.W. Becker, Joep de Hart, and J. Mens, *Secularisatie En Alternatieve Zingeving in Nederland*, vol. 24 (Rijswijk: Sociaal en Cultureel Planbureau., 1997), 178; Joep de Hart, *Zwevende Gelovigen. Oude Religie En Nieuwe Spiritualiteit.* (Amsterdam: Bert Bakker, 2011); Bernts, Dekker, and de Hart, *God in Nederland, 1996–2006*; Dekker, *God in Nederland, 1966–1996*, 27–28, 41.

[4] Karel Dobbelaere and Liliane Voyé, "From Pillar to Postmodernity: The Changing Situation of Religion in Belgium," *Sociological Analysis* 51, no. S (1990): S1–S13; Steve Bruce, *God Is Dead: Secularization in the West* (Oxford: Wiley-Blackwell, 2002); Danièle Hervieu-Léger, "Present-Day Emotional Renewals. The End of Secularization or the End of Religion?," in *A Future for Religion? New Paradigms for Social Analysis*, ed. William H. Swatos (Newbury Park etc.: Sage, 1993); Yves Lambert, "A Turning Point in Religious Evolution in Europe," *Journal of Contemporary Religion* 19, no. 1 (2004): 29–44.

[5] Émile Durkheim, "Durkheim's 'Individualism and the Intellectuals'," ed. Steven Lukes, *Political Studies* 17, no. 1 (1969): 14–30.

organisation dictates that people must remain in negotiation with each other on how to define the world, how to make sense of it, what is truth, what are the proper ways to act.

In the eyes of most people, religion moved from being basic to the structuring of society and the conduct of life to something that is perceived as an 'object', a category of practices and knowledge that can be related to. Secularization then, only describes the decline of religion in terms of organization and membership, but does not describe the ways in which it is still present in culture and society, discursively and in practice. From these considerations two main questions emerge that will guide the narrative of this book: 1) what is the location of religion in people's lives and how do they reflect on its changing location in the post-war period? 2) How do people relate to religious authority and how do they attempt to work on this relationship?

From the sweeping changes described in sociology in general and in sociology of religion to local realities can sometimes be a very big step. Do these changes in fact have the effects that they are expected to have? What can an in-depth study of a particular locality and the ways these macrolevel structural processes interact with each other and with religion teach us? This chapter will first discuss what these general theories of the changing place of religion and its expected effects are (section 2), as discussed within the secularization paradigm and later attempts to redefine the field (section 3). For an ethnographic approach, both the classic secularization theories and later attempts to redefine the field do not provide the appropriate conceptualization. Section 4 will develop a conceptualization of the subject matter based on insights drawn from general sociological and anthropological theorizing. In closing, the research on which this book is based will be presented, as well as an outline of the book itself (section 5).

2. SECULARIZATION THEORY: PREMISES AND PREDICTIONS

There are many different secularization theories that have all been finetuned in various ways. Here I will only sketch some of the basic premises that characterize the debate on secularization, and have set the terms by which present day religiosity is still considered. In brief, secularization is usually taken to refer to "...a process of transfer of property, power, activities and both manifest and latent function, from institutions with a super naturalist frame of reference to (often new) institutions operating

according to empirical, rational pragmatic criteria".[6] Generally, it indicates the loss of power of religion in societies. Theories on secularization
often include the implicit assumption that this also implies a 'secularization of consciousness' (a decline in religious beliefs) related to a decline in
church-going, or at best, relegates religion to the role of private preference.

The early Peter Berger makes this assumption explicit. In his influential
book "The Sacred Canopy", he interpreted secularization as arising out of
the tendency of monotheistic religions to simplify, codify and unify their
bodies of beliefs, in short: to rationalize them in order to make the world
a more predictable place, susceptible to human understanding.[7] The differentiation of society arising out of the advance of technology and capi-
talism furthermore results in a pluralization of life worlds. It is especially
this pluralization that Peter Berger saw as the cause of the secularization of consciousness (i.e. a decline in adherence to religious beliefs and
practices).

He saw the mechanisms of this link between pluralization and secularization as follows: First, because of the confrontation of the different
life worlds, it becomes clear that different ways of life and valuation are
possible. This realization will become part of everyday consciousness.
This means that religious worlds lose their 'taken for grantedness', their
plausibility. Second, the pluralization of life worlds means that the state
has to become a neutral entity, and this demand for neutrality is gradually extended to other institutions in the public sphere as well. With the
secularization of the public sphere, the day to day reinforcement of the
religious tradition disappears, which in turn means a lesser internalization of religion.[8]

In this theory, the secularization of society and secularization of consciousness are inextricably linked to each other. The 'causal mechanism'
the early Berger extrapolated to make his predictions is that when social
structures and organization become more differentiated, religion looses
its plausibility. In later years, Berger refuted his thesis.[9] But in the "Sacred
Canopy" he still stated confidently:

---

[6] Bryan Wilson, "Secularization: The Inherited Model," in *The Sacred in a Secular Age: Towards a Revision in the Scientific Study of Religion*, ed. Philip E. Hammond (Berkeley [etc.]: University of California Press, 1985).
[7] Peter Berger, *The Sacred Canopy* (Garden City: Doubleday & Company, Inc, 1967).
[8] Ibid., 150–151. This is linked to his view of culture as a dialectic between internalization and externalization explicated in his work with Luckmann. (Berger and Luckmann 1966).
[9] See Bruce in Linda Woodhead, Paul Heelas, and David Martin, eds., *Peter Berger and the Study of Religion* (London and New York: Routledge, 2001), 87–101 for a defense of the early Berger against the later Berger himself.

One may say, with only some exaggeration, that economic data on industrial productivity or capital expansion can predict the religious crisis of credibility in a particular society more easily than data from a 'history of ideas' of that society.[10]

Until recently, it was very much part of the thinking among social scientists to assume that the whole world was becoming increasingly industrialized, capitalist, rationalized, and therefore secularized. In these assumptions, we can recognize the pervasive influences of Weber's thoughts on the rationalization of society and the disenchantment of the world, but also of Durkheim's insights into the changing nature of social cohesion in the transition from traditional societies to modernity.

In Dutch research, the general outline of Peter Berger's secularization theory has been followed and tested by looking at the numbers of church-going people and the number of people subscribing to the 'orthodox' Christian articles of faith in several large-scale researches that have been repeated since 1966.[11] In these researches, the conclusion is obvious: the Netherlands is indeed one of the most secular countries in the world in terms of church affiliations, attendance and adherence to 'traditional' articles of faith. At the same time, these researches also show that adherence to certain beliefs has been growing again since the nineties, and many Dutch people are interested in what these researchers call 'para-cultural phenomena' such as Christian charismatic movements, alternative spiritualities and New Age.[12] However, this has not translated into a growing membership of organizations and institutions embodying these philosophies.[13] Therefore, as some scientists argue, religion is a factor that can be safely ignored as 'private'[14] or 'residual', bound to disappear soon after the melting away of the churches, of little significance to scientists interested in studying society.[15]

Although later formulations of the secularization theory confine themselves more and more to the institutional level and to Western Europe, critics of the secularization thesis still mainly address themselves to the

---

[10] Berger, *The Sacred Canopy*, 151.

[11] Becker, De Hart, and Mens, *Secularisatie En Alternatieve Zingeving in Nederland*; Dekker, *God in Nederland, 1966–1996*; ibid.; Bernts, Dekker, and de Hart, *God in Nederland, 1996–2006*.

[12] Becker, De Hart, and Mens, *Secularisatie En Alternatieve Zingeving in Nederland*, 24:17–28; de Hart, *Zwevende Gelovigen. Oude Religie En Nieuwe Spiritualiteit*.

[13] Becker, De Hart, and Mens, *Secularisatie En Alternatieve Zingeving in Nederland*, 24:177; de Hart, *Zwevende Gelovigen. Oude Religie En Nieuwe Spiritualiteit*.

[14] Wilson, "Secularization: The Inherited Model."

[15] Bruce, *God Is Dead*.

premises summarised in Wilson's definition and the early Berger: religious institutions have relinquished their power, increasing rationalization 'hollows out' religion from the inside by criticizing its own claims to truth, and the differentiation of society strains the plausibility structure of religious life worlds. To this we can add the obvious, but usually implicit, assumption in many intellectual circles, often echoed in popular thought, that scientific representations of the world contradict and undermine the plausibility of religion: as science gains authority, religious authority necessarily declines.

3. Criticisms and Attempts to Redefine the Field

In recent years, secularization theories have been subjected to a number of criticisms, and numerous attempts have been made to disprove existing secularization theories or formulate entirely new perspectives on the location of religion in Western European society, mostly in France and Britain.

Because secularization theories focus mainly on religious institutions, they do not provide any insight into actual processes of change from the point of view of the people who 'suddenly' stay away from church: the assumption that this has to do with a loss of plausibility à la Berger cannot be correct if people still do believe, and belief in miracles, reincarnation and an afterlife is even rising. To give but one puzzling example, among Catholics in the Netherlands, as many as 81% believed in reincarnation in 1996 but strangely, belief in the 'traditional' articles of faith of the Christian tradition was even lower than among the rest of the population.[16]

Furthermore, the meaning of the answers to the questionnaires used in statistical research confirming the secularization thesis is far from clear. For example, an anthropologist took the questionnaire that is used to measure secularization in the Netherlands and interviewed a group of 12 people to find the reasoning behind the answers they chose from the predefined list. She found that in some cases, people gave the same answers for widely different reasons, while in other cases, people gave different answers, but showed similar reasoning (personal communication Boudewijnse).

---

[16] Dekker, *God in Nederland, 1966–1996*, 57–58.

And finally, if we compare the place of religion in Western European societies with its place in other societies (such as the United States) that are equally modernized and differentiated, it becomes clear that modernization, pluralization of life worlds and rationalization do not necessarily predict the decline of religion. Worldwide, religions seem to increase in social relevance rather than decrease (this was already obvious before September 11, e.g. the spread of Pentecostal churches). So perhaps, rather than providing the model for developments elsewhere, the secularization of Europe should be seen as the exception.[17] The explanation for the secularization process in Western Europe would then come to lie much more in localized historical processes that cannot be extrapolated to provide a universal 'model' to predict developments in other societies.

In the international debate on contemporary religion in Western societies, the tone is set by authors such as Grace Davie, who points to the continuing importance of religious institutions, the team Paul Heelas and Linda Woodhead who published several influential books on present-day religion, and Danièle Hervieu-Léger.[18]

Davie argues that secularization should be seen in a broader perspective of social change. Rather than giving counter-examples of persisting religiosity, she shows that the decline of membership of the churches can be understood in the same light as the general decline in membership of all voluntary and civic organizations in post-war Britain. According to her, this shows that it is not a changing pattern of belief that causes secularization but rather that a different pattern of belief is the consequence of a decline in church going.

---

[17] Grace Davie, "Europe: The Exception That Proves the Rule?," in *The Desecularization of the World. Resurgent Religion and World Politics*, ed. Peter Berger (Washington D.C.: Ethics and Public Policy Center, 1996), 65–83.

[18] Grace Davie, *Religion in Britain Since 1945. Believing Without Belonging* (Oxford: Blackwell, 1994); Grace Davie, *Religion in Modern Europe: a Memory Mutates* (USA: Oxford University Press, 2000); Grace Davie, "Praying Alone? Church-Going in Britain and Social Capital. A Reply to Steve Bruce," *Journal of Contemporary Religion* 17, no. 3 (2002): 329–334; Grace Davie, Paul Heelas, and Linda Woodhead, *Predicting Religion. Christian, Secular and Alternative Futures*. (Aldershot: Ashgate, 2003); Paul Heelas and Linda Woodhead, *The Spiritual Revolution: Why Religion Is Giving Way to Spirituality* (Oxford etc.: Wiley-Blackwell, 2005); Danièle Hervieu-Léger, "The Twofold Limit of the Notion of Secularization," in *Peter Berger and the Study of Religion*, ed. Linda Woodhead, Paul Heelas, and David Martin (London New York: Routledge, 2001); Hervieu-Léger, "Present-Day Emotional Renewals. The End of Secularization or the End of Religion?"; Danièle Hervieu-Léger, *Religion as a Chain of Memory* (Oxford and Cambridge: Polity Press, 2000); Woodhead, Heelas, and Martin, *Peter Berger and the Study of Religion*; Linda Woodhead and Paul Heelas, *Religion in Modern Times: An Interpretive Anthology* (Oxford etc.: Wiley-Blackwell, 2000).

She characterizes the attitude of the British towards religion as "believing without belonging" (the title of one of her books). At the same time, people do care about the continued existence of the churches, which is why she introduces the term "vicarious religion": a small core of committed believers is implicitly supported by large sections of society.[19] Attitudes towards religion move from "obligation to consumption":

> The congregations who derive their strength from consumption—i.e. this is something that I choose to do (maybe regularly, maybe not, sometimes for long periods, sometimes for short)—display close similarities to the leisure pursuits of the secular world.[20]

At the same time, religious beliefs may actually thrive and develop in unexpected directions as the hold of orthodox religions on religious beliefs declines.[21]

More recently, she concluded in a reaction on Casanova's work that

> ...[while] the ongoing process of secularization is continuing to erode the effectiveness of religion in the private lives of many European people; conversely, religion continues to figure strongly in public discussion.[22]

This brings us to another body of literature: that which grew out of Casanova's (rather succesful) attempt to redefine the field through his influential book "Public Religions in the Modern World" and later work.[23] Apart from a very insightful discussion of the secularization thesis, in his 1994 book he showed through various case studies how religion resists the relegation to the private sphere very succesfully and discussed the conditions under which religion could play a positive role in the public sphere. This work cannot be underestimated in importance because of the ways it has enabled a shift away from the eternal debate on secularization to a focus on the ways in which religion remains important in public life. However, the conceptualization of religion in terms of 'public' and 'private' does not really work for the ethnographic approach of this book, as I will explain

---

[19] Grace Davie, "The Persistence of Institutional Religion in Modern Europe," in *Peter Berger and the Study of Religion*, ed. Linda Woodhead, Paul Heelas, and David Martin (London [etc.]: Routledge, 2001), 106.

[20] Ibid.

[21] Davie, "Praying Alone? Church-Going in Britain and Social Capital. A Reply to Steve Bruce," 333.

[22] Davie in Hubert Knoblauch et al., "I. Portrait: Jose Casanova," *Religion and Society: Advances in Research* 2, no. 1 (2011): 10.

[23] José Casanova, *Public Religions in the Modern World* (University of Chicago Press, 1994); Knoblauch et al., "I. Portrait"; José Casanova, "Public Religions Revisited," in *Religion: Beyond the Concept* (Fordham: Fordham University Press, 2008), 101–119.

below. In more recent work, he has taken up Asad's suggestion that it is 'the secular' that might need more analysis in relation to Europa's self-conception.[24] This is an interesting point that will be discussed later in this chapter, in conceptualizing the subject matter of this book.

Hervieu-Léger summarizes the failings of the secularization thesis as follows:

> The theory of secularization as an exiting from religion is entirely valid if it is applied within a religious genealogy of the autonomization of politics and of the individual in modern societies. From the viewpoint of a sociology of believing, it constitutes a local and limited theory of the deinstitutionalizing of religion. But it is altogether powerless to furnish the basis of a theory of the relationship between religion and culture in western societies.[25]

Attempts to redefine the terms of the debate on the relationship between religion and social structural change in Western Europe have pointed in four directions: (1) the limits of the disenchantment and differentiation caused by rationalization, (2) the significance of individualization (as the dominant mode of structuring societies, redefining the place of religion in social life like rationalization has redefined it) and individualism (as a complex of cultural values and beliefs). Furthermore, globalization (3) is identified as one of the structural processes influencing the whole world and the place of religion in it in several ways. Finally, several authors have pointed out gender (4) as a neglected dimension in analyzing and understanding the dynamics of religious change, suggesting that it is necessary to take a closer look at how women relate to religion.

The first direction is suggested by Hervieu-Léger, but also by authors such as Zygmunt Bauman and Van Harskamp: perhaps the rationalism that has driven modernization has exhausted itself, and runs into the contradictions that although it undermines the plausibility of all attempts to formulate ultimate answers, it cannot give ultimate answers itself.[26] In this way Hervieu-Léger attempts to understand why highly educated French are attracted to 'emotional' forms of Christian religiosity such as Pentecostalism: this kind of religiosity bases itself on an experiential reality rather

---

[24] José Casanova, "Religion, European Secular Identities, and European Integration," *Religion in an Expanding Europe* (2006): 65–92.

[25] Hervieu-Léger, "The Twofold Limit of the Notion of Secularization," 120.

[26] Zygmunt Bauman, "Postmodern Religion," in *Religion, Modernity and Postmodernity*, ed. Paul Heelas, David Martin, and Paul Alfred Morris (Oxford: Blackwell, 1998); Anton van Harskamp, *Het Nieuw-religieuze Verlangen* (Kampen: Kok, 2000); Hervieu-Léger, "The Twofold Limit of the Notion of Secularization."

than on verbalized propositions about the nature of the world and man's place in it.[27]

This argument follows the same general line of thought as the argument developed by Peter Berger, Brigitte Berger and Hansfried Kellner, in a book written after the tumultuous final years of the sixties. In this book they suggested that the anonymity, bureaucracy and alienating characteristics of modernity lead people to feel 'homeless' and to turn towards the only coherent source of meaning left to them: their own subjectivity.[28] Heelas' thesis that individual experience, a focus on the self, is becoming the paramount locus of anchoring values and cosmologies that attempt to give answers to ultimate questions also runs parallel to this line of thinking. He calls this the 'spiritual revolution', linked to a wider 'subjective turn' in Western European culture.[29] Spiritualities recognizing no ultimate authority but that of the self, he predicts, might even begin to replace religion, which he associates with an emphasis on a transcendent authority.

Like Hervieu Léger, Van Harskamp explicitly argues the position that modernity or post modernity actually 'produces' the need for religion.[30] The fragmenting forces of the rationalization and individualization of society on any kind of coherent plausibility structure, result in the shift of the locus of plausibility and legitimation from authoritative texts and religious experts to subjective experience. This ties in with the theorizing on the impact of individualization on society by authors such as Beck and Beck-Gernsheim: through individualization, the way it organizes society, we are forced to constitute ourselves as individuals.[31] This, in turn, entails a deroutinization of life. One is no longer born into a certain collectivity with all the routines, opportunities and

---

[27] Hervieu-Léger, "Present-Day Emotional Renewals. The End of Secularization or the End of Religion?".

[28] Peter Berger, Brigitte Berger, and Hansfried Kellner, *The Homeless Mind* (Middlesex [etc.]: Penguin Books, 1977).

[29] Paul Heelas, "The Spiritual Revolution: From 'Religion' to 'Spirituality'," in *Religions in the Modern World: Traditions and Transformations*, ed. Linda Woodhead et al. (London New York: Routledge, 2002), pp. 357–377; Paul Heelas and Linda Woodhead, "Homeless Minds Today?," in *Peter Berger and the Study of Religion*, ed. Linda Woodhead, Paul Heelas, and David Martin (London [etc.]: Routledge, 2001); Heelas and Woodhead, *The Spiritual Revolution*.

[30] van Harskamp, Het Nieuw Religieuze Verlangen.

[31] Ulrich Beck and Elisabeth Beck-Gernsheim, *Individualization: Institutionalized Individualism and Its Social and Political Consequences* (London and New York: Sage Publications Ltd, 2002), 4.

scripts for behaviour this entails. Rather people have to create their own 'do-it-yourself-biographies'. Lifestyle becomes a choice, the smallest details in life become of the greatest importance. According to Beck and Beck-Gernsheim "[o]ne can even say that decisions about lifestyle are 'deified'. Questions that went out of use with God are re-emerging at the centre of life. Everyday life is being post-religiously 'theologized.'"[32]

In their book on the 'spiritual revolution' Heelas and Woodhead have also argued that a "massive subjective turn" is taking place, inducing people to move away from 'religion' supporting 'life as', to spirituality, supporting 'subjective life'.[33] 'Life as' is identified with traditional societal strcutures where everybody lived out their lives according to pre-set roles. 'Subjective life' refers to the present day situation where the individualization of society is accompanied by a turn to the self as a source of meaning.

It is the necessity to constitute oneself as an individual that, according to Van Harskamp, gives rise to 'the painful question of the self': there is a collective urge to find our authentic and individual self, to figure out who we essentially are, in order to know what to do, how to plan our lives, how to direct ourselves: "only in this way can we hope to find an anchor for the different worlds in which we live, in the speeding up of time, among all the changes taking place around us".[34]

Supporting the trend in theorising where present-day forms of religiosity are seen as inextricably linked to individualization and individualism, is the increase in moral individualism that can be observed in statistical trends, which seems to be linked to detraditionalization and secularization.[35] It is even more directly borne out by a statistical analysis of data pertaining to the Dutch case testing whether 'rationalism'[36] or rather 'individualism' better explains a drawing away from traditional religion and an attraction to New Age.[37] Surprisingly, it was found that 'ratio-

---

[32] Ibid., 7.

[33] Heelas and Woodhead, *The Spiritual Revolution.*

[34] Van Harskamp, *Het Nieuw-religieuze Verlangen,* 237 my translation.

[35] Ronald Inglehart and Christian Welzel, *Modernization, Cultural Change, and Democracy: The Human Development Sequence* (Cambridge University Press, 2005); Loek Halman et al., *Traditie, Secularisatie En Individualisering* (Tilburg: Tilburg University Press, 1987).

[36] It should be noted that the authors use the term rationalization and individualisation, but since these two terms pertain to patterns of belief and convictions, and not to the structuring of society usually associated with the terms rationalisation and individualisation I prefer to use the terms 'rationalism' and 'individualism' .

[37] Dick Houtman and Peter Mascini, "Why Do Churches Become Empty While New Age Grows? Secularization and Religious Change in the Netherlands," *Journal for the Scientific Study of Religion* 41, no. 3 (2002): 455–473.

nalism' and adherence to traditional religion actually go together quite
well, whereas a higher score on individualism was positively correlated to
an interest in New Age. This directly contradicts the popular assumption
that faith in science automatically results in a loss of plausibility of the
traditional religious worldviews.

In a recent edited volume, Aupers and Houtman have explored the
'religion generating' character of present-day society to an even greater
extent, arguing that 'the sacred' is being relocated to the self and the
digital.[38] Davie has attempted to schematize the relations between religion and modernity and religion and postmodernity even more sharply,
stating that both modernity and postmodernity create problems for religion, but different problems.[39] She sees modernity as characterized by
grand narratives, whether religious or anti-religious, and secularization. In
contrast, postmodernity according to Davie is charachterized by the frag-
mentation and decentering of religious and secular narratives, an opening
up of spaces for the sacred in radically new forms and new forms of the
sacred in general.

This ties in rather well with the findings both of Houtman and Mascini
and of the authors in the abovementioned edited volume. However, it
remains to be seen when one can speak of modernity, and when one can
speak of postmodernity. Furthermore, as I found while doing the research
for this book, grand narratives might be less important for people's daily
lives than the structural frameworks generated by these grand narratives.
Even when these grand narratives have become decentered, the institi-
tional frameworks and subjectivities they have generated might remain,
and might remain important.

What many of these authors have in common is that they refer to 'the
sacred' as something that can change location. Problematic is that they
do not clearly define what they mean by 'the sacred'. Is it conceptual-
ized in a Durkheimian way, as something set apart in different ways in
different societies that can ultimately be understood in terms of 'society
worshipping itself'? Or is 'the sacred' these authors refer to essentialized
as a constant, separate domain? In this book, I will only use this word in
connection with a process of sacralization in the Durkheimian sense.[40]

---

[38] Stef Aupers and Dick Houtman, *Religions of Modernity: Relocating the Sacred to the Self and the Digital* (Leiden and Boston: Brill, 2010).

[39] Grace Davie, *The Sociology of Religion* (London, New Delhi and Singapore: SAGE, 2007), 90–91.

[40] Gordon Lynch, *The Sacred in the Modern World* (Oxford University Press, 2012).

The third direction that seeks to establish new ways of thinking about the link between structural social changes and the role and place of religion is the literature on religion and globalization.[41] Authors variously see globalization, in the form of a globalizing modernity, as triggering a defensive growth of religious identities that are labelled fundamentalist, but also see religion as one of the motors of globalization and an arena where the shaping of alternative directions for global society takes place. In the case of Catholicism, central to this ethnography, there is no doubt that it has been a motor of globalization, and that it shapes European and global imaginaries. At the same time, the case of Catholicism shows quite clearly that globalization does not necessarily mean homogenization or disembedding: Catholic practices and identities are quite often extremely well embedded locally. We will return to this issue in the next section, when we discuss 'place' in relation to globalization as a concept to approach the role of religion.

Gender is another dimension that has not yet been sufficiently explored in relation to religious change. Two authors in particular have pleaded to look at the role of gender in secularization. Woodhead points out both the role of women in the decline of religion, and in the rise of spirituality, arguing that these patterns can be explained by looking at women's relationship to their work and caring duties.[42] Brown has argued in a sweeping historical essay that the 'death of Christian Britain' has everything to do with the choices of young women: rather than stick to the roles of mother and preserver of traditions, they chose en masse for popular culture, entering the workplace and emancipation.[43] A parallel development was that the option to join the clergy lost its appeal to many young men, as was certainly the case in Dutch Catholism. As we will see, in the place

---

[41] Beyer and Beaman, *Religion, Globalization and Culture*; Simon Coleman, *The Globalisation of Charismatic Christianity: Spreading the Gospel of Prosperity*, Cambridge studies in ideology and religion 12 (New York: Cambridge University Press, 2000); Roland Robertson, *Globalization: Social Theory and Global Culture* (SAGE, 1992); Roland Robertson and JoAnn Chirico, "Humanity, Globalization, and Worldwide Religious Resurgence: A Theoretical Exploration," *Sociology of Religion* 46, no. 3 (September 21, 1985): 219–242; Nina Glick Schiller, Ayşe Çaglar, and Thaddeus C. Guldbrandsen, "Beyond the Ethnic Lens: Locality, Globality, and Born Again Incorporation," *American Ethnologist* 33, no. 4 (2006): 612–633; Peter van der Veer, *Conversion to Modernities: The Globalization of Christianity*, 1st ed. (Routledge, 1996).

[42] Eeva Sointu and Linda Woodhead, "Spirituality, Gender, and Expressive Selfhood," *Journal for the Scientific Study of Religion* 47, no. 2 (2008): 259–276; Linda Woodhead, "Gendering Secularization Theory," *Social Compass* 55, no. 2 (June 1, 2008): 187–193.

[43] Callum G. Brown, *The Death of Christian Britain: Understanding Secularisation, 1800–2000* (Taylor & Francis, 2009).

where my research took place women's roles did change greatly, although
they do not see themselves as being in the forefront of these changes and
cling to a modified conception of themselves as responsible for the care of
their family. A related body of work, departing from a historical perspective, posits that religion, especially Catholicism, has become feminized: the
so-called feminization thesis. Since the 19th century, the argument goes,
images of God have become more 'feminine' and the religious domain
provides women with the space and roles in which to develop their own
agency.[44] This thesis is much contested, but has done much to create a
greater visibility of the role and agency of women in religion.

Furthermore, anthropology has been steadily working on producing
ethnographies of religion, and have turned their attention to religion in
Europe as well. Apart from some classic ethnographies such as those of
William Christian and Larry Taylor, a body of literature has emerged on the
importance of pilgrimage and pilgrimage sites, often following a focus on
the agency of women in religious domains. For while church attendance
has declined, pilgrimage is flourishing.[45] These authors show that sites
of pilgrimage remain relevant, or become newly relevant, to people from
very different backgrounds and for very different reasons. This is fascinat-
ing research, showing the many ways in which pilgrimage sites become
linked to nationalism and the imagination of a united Europe. Religious
actors and movements use pilgrimage sites variously for establishing and
promoting conservative moral agenda's, but also as a site where feelings of
disempowerment are adressed and ritual innovation is practiced.[46]

---

[44] See e.g. Lena Gemzoë, "The Feminization of Healing in Pilgrimage to Fátima," in
Pilgrimage And Healing, ed. Jill Dubisch and Michael Winkelman (University of Arizona
Press, 2005); Tine van Osselaer and Thomas Buerman, "Feminization Thesis: A Survey of
International Historiography and a Probing of Belgian Grounds," *Revue d'Histoire Ecclé-
siastique* 103, no. 2 (June 1, 2008): 497–544, doi:10.1484/J.RHE.3.180; David S. Reynolds,
"The Feminization Controversy: Sexual Stereotypes and the Paradoxes of Piety in Nine-
teenth-Century America," *The New England Quarterly* 53, no. 1 (March 1, 1980): 96–106.

[45] E.g. Anna-Karina Hermkens, Willy Jansen, and Catrien Notermans, *Moved by Mary.
The Power of Pilgrimage in the Modern World* (Aldershot: Ashgate, 2009); Simon Coleman
and John Eade, *Reframing Pilgrimage: Cultures in Motion* (Routledge, 2004); Paulus Gijs-
bertus Johannes Post et al., *The Modern Pilgrim: Multidisciplinary Explorations of Christian
Pilgrimage* (Peeters Publishers, 1998); Anna Fedele, *Looking for Mary Magdalene. Alterna-
tive Pilgrimage and Ritual Creativity at Catholic Shrines in France* (Oxford and New York:
Oxford University Press, 2012); Deana Weibel, "Of Consciousness Changes and Fortified
Faith: Creativist and Catholic Pilgrimage at French Catholic Shrines," in *Pilgrimage and
Healing*, ed. Jill Dubisch and Michael Winkelman (Tucson, 2005), 111–134; Jill Dubisch, *In a
Different Place: Pilgrimage, Gender, and Politics at a Greek Island Shrine* (Princeton: Princ-
eton University Press, 1995).

[46] E.g. Fedele, *Looking for Mary Magdalene. Alternative Pilgrimage and Ritual Creativity
at Catholic Shrines in France*.

Perhaps surprisingly since I am writing about a formerly Catholic region, I do not pay much attention to pilgrimage. This has to do with the research strategy that I chose: rather than start with the religious and then contextualize this, I chose a context to locate the religious within it. Pilgrimage is by its nature an exceptional activity that usually takes place at most once or twice a year, and is undertaken by a limited number of people from one particular place whether in groups or as individuals. Therefore, pilgrimage did not appear as a significant activity within my research. Within my research area a major destination for pilgrimage is also located. However, for local people this place was not such an important destination, since it is in the nature of pilgrimage that it should take some time and effort to get there. Nevertheless, this research shares a many similarities with the research on piligrimage in terms of the conceptualization of the subject matter and in its focus on place, habitus and subjectivity.

4. Conceptualizing the Subject Matter

Although religion might be considered a 'private' affair in present-day western European societies, the private domain is still a socially and culturally produced domain, characterized by shared cultural notions and subject to structural forces. Whether something is public or private is both a matter of cultural agreement and social structuration. Therefore the private domain can be just as interesting to social science as the public domain (contrary to contemporary defenders of secularization theories that dismiss religion as privatized, and therefore not salient). In Limburg, both these domains can be said to exist. However, during my research, it became clear that another, intermediate domain is also of crucial importance to understand the location of religion which I will call the domain of the 'familiar'. This is the domain that people in local communities recognize they share, which is to a certain extent public, but also rests on very sharp distinctions between insiders and outsiders using language, birthplace and religious identity as boundary markers.

By distinguishing these three domains, it becomes possible to trace the shifting location of different types of religion in each of them. Historically, the Catholic church has been instrumental in constituting both the private domain of family life and the public domain. As we shall see, secularization in Limburg has meant that the church as an institution was placed at a distance from the private domain, and is under sustained attack in the public domain. At the same time, the rituals of the church remain important in reproducing the domain of the familiar: the networks of individuals, groups and families connected to a particular locale. Meanwhile, something that is now commonly called 'spirituality' has come out into the public domain, and is easily integrated into the private domain, reconstituting relationships in the domain of the familiar. However, as I will show, it does not (yet) lead to rituals that replace the role of Catholicism in the reproduction of the singularity of place and community.

How then, can we conceptualize this singularity of place in relation to the domain of the familiar? To understand how this domain can be understood in terms of the structural forces that create it and the agency it carves out for people, I must refer to a concept that has become more and more problematic, namely that of locality. Locality was the starting point of the research on which this book is based. But what is in fact a locality? Where are its boundaries? Who is local and who is not?

Globalization, Locality and the Familiar

With the increasing availability of different repertoires of meaning through books and other media, practices of signification can take on different dimensions, and become disembedded[47] from local contexts. Present-day religion is often described in terms of a supermarket, where people are free to pick and choose as they like. Through secularization the churches loose their power to define worldviews, the 'Sacred Canopy' is torn, authority becomes dispersed, and religion is privatised. At the same time, morality has lost its moorings, everything is until further notice, nothing obligates anymore, there are no lasting commitments or life-long projects. As Bauman asks: "is there a future left for morality in a world populated by vagabonds desperate for the cosiness of tribal campfires and the tourist amused by the display of entertaining tribal customs?"[48]

Without denying the importance of these processes, they might distract us from noticing the continuing *embeddedness* of much of contemporary social life, especially outside the urban areas, and how uniquely *local* horizons of meaning are maintained and valued. This emphasis on the local in my research is partly a reaction to the kind of speculative theorizing about the conditions of high or post modernity that sometimes dominate the

---

[47] The terms embedded and disembedded are used here in the way Giddens uses them to describe how social systems arise from the local, but become increasingly disconnected from local circumstances see Anthony Giddens, *The Consequences of Modernity* (Cambridge, UK: Polity Press, 1990).

[48] Zygmunt Bauman, "Morality in the Age of Contingency," in *Detraditionalization*, ed. Paul Heelas, Scott Lash, and Paul Morris (Oxford: Blackwell, 1996), 57.

debates on present day religion such as those summarized earlier in this chapter.[49] It is important to keep in mind that the processes described by social scientists in terms of modernization, the Sacralization of the self, the dis-enchantment of the world are *partial* processes. It is only certain people who have been turned into the "vagabonds" and tourists Bauman describes, always on the move, avoiding all moral proximity with the people actually living in the worlds they move through.

In this book I will argue that the 'persistence of religion' cannot be understood without looking at the production of locality and the importance people attach to it. Taking a different point of departure can afford a completely different insight into the processes that have shaped the social structures and woven the social and cultural textures of this place. For example, it will become clear that ritualization does not only emerge as a response to individualism and ontological insecurities. Instead, rituals emerge and evolve in the service of what Appadurai has named the "production of locality", in ways that have been described in countless ethnographies.[50]

Social scientists agree widely that locality is no longer the self-evident given that it once was. Localities are not bounded, not homogenous, not the self contained functional units that traditional ethnographers have described, whose categories, rituals and kinship systems have been so brilliantly described and analysed. More and more, following recognition of the forces of globalization, anthropologists have moved away from doing research in one particular place and problematize the notion of place and locality itself.[51]

Why then this rather old fashioned emphasis on locality in this study? As I said above, my interest in doing this research was to see how the rather grand theories and descriptions of what happens to religion in (post)modern societies work out in daily life, specifically in the region where I grew up. To a large extent, while growing up in this region I felt excluded from it as a locality for all sorts of reasons. The two most important ones were language (I did not speak the local dialect) and religion

[49] Zygmunt Bauman, *Postmodernity and Its Discontents*. (Cambridge: Polity Press, 1997); Zygmunt Bauman, "Consuming Life," *Journal of Consumer Culture* 1, no. 1 (2001): 9–29; van Harskamp, *Het Nieuw-religieuze Verlangen*, 200; Hervieu-Léger, "The Twofold Limit of the Notion of Secularization."

[50] Arjun Appadurai, *Modernity at Large: Cultural Dimensions of Globalization* (Minneapolis: U of Minnesota Press, 1996).

[51] Simon Coleman and Peter Jeffrey Collins, *Locating the Field: Space, Place and Context in Anthropology* (Oxford: Berg Publishers, 2006).

(I am not a Catholic). The first reason seemed self evident and natural to me. Furthermore, exposure could bridge this difference: I could understand the dialect, and everybody can also speak Dutch. The second reason however, remained a mystery to me: why was being a Catholic so important? Nobody actually went to church anymore! And above all, they did not seem to know what it meant to be a Catholic, except that it involves doing Holy Communion. I seemed to know more about the doctrines of Catholicism than my contemporaries. But somehow, they managed to make this seem completely irrelevant.

Therefore, to my mind locality and the role of religion in it represented an unsolved puzzle. Globalization and the disembedding forces of modernity, or the fragmenting force of postmodernity did not seem to have had the expected effects on the people of Limburg; community and the boundedness of locality were an obstinate reality. This does not mean that this is a study of a bounded locality, of 'my village' as anthropologists say. Some of the developments I describe here are particular to the place I did research in, most are not. Rather, I conceive of locality as a nodal point of many different processes, discourses and structures that interact, intersect and counteract each other, but also as something that has to be recreated again and again through processes of exclusion, through ritual and through constituting the domain of the familiar.

To theorize this more properly, I draw on the above-mentioned notion of the 'production of locality' and how it relates to neighbourhoods, the actual situated communities in Appadurai's book "modernity at large".[52] He argues that although it is relatively recent that localities have become a problematic notion in anthropology due to increasing attention to globalization and the reflexive turn, 'older' anthropology can insightfully be reread in the light of this problematization of locality. Many of the rituals described by anthropologists under very different headings (rituals for the house, initiation rituals) can in fact be read as concerned with one and the same thing, namely the production, reproduction and protection of locality as something that is inherently fragile.

> much that has been considered local knowledge is actually knowledge of how to produce and reproduce locality under conditions of anxiety and entropy, social wear and flux, ecological uncertainty and cosmic volatility, and the always present quirkiness of kinsmen, enemies, spirits, and quarks of all sorts.... Local knowledge is substantially about producing reliably

---

[52] Appadurai, *Modernity at Large* chapter 9.

local subjects as well as about producing reliably local neighbourhoods within which such subjects can be recognized and organized.... We might say...local knowledge is not local in itself but, even more important, for itself.[53]

This notion of locality connects very well to literature in human geography that theorize space and place as products of human interaction. Within this literature, place is seen as the product of the intersection of processes that operate on different spatial scales.[54] Thus, we can understand the locality where I did my research as the product of particular discourses within Catholicism that were shaped by the Vatican and transnational religious networks, the pillarization that became the dominant way of organizing social life according to religious affiliation, and later by processes of modernization that were shaped on a national level (see chapter 2). Within this matrix, people themselves shaped their lives in particular locales and social configurations that produce a sense of belonging, as becomes clear particularly in the chapters 3 and 4. Paradoxically, locality is produced through globalized Catholic practices.

In terms of the domains I distinguished above, this conceptualization of locality is intimately bound up with the domain of the familiar and the feeling of belonging to a particular place. The Catholic church has co-constituted this domain, and this in part explains why its rituals and the materiality of the church building as well as the Catholic identity remain important for reproducing it, even though the attitude towards the religious authority of the church and its influence on the conduct of life have undergone a sea change.

Defining Religion and Recognizing Religious Pluralism

In introducing the concept of the domain of the familiar I referred to 'spirituality' as a newcomer on the religious scene that has also entered the religious landscape of Limburg. This introduces another issue that needs to be resolved: the definition of religion.

At the time of the actual research, it was not the intention to include what is usually done under the banner of 'spiritual' in this research. However, the actual fieldwork and subsequent theoretical orientation led to

---

[53] Ibid., 181.
[54] See the overview in Brendan Bartley, Phil Hubbard, and Rob Kitchin, *Thinking Geographically* (Continuum International Publishing Group, 2004); and in particular Doreen B. Massey, *Space, Place, and Gender* (University of Minnesota Press, 1994).

the decision that in order to get into perspective how people relate to religious authority, these supposedly 'marginal' phenomena should be brought into the centre of the analysis. It is especially in these contexts that creative 'experiments' in relating to religious authority, but also with regard to themes usually thought to be 'religious' take place: life after death, the supernatural, reincarnation. These themes, as well as the foundations and limitations of authority to posess knowledge about these themes, are discussed with abandon in 'spiritual' circles. Precisely the lack of central control makes this creativity possible, although, as I will show, this does not mean that that power and authority do not play any role.[55]

What in Dutch society is called 'spirituality' these days has often been called 'New Age' within the study of religion. According to Aupers and Houtman, the study of this phenomenon is often hampered by Luckman's insistence that New Age is privatized.[56] They argue that sociologists have not done their job properly in studying New Age spirituality, looking critically at the discourse, analysing how it is transmitted and reinforced, and how, why and with what consequences it enters the public domain.

The increasing attention for New Age/spirituality in sociology ties in with a development within religious studies to reconceptualize European cultural history in terms of religious pluralism, including a strong esoteric tradition.[57] Other authors suggest that in understanding present-day religiosity, especially the apparent link between individualism and an interest in alternative spiritualities, the historical contribution of the Romantic tradition should be recognized to a greater degree. As Hanegraaff shows, many present day forms of alternative spiritualities can be understood as a transformation of the esoteric tradition in Western Europe, inspired by the Romantic criticism of the Enlightenment.[58] Charles Taylor, in his monumental work on 'sources of the self', has also argued convincingly that our present day value-orientations are to a great extent indebted to the Romantic tradition.[59]

---

[55] See also Anna Fedele and Kim Knibbe, eds., *Gender and Power in Contemporary Spirituality: Ethnographic Approaches* (London and New York: Routledge, 2013).

[56] Aupers and Houtman, *Religions of Modernity*, 9.

[57] Kocku von Stuckrad, *Western Esotericism: A Brief History of Secret Knowledge* (translation of *Was ist Esoterik? Kleine Geschichte des geheimen Wissens*) (London: Equinox, 2005).

[58] Wouter J. Hanegraaff, *New Age Religion and Western Culture: Esotericism in the Mirror of Secular Thought* (Leiden and Boston: Brill, 1996); Wouter Hanegraaff, "New Age Spiritualities as Secular Religion: a Historian's Perspective," *Social Compass* 46, no. 2 (1999): 145–160.

[59] Charles Taylor, *Sources of the Self; the Making of the Modern Identity* (Cambridge, Mass.: Harvard University Press, 1992).

Despite this increasing acceptance of 'spirituality', 'new age' or 'the esoteric tradition' as legitimate subjects for the sociology of religion and the
study of religion, the argument about what religion is, or should be, is
ongoing and has high societal stakes: to be defined as a religion can have
all sorts of advantages, but also disadvantages. I follow the understanding
that has emerged within anthropology and religious studies that resists
the adoption of a strict a-priori or essentalist definition of religion. An
anthropological critique of 'religion', 'the religious' or 'religiosity' would
first problematize whether these terms refer to a universal category or
characteristic of humanity, and point out that in many societies, religion
cannot be distinguished from general ways of ordering the world, that the
distinction between the 'sacred' and the 'profane' is not universal either,
as well as the distinction between the 'natural' and the 'supernatural'.[60]

It makes more sense not to see 'religion' as a universal category: at
least in the sense of a system of beliefs pointing to the sacred or the transcendent it can only refer to a localized identification of a phenomenon.[61]
In the research presented here, I have used the term religion in this
way: as something set apart by Dutch society as different from common
sense notions about the world because it uses transcendent explanations to make sense of life, the world, death, etcetera.[62] In Dutch society,
religion is understood to involve 'beliefs' and practices that go beyond
common sense and mediates the 'transcendent' or radically 'other'. Or,
to put it in even more general terms: both the term religion and more
recently the term spirituality have become anchoring points for specific
discourses and practices. People who call themselves spiritual usually do
so by referring to religion, sometimes calling themselves 'spiritual but not
religious', sometimes as religious *and* spiritual. In our introduction to an
edited volume on gender and power in spirituality, Anna Fedele and I
argue that we might think of the pair 'religion-spirituality' along the same
lines as suggested by Asad for the pair religion-secularity.[63] As van der
Veer argues the spiritual and the secular are "produced simultaneously as

[60] See e.g. Talal Asad, "The Construction of Religion as an Anthropological Category,"
in *A Reader in the Anthropology of Religion*, ed. Michael Lambek, Blackwell Anthologies in
Social and Cultural Anthropology (Malden [etc.]: Blackwell Publishing, 2002), 114–132.
[61] But see Hervieu-Léger for a very interesting suggestion on how to identify what is
'religious' about religion (Hervieu-Léger 2000).
[62] See also Robertson's account of how the concept of religion arose as a separate category in Western cultures (Robertson 1993).
[63] See the Introduction in Fedele and Knibbe, *Gender and Power in Contemporary Spirituality: Ethnographic Approaches.*

two connected alternatives to institutionalized religion in Euro-American modernity".[64]

Although 'religion' and 'spirituality' cannot be thought of as universal, timeless categories, still, as Casanova has pointed out:

> In fact, we now find ourselves within a global secular-religious system of classification, in which the category of religion has to do extra work and serve to articulate and encompass all kinds of different 'religious' experiences, both individual and collective; all kinds of magical, ritual, and sacramental practices; all kinds of communal, ecclesiastical, and institutional arrangements; and all kinds of processes of sacralization of the social, be it in the form of religious nationalism, secular civil religions, or the global sacralization of human rights.[65]

Often, the discourses and practices to which religion and spirituality refer have something to do with the dynamic of balancing between certainties and uncertainties that the anthroplogist Jackson identifies as basic to human meaning making:

> …in every human society concepts such as fate, history, evolution, God, chance, and even the weather signify forces of otherness that one cannot fully fathom and over which one can expect to exercise little or no ultimate control. These forces are given; they are in the nature of things. In spite of this, human beings countermand and transform these forces by dint of their imagination and will so that, in every society, it is possible to outline a domain of action and understanding in which people expect to be able to grasp, manipulate, and master their own fate.[66]

According to Jackson, constitutive to all human action is this balancing between the domains one can control, and those one cannot control, and the negotiation of the boundaries between those domains.

Discursive Power, Habitus and Ritual

Although this is not explicitly part of Jackson's conceptualisation, it follows that implicitly or explicitly, ontological and epistemological assumptions are an important underlying determinant in the negotiation of boundaries: to be able to decide what is within or outside one's control one needs knowledge about the world, its nature, the way it works, the limits

---

[64] Peter Van der Veer, "Spirituality in Modern Society," *Social Research: An International Quarterly* 76, no. 4 (2009): 1097.

[65] Knoblauch et al., "I. Portrait," 31.

[66] Michael Jackson, *Minima Ethnographica: Intersubjectivity and the Anthropological Project* (University of Chicago Press, 1998), 19.

of human action and power, and the extent of the power of other people, institutions and Gods.[67] In the ethnographic descriptions and interpretations presented in this book, I have expanded on Jackson's analysis of human life as a balancing act to describe the role of religion, power and authority in this balancing. In short, I have connected it to a discursive understanding of the ways power works: not in the hands of persons, but as embedded in discursive formations.[68]

Although the delineation between certainties and uncertainties can be seen as an ongoing activity, this does not mean that we should assume that people are continuously aware of the kind of ultimate questions formalized religions try to answer or the underlying ontological and epistemological assumptions of these answers: as long as their habitual practices and attitudes are sufficient to address the daily problems of life, there is no need to dive beneath the surface to take a look at the foundations of these habitual practices and attitudes. Usually, it is only at times of crisis that the self-perpetuating nature of the daily making sense of things might be called into question. At a time like that, ultimate questions may become a concern, and may prompt people to reflect on them and formulate answers. It is not to be expected that these answers will become a part of a coherent 'theology' that informs all of life. It is therefore all the more important to situate interpretations of present-day religiosity within an understanding of the social structures and processes that shape the world people live in.

This focus on practice and routines is strongly inspired by the practice approach pioneered by Bourdieu and developed by authors such as Ortner.[69] Of particular importance for this study is Bourdieu's conceptualisation of habitus as the individually embodied structures, dispositions, tastes and attitudes that guides people's sense of their place in the world. This allows us to conceptualize the domain of the familiar not as an 'empty' domain delineated by boundary-markers such as the local dialect and

---

[67] Cf. Kim Knibbe, "The Role of Religious Certainty and Uncertainty in Moral Reasoning in a Catholic Province in the Netherlands," *Social Compass* 55, no. 1 (2008): 20–31.

[68] Michel Foucault, *Archaeology of Knowledge* (Routledge, 2002), 129–130; Margaret Wetherell, *Discourse Theory and Practice: A Reader*, ed. Simeon Yates and Stephanie Taylor (SAGE, 2001) chapter 7.

[69] Pierre Bourdieu, *Outline of a Theory of Practice.* (*Esquisse D'une Théorie De La Pratique*). *Transl. by Richard Nice.* (*Repr.*) (Cambridge: Cambridge University Press, 2003); Sherry B. Ortner, *Anthropology and Social Theory: Culture, Power, and the Acting Subject* (Durham: Duke University Press, 2006); Pierre Bourdieu, *Distinction: A Social Critique of the Judgement of Taste* (Cambridge: Harvard University Press, 1984).

a nominal Catholic identity, but as unified through shared dispositions, a shared 'bodily hexis'. As we will see, the organizations of the Catholic pillar put much effort into creating the habitus of a 'good Catholic' and this habitus does not change overnight. Even across generations, particular dispositions are passed on, even though the organizations inculcating these attitudes do not exist anymore, or, to the extent that thay still do exist, are not very powerful anymore. This becomes particularly clear in the discussion on chastity in chapter 3, and in the discussion of the 'burden of the past' in chapter 6.

In a recent summary, Bourdieu describes habitus as "a system of dispositions, that is of permanent manners of being, seeing, acting and thinking, or a system of *long-lasting* (rather than permanent) schemes or schemata or structures of perception, conception and action".[70] He emphasizes that the term 'system' does not refer to a logical system, rather it refers to a practical system that could also be called a lifestyle. As he has shown in his work Distinction,[71] the ways in which people distinguish themselves are often aesthetic.

Often, discussions of Bourdieu's concept of habitus have focused on the presupposed static nature of this term: since it eludes everyday consciousness and is "political ideology embodied", it seems that our habitus convicts us to our position in society. Yet many religious and spiritual practices have precisely this as their aim: to work on embodiment, the ways in which we experience the world and our place in it. In her study of pietist Islam in Egypt, Mahmood has insightfully paired the concept of habitus to Foucault's notion of subjectification and techniques of the self.[72] Similarly, I understand the religious practices in the two contexts described in the last two chapters as conscious efforts to work on the embodiment of habitus, in the sense that in both contexts the relationship of the individual with religious knowledge and religious authority, but also the ways in which particular dispositions tie us to particular positions in society, are a major area of exploration.[73]

---

[70] Pierre Bourdieu, "Habitus," in *A Sense of Place*, ed. Jean Hillier and Emma Rooksby, second edition (Aldershot: Ashgate, 2005), 43.

[71] Bourdieu, *Distinction*.

[72] Saba Mahmood. "Rehearsed Spontaneity and the Conventionality of Ritual: Disciplines of Şalat." *American Ethnologist* 28, no. 4 (2001): 827–853. doi:10.1525/ae.2001.28.4.827.

[73] Cf. Kim Knibbe, "An Ethnography of a Medium and Her Followers: How Learning Takes Place in the Context of Jomanda," in *Meister Und Schüler in Geschichte Und Gegenwart: Von Religionen Der Antike Bis Zur Modernen Esoterik*, ed. Almut Barbara Renger (Göttingen: V&R unipress, 2012), 383–398; Kim Knibbe, "Obscuring the Role of Power and

An important consequence of the focus on practice and habitus for the approach in this book is that religion is not studied in terms of 'belief'. Sociological surveys often measure beliefs, Weber characterized the world religions according to soteriology, Geertz characterized religion as belief systems. However, following Bourdieu, it becomes possible to think of religion as located not (only) in the minds of people, but in their acts, in the material culture to which they relate, and the rituals they find necessary to perform. The church building that is central to a village, the act of lighting a candle, the urgency of the last rites, an aura-reading: these do not necessarily have anything to do with explicit, well reflected on beliefs.

Rather, these acts, rituals and things are present, to draw on when it becomes necessary. Ritual in particular seemed to have primacy over belief. Following Humphrey and Laidlaw, we can conceive of rituals as 'things', or cultural artefacts, that have become unmoored from the original intentional action through which they were created.[74] As Humphrey and Laidlaw show, people often do not know the meaning of ritual, but perceive it as something which must be performed. This, then, also provokes the need to resignify these rituals, both on the part of the institution (in this case, the Catholic church) and on the part of the people who feel these rituals must be performed. Often, people I spoke to said they surprised themselves by reaching for religious ritual at certain points in their life, while they thought they were not 'a religious person'. Most people in Limburg do not go to mass on a regular basis, yet they still find it important that there is a church in their village, and that mass can be said when it is necessary. It seems these rituals are a necessary instrument for the creation of the domain of the familiar, Yet, as we shall see in chapter 4, it is precisely through ritual that people are confronted with a type of religious authority that they are not willing to accept anymore, resulting in an ambivalent attitude towards the Catholic church and religion in general that is crucial to understanding the role of religion in present-day society.

5. Description of the Research

The research on which this book is based was not an exhaustive study of the range of religious repertoires and institutions in the region of the

---

Gender in Contemporary Spiritualities," in *Gender and Power in Contemporary Spirituality: Ethnographic Approaches*, ed. Anna Fedele and Kim Knibbe (Routledge, 2013).

[74] Caroline Humphrey and James Laidlaw, *The Archetypal Acts of Ritual, a Theory of Ritual Illustrated by the Jain Rite of Worship* (Oxford: Clarendon Press, 1995).

south of Limburg: in this study there are no protestant churches, no evangelicals, and no charismatic Catholics. These options were present, but not as part of 'mainstream' culture and no one in the village where I started out directed me towards these places. The various more upscale New Age centres in the region are not included either. These centres cater to a public from all over the Netherlands, Germany and Belgium and are relatively 'disembedded' from the region where they happen to be located. Besides, the field of the study of alternative spiritualities already has these kinds of centres well within its sights also in the Netherlands.[75] My interest was primarily to investigate the religious practices more firmly part of the production of locality within the local context, so I went where my informants pointed me.

Before starting on my fieldwork, I had not established where I would do my research except in terms of geography: I started by contacting the headmaster of a local elementary school in the village of Welden,[76] located in a rural area bounded by three cities in the south of Limburg. My original plan was to confine my research to participant observation and in-depth interviews within the boundaries of this village. Soon, it became clear that this was an unrealistic plan, since many people participated in religious contexts outside the boundaries of their village and parish, although close by. By following the leads from Welden to other religious contexts, my research turned out to include two religious contexts located within the same municipality: a 'spiritual society' (described in chapter 5) and a (Catholic) pastoral centre (described in chapter 6).

During the fieldwork period, funerals and other rituals around death and dying emerged as an issue where all the changes and differences between the different generations, between the church and lay people have to be negotiated. Following up on this theme, I interviewed several priests and undertakers about this issue, as well as someone connected to the humanist society. The findings of this line of inquiry are integrated into chapter 4.

Chapters 2 and 3 describe religious change from two perspectives: from the perspective of (often Catholic) historians and from the perspective

---

[75] Stef Aupers and Anneke van Otterloo, *New Age; Een Godsdiensthistorische En Sociologische Benadering* (Kampen: Kok, 2000); Martin Ramstedt, "Metaphor or Invocation? The Convergence Between Modern Paganism and Fantasy Fiction," *Journal of Ritual Studies* 26, no. 1 (2007): 1–15.

[76] This is a pseudonym to protect the anonymity of the people who helped me with my research.

of the life histories of the people I interviewed in and around Welden. Because of the focus of historians on organizations and key figures within Catholicism, this means that chapter 2 describes how a particular Catholic elite has attempted to produce 'good Catholics' and instigate reforms that ultimately led to the crumbling of the Catholic pillar, while chapter 3 describes how these 'good Catholics' themselves experienced the crumbling of this pillar.

In doing research, I departed from the premise that there is no such thing as 'data' waiting to be uncovered and collected. Rather, the ethnographic approach I took is dependent on the recognition that 'data' emerge out of the interaction between researcher and researched, my notes and reports. Denzin and Lincoln describe qualitative research in the following way:

> qualitative research is a situated activity that locates the observer in the world. It consists of a set of interpretative, material practices that make the world visible. These practices transform the world. They turn the world into a series of representations, including field notes, interviews, conversations, photographs, recordings and memos to the self. At this level, qualitative research involves an interpretative, naturalistic approach to the world. This means that qualitative researchers study the things in their natural settings, attempting to make sense of, or interpret, phenomena in terms of the meanings people bring to them.[77]

This understanding of research follows from the many discussions of the 'reflexive turn' and a constructionist understanding of social reality: a researcher is not an independent, cool observer but part of the reality he or she studies, positioning herself in certain ways and being positioned by others, creating data out of everyday life. I started out with a minimal research agenda, constantly adapting it as I learned more about the context of my research.

Three activities have generated most of the material for this book: interviews with key informants and life history interviews with lay believers in Welden, (participant) observation in the courses and discussion groups of a local (Catholic) pastoral centre and (participant) observation in a Spiritualist/New Age association. Geographically, the parish, the pastoral centre and the spiritual society were located close to each other, although not in the same village. The people frequenting the pastoral centre and

---

[77] Norman K. Denzin and Yvonna S. Lincoln, *The SAGE Handbook of Qualitative Research* (SAGE, 2005).

the spiritual society were mostly local, and the few 'imported' people participating in these contexts had been living in the area for a long time or were committed to become part of their local community. The difference between 'locals' and 'import' is usually keenly felt, but of course this difference fades over time as people get used to each other. Other differences were just as important in the two contexts: the difference between lay people and priests, between lay pastors and priests, between professionals and priests, between spirit mediums and those who were 'unawakened', between those with a higher education and those without, between city-people and rural people, between neo-conservatives and progressives.

Right at the start of my fieldwork, it became clear that doing participant observation in the parish life of Welden would be difficult because of the history of polarization between a 'neo-conservative' priest and 'progressive' Catholics in that parish. This polarization had affected the whole community: most people felt that after the polarization, 'it was never the same again' and the parish church was not 'their' church anymore. They referred me to the pastoral centre two kilometres away from Welden instead. They felt I would be better off with the people of the pastoral centre, because in contrast to the parish priest, the pastoral centre had 'kept up with the times'. Even the parish priest (who had, supposedly, not 'kept up with the times', and had a problematic relationship with this centre) referred me to them. His argument was that his (neo-conservative) brand of Catholicism did not make for a very lively parish life, so there would not be many interesting things for me to observe. It was also clear that my presence was not comfortable to him, since I was not a Catholic and he supposed I did not share his neo-conservative views on morality. At first, this made him wary; although after the interviews I had with him it seems this wariness lessened.

Although I had some confidence that we could have established a working relationship, the rift his style and views had caused in the local community was a significant obstacle to getting cooperation for my research: people were afraid that my research, because it focused on religious life, would open old wounds and rivalries. So I had to tread carefully: clearly local parish and community life did not amount to an environment that I could hope to navigate safely with just one year of participant observation if I was doing research on religion. The different factions had each cut their losses, and settled down into a status quo that minimized contact and conflict between them. To gain an impression of parish life therefore, I stuck to doing interviews with individuals.

In contrast, the people of the pastoral centre welcomed my research and were very interested. Although this was very nice, it also made things difficult for me. First of all, there were issues of confidentiality: they had to trust me not to tell anything damaging to 'religious rivals' (neo-conservative clergy), and I had to be careful not to tell them too much about their 'religious rivals' as well (neo-conservative clergy and the spiritual society). Second, although on the face of it, the people of the pastoral centre and the background I come from are similar in values and general outlook on life, and the professional staff shared a strong sociological interest with me, this sometimes made me even more aware of the differences between them and myself: I was not a Catholic, not even baptised, and I did not want to become a Catholic either.

This tension between mutual recognition and familiarity and the underlying differences was reinforced by the very inclusive ideology of the pastoral centre. This ideology made me feel that I would be spoiling the atmosphere if I would insist on signalling that I was not the same, I did not belong to them, was not a Catholic. When people are constantly telling each other and themselves that the message of Jesus was that every person counts and therefore they should not exclude anyone, it feels sort of impolite to voluntarily exclude yourself mentally and to some extent also emotionally, while at the same time sticking around physically. Besides, this inclusiveness was to the advantage of my research because it facilitated access to the courses and discussion groups.

The place that seems to come closest to taking advantage of the 'new' situation where repertoires seem to be freely available was the Spiritual society of the Hills, where I also did participant observation. In the spiritual society, any new information, practice, and ideas would be received with interest and curiosity, discussed at length and immediately applied and tested. In this context, I was classified as a 'seeker' and easily included as such. I tried to explain many times that I was doing a PhD and that this would not be so much about my personal views on spiritual matters, but more on their views on them, yet this did not really seem to sink in. I was a seeker; I was younger than most of the other people there, and therefore like any newcomer, the object for much unsolicited advice. Which was of course convenient for me as a researcher.

Methodological reflections are integrated into the introductions to all the chapters. They are of such a diverse nature that it does not make much sense to summarize them here. However, recent events have given rise to another methodological question. About two years ago, it became clear that also in the Netherlands, sexual abuse within Catholic institutions had taken place on a large scale. A committee was set up to investigate the scale and nature of this abuse, resulting in a detailed study that was shocking not only through the nature of the crimes described, but also because of the attempts of the church, orders and congregations to consistently cover up these crimes. Organizations of victims wonder why historians of Catholicism have never paid attention to these issues, have not pointed out the systematic nature of the abuse taking place on Catholic-run boarding schools and the systematic abuse of power. This has become a matter of conscience in current discussions about the Catholic church (personal communication Monteiro). To what extent are scholars of Catholicism complicit in the culture of covering up these crimes if they do not address them in their work?

This is a legitimate question that deserves serious thought. In my own research, I did encounter some stories of sexual abuse and sexual misbehaviour of priests. In the cases where sexual abuse was related as a personal experience, it had happened many years ago. A large part of my respondents were very old. As a young researcher I felt I had no right to probe further into these stories and perhaps revive trauma's. Without being able to commit therapeutic counseling, it would have been irresponsible to try to find out more about this. I am not a therapist, and I already had to struggle with the therapeutic nature of the interviews (this is further described in chapter 3).[78] The recent scandals and the stories I heard during fieldwork all justify a more rigorous research set-up where the workings and abuse of and power over children in Catholic institutional settings is the focus of research. However, this implies a research design where ethical considerations are carefully thought out beforehand and therapeutic support is available.

More generally, I do pay attention to the workings and abuse of power in the Catholic 'clerocracy' of local village life until the 1960s through what I call 'the mechanism of the sacraments', especially in regulating sexuality and denying women reproductive rights (or at least making it very traumatic to claim reproductive rights). This is remembered vividly by the narrators of chapter 3 and described in detail in the chapter that now follows.

[78] See also Kim Knibbe, "Secrets, Gossip and Betrayal: Doing Fieldwork on the Role of Religion in Moral Orientation in a Dutch Catholic Province," *Fieldwork in Religion* 6, no. 2 (2011): 151–167.

CHAPTER TWO

MORAL DISCOURSES IN DUTCH CATHOLICISM:
FROM PILLARIZATION, VIA LIBERATION TO POLARIZATION

1. INTRODUCTION

This chapter describes the changes in discourse on morality within Dutch Catholicism since the Second World War. The organization of the Catholic segment of Dutch society extended right down to the grass roots level through the uniquely Dutch phenomenon of pillarization.[1] In Limburg, the Catholic pillar was in fact not one of the pillars, but encompassed the whole of social life. The tenet: 'no salvation outside the church' was a literal description not only of spiritual but also of social reality in Limburg. This has had a lasting impact on the habitus of Limburg Catholics. In order to understand their narratives, it is necessary to understand the ways in which the organizations of the Dutch Catholic pillar strategically attempted to mold people into good Catholics. In the post-war years, the programme developed by the intellectual elite of the Catholic pillar was evaluated critically and changed radically as a result.

The political history of the Netherlands in the nineteenth century and the beginning of the twentieth century is marked by a struggle between different denominations and ideologies for equal rights, resulting in the uniquely Dutch organization of society in different 'pillars'.[2] This process was taken up and completed after WWII.[3] A pillar has been defined as a network of organizations covering different domains of life, such as politics, unions, recreation, health care, schooling and religion that shape the corresponding subculture and give it its identity.[4] These identities were sharply demarcated from each other, and on an everyday level, interaction

---

[1] For an English language description of this process see John Coleman, *The Evolution of Dutch Catholicism, 1958–1974* (Berkeley and Los Angeles: University of California Press, 1978).

[2] Peter Van Rooden, "Long-term Religious Developments in the Netherlands, 1750–2000," in *The Decline of Christendom in Western Europe*, ed. McLeod, Hugh and Ustorf, Werner (Cambridge University Press, 2002), 113–29.

[3] Coleman, *The Evolution of Dutch Catholicism, 1958–1974* chapter 2.

[4] Staf Hellemans, "Verzuiling En Ontzuiling Van De Katholieken in Belgie En Nederland, Een Historisch Sociologische Vergelijking," *Sociologische Gids* 35, no. 1 (1988): 43.

between people of different pillars was discouraged or actively forbidden: Catholics, socialists, protestants of different churches and humanists; all had their own organizations, political parties, church buildings, radio broad casting services, swimming pools, schools, cemeteries etc.

The sixties and seventies saw the gradual crumbling of these pillars, as the state took over many of the functions of the pillarized organizations, countercultural movements criticized and shook up 'the establishment', and the churches started to empty at an unprecedented rate. However, it would be wrong to assume that the Catholic pillar disintegrated only as a result of outside forces such as modernization, and the consequent out-flux of lay believers who did not see Catholicism as a plausible worldview anymore. A review of the literature shows that many changes were insti-gated from *inside* the Catholic pillar. Long before believers stopped going to church regularly, church officials recognized and tried to answer to the challenges of modernity, lay believers emancipated and pushed for more democratic relations within the church, and insights from psychology and the social sciences were applied to the organization of belief.[5]

In the Netherlands, the original impetus for the organization of the Catholic pillar starting in the 1920s was a fear of what the church saw as the 'dangers of modern society'. At the same time, modernity also cre-ated the conditions for the Catholic pillar to organize itself effectively, reaching not only the cultural elites but down until the lowest classes.[6] The Catholic church saw it as its duty to keep its flock together, safely shepherded by a large and active clergy. This care extended from cradle to grave, into every detail of daily life. The organization of the pillar of Dutch Catholicism was hugely successful. It enabled Dutch Catholics to become very influential politically, and it enabled the Catholic church to keep a very tight rein on the spiritual and moral life of Catholics: schools were run by congregations, on the board of every Catholic organization priests and chaplains usually had the largest say, and local authorities cooperated with the clergy in guarding against 'moral decay', especially in Limburg.

---

[5] Coleman, *The Evolution of Dutch Catholicism, 1958–1974*, 85; Ed Simons and Lodewijk Winkeler, *Het Verraad Der Clercken: Intellectuelen En Hun Rol in De Ontwikkelingen Van Het Nederlandse Katholicisme Na 1945* (Baarn: Arbor, 1987); James Kennedy, "Nieuw Babylon in Aanbouw," *Nederland in De Jaren Zestig* (1995): 12.

[6] Coleman, *The Evolution of Dutch Catholicism, 1958–1974*, 85; Hellemans, "Verzuiling En Ontzuiling Van De Katholieken in Belgie En Nederland, Een Historisch Sociologische Vergelijking," 44; Simons and Winkeler, *Het Verraad Der Clercken: Intellectuelen En Hun Rol in De Ontwikkelingen Van Het Nederlandse Katholicisme Na 1945*.

The discourse against 'moral decay', represented by enemies such as socialism (no respect for authority) and 'neo-Malthusianism' (proponents of birth control) is the subject of section 2 of this chapter. The pre-war generation whose narratives are central to the next chapter grew up and had their first children during the height of this discourse.

In section 3, I discuss the changes in the discourse within the church and associated Catholic organizations that hesitantly started among Catholic intellectuals in the late fifties. The ideas developed in these circles influenced key decision makers within the Catholic church and came out into the open in the sixties. Especially after the Second Vatican Council this discourse radicalized and caught up many believers in its zeal for reform. In those days, the Dutch Catholics made world news with their proposals for new ways of 'being a church'. Paradoxically, the high degree of organization of Dutch Catholicism that was once so highly praised in Rome, also made sure that these ideas were much more swiftly implemented than Rome could keep track of developments. The post-war generation whose views are discussed in chapter 4 came of age during this period.

In section 4 I discuss the main events during the remainder of the twentieth century with regard to the Catholic church and Catholicism in general in the Netherlands. The history of Dutch Catholicism after the 1970s is marked by polarization: Rome reacted to the Dutch zeal for experimenting and democratization by installing as many conservative bishops as they had the opportunity to install. At the same time, the Catholic organizations that had made up the Catholic pillar became more independent from the church and secularized. The specific history of the Catholic church and the Catholic pillar in Limburg is the subject of section 5. In this section, I focus less on changes in discourse (they largely followed the national trends) and more on the social presence of the church on the local level.

Note on the Literature

Insiders, active Catholics, have written much of the history of Dutch Catholicism of the past 50 years and also of the history before that. In some cases, they even played a leading role in the changes they were describing.[7] To these academics, writing the history of change was often

---

[7] E.g. Walter Goddijn, Hans Wewerinke, and Fons Mommers, *Pastoraal Concilie (1965–1970): Een Experiment in Kerkelijk Leiderschap* (Baarn: Nelissen, 1986); Walter Goddijn, *De Beheerste Kerk: Uitgestelde Revolutie in Rooms-Katholiek Nederland* (Amsterdam: Elsevier,

partly a reflexive exercise as a committed participant.[8] Even when this was
not the explicit goal of the undertaking of writing history, the concerns of
these authors often revolve around the same issues that dominated the
debate in Dutch Catholicism: the decline of church going, changes in moral
discourse and beliefs, Catholicism and social justice, the role of women and
lay believers, the future of celibacy, democratization within the church.
Hope for the future of Catholicism in the Netherlands is held out or denied
based on the answers to questions such as: were the changes taking place
during the sixties too radical, or were they justified and is Rome simply
'lagging behind'? Does the dwindling number of committed believers and
callings to the priesthood mean that Catholicism is slowly 'dying out' in the
Netherlands? Is Catholicism relevant to the present day and age?

Thurlings describes three generations of researchers of Dutch Catholicism: the first generation, mainly historians, looked at Dutch Catholicism
as an oppressed minority within the Dutch political landscape and
described their history in terms of social en cultural emancipation. The
epitome of this generation, according to Thurlings, is Rogier's work significantly titled: 'Reborn into Freedom' (In Vrijheid Herboren). The second
generation, in contrast, assumed that Catholics in the Netherlands were
dominantly motivated by the drive to defend themselves against the dangers of modernity, and to refine measures of internal control. They were
very critical of the benefits of the Catholic pillar. Goddijn is an important
figure in this second generation. The third generation Thurlings recognizes uses the sociological model of 'movements' to understand Dutch
Catholicism. History should be seen as a process by which charismatic
leaders, supported by an elite, manage to mobilize large groups of people
for their ideas.[9]

The historical sketch presented here is mainly based on authors who
use, implicitly or explicitly, this last model to present their findings. The
changes within Dutch Catholicism are then seen as part of a movement
that undergoes several stages: a charismatic leader, supported by a powerful elite, mobilizes the anxiety of the masses. During the next stage, there

---

1973); Walter Goddijn, Jan Jacobs, and Gérard van Tillo, *Tot Vrijheid Geroepen: Katholieken
in Nederland: 1946–2000* (Baarn: Ten Have, 1999).

  [8] Paul Luykx, *Andere Katholieken. Opstellen over Nederlandse Katholieken in De Twintigste Eeuw* (Nijmegen: SUN, 2000), 209.

  [9] Jan Thurlings, "Verzuiling En Beweging. Over Nut En Onnut Van Het Bewegingsmodel," *Trajecta. Tijdschrift Voor De Geschiedenis Van Het Katholiek Leven in De Nederlanden* 13 (2004): 18–20.

is militant action and a great enthusiasm for organization, culminating in a phase of triumphalism: the Catholic pillar at its height during the centennial of the restoration of the hierarchy in 1953 (section 2). This becomes the prelude to a phase of internal factionalism and critique: the forces of renewal, spurred by the Second Vatican Council, versus the conservative Rome-oriented Catholics (section 3).

Even when their role was not very active, the position of most of these historians and social scientists is usually one of sympathy with the forces for renewal, even in those cases where nostalgia for the 'rich Roman life' of the years before Vatican II is freely admitted. This overrepresentation of progressive Catholics in sociological and historical descriptions leaves us with much insight into the motivations and discourses of the actors that were pushing for radical changes, but with less insight into the motivations and discourses of the neo-conservative faction in Dutch Catholicism,[10] let alone, lay Catholics at the grassroots level. However, it is the faction of neo-conservatives that has now gained the upper hand in terms of church politics in the Dutch Catholic church. Concerning the literature on Limburg, it was well known that the neo-conservative bishop Gijsen of Limburg did not have much time for social scientists. He was a historian himself, and he saw the radical changes in Dutch Catholicism as no more than a slight ripple in the history of the Catholic church. The literature on Limburg is even more characterized by a progressive spirit, a drive to 'unmask' the representations of Gijsen, than the writing on Dutch Catholicism in general.

Because of the 'progressive' bias in the perceptions of the historians and sociologists of Dutch Catholicism, there are more than enough good studies to give an insightful sketch of the changes in discourse, the heady atmosphere of change that gripped Dutch Catholics at a certain point and the clamour this zeal for change gave rise to. The descriptions below are based on studies such as the detailed books by Westhoff, Simons and Winkeler and Van Schaik,[11] fleshed out with studies such as those by

---

[10] See also ibid., 37.

[11] Ton. H.M. van Schaik, *Alfrink. Een Biografie* (Amsterdam: Anthos, 1997); Simons and Winkeler, *Het Verraad Der Clercken: Intellectuelen En Hun Rol in De Ontwikkelingen Van Het Nederlandse Katholicisme Na 1945*; Hanneke Westhoff, *Geestelijke Bevrijders. Nederlandse Katholieken En Hun Beweging Voor Geestelijke Volksgezondheid in De Twintigste Eeuw* (Nijmegen: Valkhof, 1996).

Luyckx, Nissen[12] and general historical overviews of the changes in Dutch society as described by Kennedy[13] and in Limburg, as described by Ubachs.[14]

2. CATHOLIC IN EVERYTHING: TRIUMPH AND MORAL ANXIETY

From the time when the Catholic hierarchy was re-installed in the Netherlands in 1853 until the time period under review in this chapter, the Dutch Catholic church was characterized by a policy of strong ultramontanism. This ideology took Rome and the pope as its centre, and although it accepted the separation between church and state, it refused to see the church as subservient to the state, and resisted any interference from the state in religious affairs, especially from a state dominated by Protestants and liberals, as was the case in the Netherlands. This ultramontanism of Dutch Catholicism was reinforced by the announcement of the dogma of the infallibility of the pope in 1870, consolidating his power and creating an opposition between the 'absolute' power of the church and the fallible, democratic power of the state. It also contrasted sharply with the tradition of Dutch Protestantism, in which the independent reading of the Bible was an important element. The Dutch Catholics were proud that at least they did not have endless discussions, uncertainties and schisms in their church: they had the certainties proclaimed by the pope.

The boundaries towards Protestantism were further reinforced by the dogma of the immaculate conception of Mary, emphasizing her central importance to Catholics and sparking off new devotional traditions such as those centring on Lourdes. The ideology of ultramontanism was also explicitly anti-modern, and feared the influence of both liberalism and Marxism. The Catholic historian Roes has characterized ultramontanism as a modern movement with three distinct aims: (1) the disciplining and subjection of all Catholics (from lay believers, to priests and bishops) to the infallible authority of the pope, (2) the promotion of the sovereign

---

[12] Luykx, *Andere Katholieken. Opstellen over Nederlandse Katholieken in De Twintigste Eeuw*; Peter Nissen, "Confessionele Identiteit En Regionale Eigenheid," in *Constructie Van Het Eigene. Culturele Vormen Van Regionale Identiteit in Nederland*, ed. Carlo Van der Borgt, vol. 25 (Amsterdam: P.J. Meertens-instituut, 1996); Peter Nissen, "Constructie En Deconstructie Van Het Katholieke Limburg," *Studies over De Sociaal-economische Geschiedenis Van Limburg* XLV (2000): 79–97.

[13] Kennedy, "Nieuw Babylon in Aanbouw."

[14] P.J.H. Ubachs, *Handboek Voor De Geschiedenis Van Limburg* (Hilversum: Verloren, 2000).

legitimacy of the central church authorities based on tradition and (3) the systematic penetration of daily life through the promotion of devotions and other regular religious practices.[15]

In order to achieve these goals, Dutch Catholicism organized itself very effectively. The main drive towards this organization started in the 1920s. In this history, the Second World War was no more than an interlude. However, for Catholic intellectuals and politicians, this interlude provided a shared experience that laid the foundations for later changes. The late forties and early fifties are usually described as a time when everybody in the Netherlands was working hard to rebuild pre-war society after the destruction of WWII. The Catholics joined in this spirit in their own way, by strengthening their own organizational structures. Church attendance and membership of Catholic organizations was exceptionally high. Because of their obedience and adherence to devotions, the pope often mentioned the Dutch Catholics as an example to Catholics in other countries. This self-conscious Catholic identity and frontier mentality was further proven by the exceptionally high level of callings to the priesthood[16] as well as the tremendously high birth-rate.

Depending on who is speaking, the fifties are represented as both the height of a quiet, hardworking and solid period, but also as charactererized by a stifling atmosphere and narrow-mindedness. The ideal was to rebuild society the way it was, but better and more prosperous. Discipline, obedience and asceticism were prized. The pillarization of Dutch society was perfected.

At the same time, there were people hoping for a 'breakthrough' ('doorbraak' in Dutch) between the rigidly segregated pillars. During the Second World War, people from different pillars had worked together in the resistance movement against the German occupation. This experience gave rise to a belief that the old enmity between Catholics and Protestants, and between Catholics and the 'reds' (communists and socialists), could be left behind. The Catholic clergy however, opposed this breakthrough, seeing it as a threat to the moral integrity and Catholicism of their flocks.

---

[15] Erik Borgman et al., *Katholieken in De Moderne Tijd: Een Onderzoek Door De Acht Mei Beweging* (Zoetermeer: De Horstink, 1995), 46.
[16] Nissen, "Constructie En Deconstructie Van Het Katholieke Limburg," 84; Hans Knippenberg, *De Religieuze Kaart Van Nederland, Omvang En Geografische Spreiding Van De Godsdienstige Gezindten Vanaf De Reformatie Tot Heden* (Assen/Maastricht: Van Gorcum, 1992), 171.

It was a time when Dutch Catholics felt they had finally come to achieve the emancipation they had strived for in the previous centuries. In the years following the declaration of the Batavian Republic in 1796, Catholicism slowly rebuilt its institutional presence in the Netherlands, culminating in the re-instalment of the territorial hierarchy of bishops and parishes in 1853. The rhetoric used in 1953, at the celebration of the centennial of this important event, had a decidedly triumphant ring to it, speculating on the chance that in a few years Catholics would make up more than half of the Dutch population. Their political influence had been rising steadily and was still rising, and they were tightly organized. Furthermore, almost every Catholic family was eager to contribute at least one son to the clergy, or a daughter to one of the many orders. This meant that there was an abundance of priests, friars and nuns to staff parishes, schools and the many Catholic organizations. In Limburg, the attraction of the secular clergy was particularly strong, so that many parishes had at least one priest assisted by several chaplains.[17] This meant that the diocesan hierarchy had enough manpower to serve as spiritual advisors on the boards of the many flourishing Catholic organizations with all their local chapters. The clergy, nuns and friars were not only omnipresent in social life in Limburg, they actually shaped it.

This clergy promoted an awareness of the many threats to be combated and the need for Catholics to close ranks against these threats: communism, socialism, modernism, freemasonry, Neo-Malthusianism and, of course, the old time enemy of Protestantism. The threat of withholding the sacraments (and thereby withholding salvation as well as social acceptance) was used to keep people in line, on the level of village life but also on a national scale. However, on this level the attempt to control Catholics worked as a boomerang, as illustrated by the indignation caused by a joint episcopal letter published by the Dutch bishops in 1954.[18] In this letter Catholics were admonished not to listen to non-Catholic and especially socialist or humanist radio broadcastings, not to trade with non-Catholics, not to read non-Catholic newspapers:[19]

---

[17] Nissen, "Constructie En Deconstructie Van Het Katholieke Limburg," 86.

[18] J.d. Jong et al., "De Katholiek in Het Openbare Leven Van Deze Tijd: Bisschoppelijk Mandement 1954," 1954.

[19] 'Wij handhaven de bepaling dat de Heilige Sacramenten moeten geweigerd worden—en als hij zonder bekering sterft, ook de kerkelijke begrafenis—aan de katholiek van wie bekend is dat hij lid is van een socialistische vereniging of dat hij, zonder lid te zijn, toch geregeld socialistische geschriften of bladen leest of socialistische vergaderingen bijwoont'.

We enforce the rule that the holy Sacraments should be refused—and if he dies unrepentant must be refused a Catholic burial—to the Catholic of whom it is known that he is a member or that he, without being a member, still regularly reads socialist writings or magazines or attends socialist meetings'.[20]

Among protestants and socialists, this episcopal letter was received with indignation, and those Catholics who had organized themselves within the socialist party were particularly affected. Generally, historians agree that most Catholics ignored the admonitions.[21] Change was in the air, and it was thought to be inevitable. Because of the many protests, and because of the respected positions those who protested occupied, openness towards cooperation with non-Catholics became a topic that could not be avoided anymore and even came to be articulated as a necessity among Catholic intellectuals. Especially openness towards the other Christian churches was felt to be desirable. And the VARA, the 'socialist' radio station alluded to in the letter, seemed to become even more popular among Catholics.[22]

Moral Renaissance

The rebuilding of the Catholic pillar after WWII went hand in hand with an effort towards a moral renaissance and a very well developed and detailed reasoning on 'morality', a subject that seemed to be almost synonymous with 'sexuality'[23] at the time. Nationally and in Catholic circles, the immediate post-war period was a time of concern over the loosening of morals that was perceived to be the aftermath of the war, encouraged by 'the mass media' (film, dance and music). The many Catholic organizations that concerned themselves with the education of youth produced numerous booklets, folders and courses for the young. These materials prescribed exactly, in meticulous detail, what was and what was not allowed in terms

---

[20] Jong et al., "De Katholiek in Het Openbare Leven Van Deze Tijd: Bisschoppelijk Mandement 1954," 43.

[21] Kennedy, "Nieuw Babylon in Aanbouw"; Coleman, *The Evolution of Dutch Catholicism, 1958–1974*, 55–56.

[22] Jacobs in Borgman et al., *Katholieken in De Moderne Tijd: Een Onderzoek Door De Acht Mei Beweging*, 30–31.

[23] The description of the post-war concern with morals and in particular chastity and the efforts of Catholic intellectuals to promote a different way of dealing with these issues discussed in the next section is based for the most part on the historical monograph of Hanneke Westhoff unless otherwise indicated: Westhoff, *Geestelijke Bevrijders. Nederlandse Katholieken En Hun Beweging Voor Geestelijke Volksgezondheid in De Twintigste Eeuw*.

of dress, relationships between the sexes, music and dancing. In schools
and Catholic societies where young people could go for entertainment,
all behaviour and thought that could be even remotely related to sexuality was the subject of intense scrutiny and worry for the educators. Lists
of questions were published to help a priest along in taking confessions
(obligatory every fortnight) and hold the sexual lives of young people to
the light: masturbation, kissing, holding hands and the exact feelings this
aroused were all subjects a priest could, and should, enquire into. This
information could then be fitted into an elaborate classification of sins,
with which the penitence called for could be calculated.

The argument was that young people were allowed to develop a bond
of love, but that a sexual bond was preserved for marriage, partners
should 'save themselves', keep their love pure and chaste. Anything that
aroused sexual feelings could be an occasion for sin and should therefore
be warned against and prohibited.[24]

The more these rules were refined, the more the clergy was confronted
by the fact that their discourse was mystifying to many young people:
the censure of everything to do with sexuality was so effective that many
young people did not have a clue what they were being warned against.
After all, education on sexual matters was thought to be unnecessary for
the young, so it was usually the priest who informed a couple about to
be wedded of the right way of 'fulfilling' their marriage and warn them
against the sin of trying to prevent conception.[25]

One can imagine that the ambiguity about sexuality (one should not
know about it, and at the same time one was constantly warned against
its pitfalls) produced an atmosphere of tension and confusion around the
subject. Until the time of marriage, the subject of sexuality was necessarily
clouded by an aura of sin and taboo. After marriage, sexuality remained
an area of life the church wanted to control, right into the most intimate
details, to root out the grave sin of 'Neo-Malthusianism' (birth control).
In the papal encyclical Casti Connubii, Pope Pius XI had left no doubt
about what he saw as the right way of having marital relations and that
procreation was the primary aim of the conjugal act:

---

[24] Examples of the anxiety about sexuality and the level of detail of the proscriptions
for chastity are collected in a book titled 'The Desert of Morals' (Kroon 1965). At the time of
publication of this book, all these prohibitions and rules were apparently already seen as
something strange and exotic, and more importantly, a testimony to the small-mindedness
of Catholic clerics.

[25] Westhoff, *Geestelijke Bevrijders. Nederlandse Katholieken En Hun Beweging Voor Geestelijke Volksgezondheid in De Twintigste Eeuw*, 132.

> Since, therefore, the conjugal act is destined primarily by nature for the begetting of children, those who in exercising it deliberately frustrate its natural power and purpose sin against nature and commit a deed which is shameful and intrinsically vicious.[26]

This was interpreted in such a way that anything preventing the conception of children was seen as a sin that could not be absolved until the couple involved repented and promised to resume normal marital relationships.

Since the beginning of the 1920s, the moral instructions for marital life had received much attention in the training of the clergy preparing for a pastoral role.[27] Priests had explicit instructions to ask probing questions about the details of a couple's sexual relations, because the sins of preventing conception were deemed so grave that it could not be left to the initiative of the confessant to confess them voluntarily. According to the testimony of both priests and lay believers, many (although not all) priests followed these instructions to the letter in their role as confessor.[28] Furthermore, priests and chaplains visited the homes of families in their parishes regularly, to inquire when the next child would be due and admonish couples that were slow to produce children. If no children were born for a while, a priest was encouraged to probe for 'sinful' behaviour. Periodic retention to limit the number of births would only be 'allowed' under special circumstances, on the advice of the family physician. In that case, a priest could give a couple 'dispensation'.

In many cases however, the family doctor was unhelpful in providing the necessary medical legitimation for this dispensation. The society of Catholic family doctors was a strong force helping in maintaining the 'right matrimonial relationships'. Initially, they opposed the use of periodic retention as much as possible. In the thirties, a family doctor from Brabant had published a booklet detailing the calculations necessary to know when a woman was fertile. At the time of publication, this had caused much discussion. The general opinion among Catholic physicians and priests was that practicing this method of birth control was only

---

[26] Pius XI, "Casti Connubii," 1932, para. 54.

[27] Westhoff, *Geestelijke Bevrijders. Nederlandse Katholieken En Hun Beweging Voor Geestelijke Volksgezondheid in De Twintigste Eeuw*, 132.

[28] See for narratives of women on how this control was exercised Marga Kerklaan, ed., *Zodoende Was De Vrouw Maar Een Mens Om Kinderen Te Krijgen, 300 Brieven over Het Roomse Huwelijksleven.* (Baarn: Ambo, 1987).

permitted if there were very grave circumstances that made it advisable that a woman should not bear children.

According to the discourse dominating Dutch Catholicism at the time, birth control was sinful for two reasons. First, because it endangered the primary aim of marriage. Second, it promoted selfishness and wanton behaviour since apparently the couple engaging in sex was not prepared to carry the responsibility of the natural result of this act. The sexual act thereby became 'unchaste' and sinful, instead of 'chaste' and loving. Another argument used against periodic retention was that it introduced a measure of calculation into marital life that was not conducive to a loving relationship.

The doctrine of confession, repentance and absolution to restore people to a life in a 'state of grace' was an important mechanism in enforcing this moral discourse. A woman confessing to the wish not to have more children would usually be severely reprimanded by her confessor. Unless she agreed to have more children she would not be absolved. In popular language, this was described as 'getting the shutter': the little window between priest and confessant would be slid shut, effectively dismissing her and her concerns, leaving her in a 'state of sin' (in Dutch: 'het schuifje krijgen'). It also meant that one could not participate in the Holy Communion during church services.

Of course, many women found a way around these obstacles by picking a priest that they knew to be permissive, or by finding a doctor who did not require a permission slip. However, especially in rural areas these alternate routes were not accessible to women.[29] As mentioned before, the birth rate among Catholics was astonishingly high until well into the fifties, so it seems that all these measures provided the expected results.[30]

In this case we can see clearly how the church controlled what people knew; decided how much was good and right for them to know, and decisively impacted on the infrastructure of options available through its domination of education, the libraries, and in this instance the organization of Catholic physicians. It also shows to what extent they were able to mobilize the cooperation of professionals and authority figures. Through strictly defining the boundaries of a 'good' moral life, the church attempted to block alien ideas as much as possible. Within these

---

[29] Westhoff, *Geestelijke Bevrijders. Nederlandse Katholieken En Hun Beweging Voor Geestelijke Volksgezondheid in De Twintigste Eeuw*, 132–133.
[30] Monique Schoonheim, *Mixing Ovaries and Rosaries. Catholic Religion and Reproduction in the Netherlands 1870–1970* (Amsterdam: Aksant, 2005).

boundaries, the focus of control was the regulation of sexuality and the promotion of a consciousness that aimed to be 'Catholic in everything'. In later years, many aspects of the Catholic regime were criticized, but it was especially the aura of taboo and the strictness of the rules surrounding sexuality that were to come under fire.

3. FROM MORALIZING TO PSYCHOLOGIZING

Despite the episcopal letter of 1954, the discussions within Dutch Catholicism persisted, and young Catholic intellectuals continued to take inspiration from sources outside Catholicism, such as socialism, psychology and sociology, as well as from radical theological debates such as the 'Nouvelle Théologie' from France. But it was especially the discussion about the Catholic morality on sexuality that busied the hearts and minds of many Catholic intellectuals during the late fifties.

This discussion was put on the agenda with a vengeance by the Catholic Movement for general mental health (KNBGG).[31] This movement was inspired by ideas about mental hygiene that were developed in the beginning of the twentieth century in the U.S. Originally, the aim of this movement was to improve the conditions in psychiatric hospitals but later it shifted its emphasis towards the prevention of mental illness. After the Second World War it developed into a full fledged and influential movement for the promotion of the general mental health of Dutch Catholics. Because of their catalysing role in changing the way Catholics thought about sexuality, authority and punishment, the (mostly) men of this movement have been characterized as 'spiritual liberators'[32] by their historian, Hanneke Westhoff, a characterization they would not have objected to.

According to some prominent figures in the Catholic mental health movement (notably the physician Buytendijk),[33] the small-mindedness of Catholic regulations concerning morality was the source of many psychological problems, a higher delinquency among Catholics due to a not fully grown personal conscience, and a high rate of sexual delinquency. Catholic moral education and the social and spiritual 'mechanism of the

---

[31] Katholieke Nationaal Bureau voor Geestelijke Gezondheidszorg, later KCV: Katholieke Centrale Vereniging voor Geestelijke Volksgezondheid.

[32] In Dutch: geestelijke bevrijders.

[33] Interestingly, Buytendijk was a convert to Catholicism, perhaps one reason why he was able to develop such a radically new perspective on sexuality and psychology.

sacraments' emphasized what would happen if one 'broke the rules'. According to Buytendijk and other spiritual liberators, Catholic moral teaching should focus on *inspiring* believers to live a morally good life, whereas now it in fact *prevented* believers from developing fully as independent adults. Catholic morality as it was enforced at that time, according to the spiritual liberators, forced Catholics to live in constant fear of sin.

The spiritual liberators perceived the relationship between the church regulations and the sexual life of many Catholics as especially problematic. Instead of promoting 'chaste and pure' love, these rules promoted an atmosphere of ignorance, taboo and intense psychological suffering and neurosis. The aim of the spiritual liberators was to develop a discourse and practice within Dutch Catholicism that would make the "fears, vulnerabilities and constraints"[34] of Dutch Catholics disappear.[35]

At first, the discussions on Catholic morality concerning sexuality took place behind closed doors. Anything intended for public use was controlled and censored by the hierarchy of the Catholic church (it was the practice to ask the bishop for an 'imprimatur' for all publications of Catholic organizations and intellectuals). But gradually, the censorship of the church loosened and sexuality and birth control became an openly discussed topic in the Catholic media: first some Catholic magazines, later the radio and finally, television. In Amsterdam, the psychiatrist Trimbos set up a 'school' for marriage. The aim of this school was to help couples not to 'control' their sexuality, but rather to develop it. The school was hugely successful, convincing the spiritual liberators that they were addressing a real need. In weekly radio talks on the Catholic broadcasting service (KRO), Trimbos also discussed the subject of marital sexuality, sexual education and birth control quite openly. The spiritual liberators argued that it should not be the clergy that advised a couple about their sexual relations, but that it was rather a subject for mental health, to be managed by professionals trained in psychology. Within a few years, a paradigm shift occurred within the Catholic pillar:

> ... the 'psychological' aspect of being human emerged as an area of concern *preceding* religious and ethical concerns. A healthy psychology was a prerequisite to a good moral and religious life. The question to be asked changed from 'is it right?' to 'is it healthy?'.[36]

[34] Zodat "die angsten, kwetsbaarheden en onvrijheden zouden verdwijnen".
[35] Bartels, one of the foremen of this movement, quoted in Westhoff, *Geestelijke Bevrijders. Nederlandse Katholieken En Hun Beweging Voor Geestelijke Volksgezondheid in De Twintigste Eeuw*, 261.
[36] Ibid., 120.

'Official' Catholic morality, more specifically Casti Connubii, remained the primary moral source to the spiritual liberators. In their zeal to bring about a 'healthier' moral development among Catholics, they remained, at least in their own eyes, loyal to traditional Catholic morality. This was explained in sophisticated and flowery language that bridged the old discourse of chastity and the new discourse of psychological health quite easily. For example, they often referred to a 'sensus Catolicus', a supposedly typically Catholic receptivity to direction by the Holy Spirit and the church as the body of Christ. It was on this 'sensus Catolicus' that they relied to make their efforts to improve the mental health of Catholics not just a neutral professional effort, but a truly Catholic endeavour that would promote the liberating message of Jesus Christ.[37]

Nevertheless, Casti Connubii was reinterpreted in such a way that the role of sexual relations in the 'primary' (procreation) and 'secondary' (a loving relationship) aims of marriage came to be seen quite differently. The reasoning went as follows: from a psychological point of view, good sexual relations are not only important to procreation, but also to the loving fulfilment that according to Casti Connubii is the secondary aim of marriage. Therefore it is conceivable that it could be better *not* to have more than a certain number of children, since this would put unnecessary strain on marital relations, the happiness of the couple and the attention and love they would be able to give to the children they already have. Therefore, if a couple already have some children, it should be all right for them to use ways to prevent having more children, since the primary aim of marriage has already been fulfilled.

Topics such as homosexuality and masturbation, previously sources of much anxious rule making,[38] were also repositioned. They came to be seen as psychological problems, which were blocking the path to happiness and a spiritual life, rather than as sins, which are the result of morally wrong choices. After all, how could one speak of a 'choice', if the morally wrong behaviour was caused by a psychological problem? Furthermore, the extent to which a couple should be allowed to explore their sexuality before marriage was much debated. Sexuality and even morality in general became a topic for psychologists and mental health workers, and not for the clergy. Persuaded by this reasoning, the church hierarchy

---

[37] Ibid., 314–315.
[38] Especially in boarding schools the nuns and friars concerned themselves with the dangers of homosexuality and masturbation: hands above the blankets, bathing with a dress on, discouraging 'special friendships' etc.

relinquished much of its control over the minds and emotions of their flock to (usually lay) professionals.

At first, this shift in discourse took place mainly in the 'top' layers of society, among the more educated people, the young people being educated at that time, and the clergy. They read the magazines where these things were discussed openly, they witnessed the changes in curriculum in the education of priests and universities, they were studying at the university of Nijmegen at the time of the controversial psycho-analytical practice of dr. Anna Terruwe, who was eventually reprimanded by Rome for her supposedly 'immoral' advice to young priests with sexual problems. These groups had a special interest in reconciling the intellectual, political and practical developments of modernity with their Roman Catholic affiliations.

In time, lay Catholic professionals implemented these ideas in the many institutions and organizations of the Catholic pillar: from kindergarten to university, from the first experiments with co-education to the re-organization of the training of priests in open institutes mixed with the training for lay pastors. Furthermore, due to radio and television, 'the public' at large was also drawn into the discussion. And since it concerned issues very close to their heart, this public listened avidly.

The Emancipation of Individual Consciousness and the Democratization of the Church

The point when church control over marital relations was openly, although almost unintentionally, given up, could be situated in 1963. All the discussions opened up by the spiritual liberators and in other segments of the Catholic pillar had raised many questions around authority, morality and the extent to which people should be allowed to follow their 'own consciousness' in matters concerning sexuality. At the same time, oral contraceptives were becoming available. A tension was arising between these debates and their inevitable conclusions, and the conservative policies on chastity and birth control implemented within the Dutch church and the Catholic pillar. Within the church-hierarchy, the clergy expected that the Second Vatican Council, still not concluded at the time, would create more clarity. After all, the main aim of this council, as summarized by the term 'aggiornamento' introduced by pope John XXIII, was to bring the church up to date.

However, a statement made on television in 1963 by bishop Bekkers of Brabant, foreshortened this process. This statement was made long before the Second Vatican Council was concluded, and long before the pope made any pronouncements on the use of oral contraceptives or other methods of birth control. Bekkers' pronouncements gave the process through which the relationship between lay people and clergy in the Netherlands was fundamentally restructured a momentum that made subsequent developments seem inevitable.

Bishop Bekkers was a popular bishop, who often appeared on television and had a large audience. He was considered to be an example of the new developments within the Catholic church. In one of the short television speeches that he often made at the end of a news programme on the Catholic Broadcasting Service (KRO), he declared that the decision on the number of children to have should be left to the individual consciousness of the couple involved. According to the biographer of Alfrink, the Dutch archbishop at the time, Bekkers made this statement without first consulting with his colleagues. Alfrink actually disagreed with Bekkers, but felt he could not do so publicly.[39] Bishop Bekkers was immensely popular with the majority of Dutch Catholics and even likened to the charismatic pope John XXIII.

In general, Bekkers' comments during these television broadcasts emphasized that the church had perhaps been too repressive in the past, fostering fear and grief rather than belief. In these kinds of pronouncements the influence of the spiritual liberators was evident. But because he was a bishop, his pronouncements were not only a watershed with regard to sexuality, but also with regard to the use of sanctions and fear to keep the Catholic flock in line. To the generations growing up during the sixties, especially the 'professionals' who took over many functions from the clergy, nuns and friars in schools, hospitals and mental institutions, the whole 'mechanism of the sacraments' underlying the social and psychological control of Catholics, came to be seen as something immoral in itself.

Bekkers' statement came at precisely the right time. He was aware of this, as we can read in Van Schaik,[40] and nervous about the pronouncements he was going to make, but convinced he was only taking a position that would be commonplace within the church very soon. Although Alfrink did not agree with him, this position became a fait accompli, accepted as

---

[39] Van Schaik, *Alfrink. Een Biografie,* 347.
[40] Ibid.

the official position of the church, at least within the Netherlands (and most believers did not look further than the borders of the nation).

To emphasize the revolutionary nature of this statement from yet another angle: Bekkers did *not* say anything about birth control, which methods were allowed and which were not.[41] Statements on do's and don'ts were the kind Catholics were used to, and the kind of statements the clergy expected itself to be making after ample deliberations and consultations with the approved authorities on the subject in question. Instead, Bekkers' statement effectively removed an *entire area of life* outside the control of the church. The statement that such an important area of life was an issue of individual consciousness where the church had no business, made by a bishop to such a large and attentive audience, opened up the field of discussion in a way that was unprecedented. Within the church, like in Dutch society in general, the authorities felt that change was inevitable, and did not make it difficult for those seeking radical reforms.[42]

In the years to follow, virtually everything that had previously been taught as the eternal and true teachings of Catholicism came under the scrutiny of the democratic spirit that arose after Vatican II.

4. THE LOCAL CHURCH VERSUS PAPAL POWER PLAY

One of the things historically setting the Dutch Catholics apart from their countrymen was their obedience and loyalty to the Roman church and its hierarchy. Partly in reaction to their marginalization in a country dominated by Protestants, Dutch Catholics had developed a very 'Rome-oriented' Catholicism. The efforts of pillarization had produced a Catholic 'flock' that seemed to follow their pastors enthusiastically or meekly, but in any case obediently.[43] Other authors have emphasized the voices of protest that could also be heard in these years.[44] In general however, until the late 1950s, Dutch Catholics were (supposed to be) oriented towards

---

[41] Ibid., ibid.

[42] James C. Kennedy, "Building New Babylon: Cultural Change in the Netherlands During the 1960s" (University Microfilm International, 1995), 413–422.

[43] Roes in Borgman et al., *Katholieken in De Moderne Tijd: Een Onderzoek Door De Acht Mei Beweging*, 51–52.

[44] Tjitske Akkerman and Siep Stuurman, *De Zondige Riviera Van Het Katholicisme. Een Lokale Studie over Feminisme En Ontzuiling 1950–1975* (Amsterdam: SUA, 1985); Luykx, *Andere Katholieken. Opstellen over Nederlandse Katholieken In De Twintigste Eeuw*.

Rome as their main authority. In the fifties, the complaints of active Catholics and priests were gathering steam: according to them, many Catholics were not very interested in the substance of what the church had to offer them, they just followed the rules and tried to stay out of trouble. Among the younger clergy and lay professionals, the need for pastoral redirection was becoming urgent.

From the late fifties onwards the 'integrity of the individual consciousness' became a key concept to Catholics, publicly formulated in Bekkers' statement. This key enlightenment value, well developed among Protestants, proved to be a catalyst of many changes. Some have called this the 'second emancipation': after the emancipation of the Catholic population as a whole within the Dutch nation came the emancipation of the laity vis à vis the church as a hierarchical institution. Others have noted that this emancipation concerned more the lower clergy and regulars: lay Catholics could simply walk away, but clergy and regulars couldn't, except by 'jumping the wall' (i.e. breaking their vows).[45] However, since lay professionals found their work within the Catholic pillarized organization, the second emancipation was also powered by their agenda.

During the same time period, the Second Vatican Council positioned the Catholic church in a dialogue with other religions, and declared for the first time that salvation outside the church was a possibility. Theologians such as Karl Rahner, Hans Küng and Edward Schillebeeckx were bridging differences between Catholics and non-Catholics. The 'aggiornamento' announced by pope John XXIII produced a heady atmosphere among the intellectuals of the Catholic church. The years after Second Vatican Council became a time of experiments, democratization, the 'breaking of taboos' (a national hobby at the time) among Dutch Catholics. There was a general expectation that everything would be different in the years to come, that they were only now truly liberated to unite as Christians with other believers, to conceive of themselves and others as 'God's people' in transit (Gods volk onderweg).

The New Catechism (Nieuwe Katechismus) that appeared in 1966 exemplifies this new élan. Instead of a set of questions and answers which taught the central tenets of Catholic belief, this Catechism expounded in general and very optimistic term on the nature of Man, God, Christ, forgiveness, and love. Although this Catechism is not promoted by the

---

[45] Roes in Borgman et al., *Katholieken in De Moderne Tijd: Een Onderzoek Door De Acht Mei Beweging*, 52–53.

Catholic church in the Netherlands any more, many Catholics who were active at that time keep a copy at home and feel that it expresses their beliefs better than the Catechism approved by pope John Paul II that was published in 1992.

We Are the Church

This enthusiasm came to a peak during the pastoral 'council' (the name, and therefore its status, was controversial) in Noordwijkerhout. This pastoral council took place in several sessions from 1966 to 1970. In the spirit of democratization prevalent in Dutch society at the time, the church hierarchy had little say in the overall proceedings, but were rather instructed to listen carefully to the views developed during these sessions by the enthusiastic lay believers and young priests. The aim was to give shape to the local Dutch church, the next step in bringing the church up to date. During the Second Vatican Council, archbishop of the Netherlands Alfrink had played a key role in formulating the importance of the local church as relatively independent from Rome: the pope should be no more than the first among equals rather than the source of infallible pronouncements that should be followed by all Catholics everywhere.[46] In each country, the Catholic church should find its own way of interpreting Christianity in accordance to their needs and insights. In keeping with this spirit, active lay Catholics combining forces with the younger clergy were claiming speaking time in this process.

During this pastoral council, the long awaited papal pronouncements on sexuality and birth control were published in the encyclical Humanae Vitae (1968). For the Dutch Catholics gathered in Noordwijkerhout, this encyclical was a terrible disappointment. It went against the practice and ideas that had developed in the previous years in the Netherlands, of considering sexuality in the light of sound psychology and personal responsibility rather than in terms of sin and prohibitions. It explicitly forbade the use of contraceptives and condemned homosexuality, sex before or without marriage etc. although the language used is less condemning towards other ways of life than Casti Connubii,

> The church, nevertheless, in urging men to the observance of the precepts of the natural law, which it interprets by its constant doctrine, teaches that

---

[46] Van Schaik, *Alfrink. Een Biografie* chapter 9.

each and every marital act must of necessity retain its intrinsic relationship to the procreation of human life.[47]

Nevertheless, the participants of the pastoral council continued on their path to organize the Dutch church according to their own insights, referring to the primacy of the 'local church' doctrine developed during the Second Vatican Council.

The discussions and turbulence generated at the pastoral council in Noordwijkerhout caught the attention of Catholics worldwide and prompted pope Paul VI to write a concerned letter to archbishop Alfrink, asking the bishop what Rome could do to help reinforce his authority.[48] The Catholics gathered in Noordwijkerhout were supremely confident: they were putting the ideas of Second Vatican Council in practice, they were forging their own, democratic, open and inspired local church. Such was their confidence that they sent archbishop Alfrink on a mission to Rome with the message that the Dutch thought it was high time to change the obligation of celibacy for priests.

Alfrink went, against his own personal best judgement but in keeping with his views that each province of the church should develop its own way of interpreting Catholic doctrine. Rome received his message frostily and promptly developed a policy of appointing the most conservative bishops it could find to administrate the rebellious Dutch province.

Roman Machinations and Political Activism

The first of these appointments (1971) was that of bishop Simonis to Rotterdam, who in 1983 moved on to become archbishop of Utrecht. The second of these, and with drastic consequences for the Netherlands as a province of the Catholic church and especially the diocese of Roermond (Limburg), was the appointment of Gijsen. If Alfrink and Dutch Catholics in general could still think of the first appointment as an unfortunate incident, with the second the message was becoming clear: Rome did not like the direction Catholicism in the Netherlands was heading.

After his appointment, Gijsen speedily developed a policy of marginalising all 'progressive' Catholics in his diocese and dismantling the results of the process of democratization. The relations within the college of Dutch bishops became severely disturbed. Gijsen and Simonis, backed by

---

[47] Paul VI, "Humanae Vitae. Encyclical of Pope Paul VI on the Regulation of Birth," 1968, para. 11.

[48] Van Schaik, *Alfrink. Een Biografie*, 435.

Rome, usually managed to get things done in a way that was contrary to the insights and wishes of the other bishops. The Dutch Catholic church became a hopelessly polarized church at least on the level of the formal hierarchy.[49]

Despite the growing polarization, and the frosty attitude of Rome towards Dutch Catholicism, the democratic spirit of the pastoral council led to a growing political awareness among active Catholics. This awareness gave rise to many organizations and even political parties that were characterised by a commitment to pacifism and social justice (e.g. Pax Christi and PPR).[50] These grassroots organizations moreover were fed by the growing Catholic Ecclesiastical Base Community movement inspired by liberation theology in South America. The spirit of 'aggiornamento' that had gripped Dutch Catholics during the pastoral council (despite Humanae Vitae) intermingled with the political notions of change that motivated many people and social movements at the time. The welfare state was at its height, and this led to the expectation that with a concerted effort 'social ills' such as national and international inequality, warfare, sexism and racism could soon be a thing of the past. It was simply a matter of raising awareness and empowering and organising the oppressed. Among active Catholics, liberation theology became an influential framework to formulate a global connectedness uniting against social ills and fighting for justice and equality. It has been said that at this time, the church might have been emptying at an alarming rate (in 1979, 30% of those who had been raised Catholic had left the church,[51] but at the same time there was a tremendous proliferation of small groups where lay Catholics, lay pastors and progressive priests would get together to organize celebrations, educate themselves, raise awareness and promote causes such as feminism, world peace, and social justice.

The Catholics committed to these ideals saw themselves as the vanguard of the future, a force for progress, whereas the neo-conservative faction within the church in their eyes represented an understandable but

---

[49] See the sometimes emotional descriptions in Richard Auwerda, *De Kromstaf Als Wapen: Bisschopsbenoemingen in Nederland* (Baarn: Arbor, 1988); Borgman et al., *Katholieken in De Moderne Tijd: Een Onderzoek Door De Acht Mei Beweging*; Henri Haenen and Hugo Verweij, *De Verscheurde Katholieken* (Weesp: De Haan, 1985).

[50] 'Politieke Partij Radicalen', a party founded by radical Christians in 1968. In 1990 they became part of the Green leftist party, Groen Links. Bert van van Dijk, Liesbeth Huijts, and Trees Verstegen, *Katholieke Vrouwen En Het Feminisme: Een Onderzoek Door De Acht Mei Beweging* (Amersfoort: De Horstink, 1990); van Schaik, *Alfrink. Een Biografie*, chap. 10–11.

[51] Dekker, *God in Nederland, 1966–1996*, 52.

unrealistic attempt to return to the past, backed by a Vatican, especially the Roman Curia, that they perceived as perpetually a few *hundred* years behind current affairs. They expected that the polarization in the church would resolve itself once the reactionary forces saw the inevitability of progress. According to Winkeler the polarization within Dutch Catholicism only came to be fully expressed at all levels and a prevalent issue in the consciousness of lay Catholics with the visit of the pope in 1985: many Catholics boycotted this visit because only the neoconservative faction was given speaking time during this event. Consequently, the pope waved at empty streets while thousands of active Catholics gathered at the Malieveld.[52]

After the shift from 'moralizing to psychologizing', we might summarize the shift in the dominant discourse in Dutch Catholicism that took place afterwards as a move away from the ideal of a hierarchical church and society underpinned by a 'timeless' theology based on 'natural law'. In its place came the ideal of a 'democratic' church and society, legitimated by a historically situated approach to theology and the bible as exemplified in the work of Schillebeeckx and linked to the emergence of movements for greater social justice worldwide. At the same time, forces for restoration within Dutch Catholicism were organized into a distinct church-political faction backed by Rome.

The Visit of the Pope and the Emergence of a Distinct Countermovement

In accounts of the visit of John Paul II to the Netherlands in 1985, it is often contrasted with the visit of the pope in 1953, celebrating the centennial of the re-instalment of the official hierarchy of the church in the Netherlands. In 1953, the streets were full, and the church presented itself in its most magnificent splendour. In 1985, the streets the pope drove through were conspicuously empty, while liberal Catholics gathered by the thousands on the Malieveld[53] in The Hague. They had organized this gathering to protest against the preparations of the papal visit. During these preparations, any attempt by progressive Catholics to present their concerns to the pope was stifled. After more than a decade of polarization following the appointments of Simonis and Gijsen, they wanted a chance to present

---

[52] Winkeler in Borgman et al., *Katholieken in De Moderne Tijd: Een Onderzoek Door De Acht Mei Beweging*, 95.

[53] The Malieveld was the site of many large demonstrations in those years, notably against nuclear weapons.

their concerns to the pope: the stalling process of democratization in the church, the ordination of women, the obligatory celibacy of priests, lay participation in mass, the conservative Catholic teachings on sexuality and ecumenism. After being marginalized during the preparations, they decided to hold their own impromptu meeting, to show the pope 'the other side' of the church in the Netherlands. Out of this gathering the '8th of May Movement' (8 mei beweging) was born. For many years, this movement bundled progressive forces within Dutch Catholicism.

During the years after the visit of the pope, it became more and more clear that the pleas of the 8th of May Movement, although it could count on the sympathy of many Catholics, were falling on deaf ears within the hierarchy of the church. Dutch bishops were primarily held account- able to *Roman* policies, while the topics close to the heart of progressive Catholics who wanted to bring the church 'up to date' were forced to the margins of the church as an institution. The gap between the Catholic church and the general moral outlook and worldview of Dutch Catholics became ever bigger. In 1996, Dekker et al. came to the conclusion that Dutch Catholics were actually *less* orthodox in their beliefs, had less trust in their church and did not think the Christian tradition was very impor- tant for the safeguarding of morality and were much more liberal in their moral outlook than the general Dutch population.[54]

In 2003, the 8th of May Movement disbanded due to a lack of volunteers and young people willing to take over. When he announced the news, chairman Henk Baars admitted that on the level of church politics, their movement had not had a lot of success. According to Baars, the forces of restoration have gained the upper hand in determining church policy in the Netherlands and worldwide.[55]

5. CATHOLICISM IN LIMBURG

There is not a lot of research on the history of Catholicism in Limburg. Generally, the developments within Dutch Catholicism were followed or even instigated in Limburg. Since the Catholic pillar encompassed practi- cally the whole social world of people in Limburg, the changes within this pillar had a big impact on the local landscape. Historical descriptions

---

[54] Dekker, *God in Nederland, 1966–1996*, 57–76.
[55] http://www.katholieknederland.nl/archief/actualiteit/nieuws/index_archief_ juni_2003_17658.html as accessed on 7th october 2005.

of the developments within the church as an institution such as those compiled by Nissen and Ubachs had to rely primarily on the biographies of individual clerics.[56] The summary of developments of Catholicism in Limburg below is based primarily on their overviews, as well as on journalistic accounts and publications in folklore studies.[57]

The diocese of Roermond, geographically equivalent to the present day province of Limburg, emerged out of the diocese of Liège (nowadays situated in Belgium) when Limburg was split up between the Netherlands and the new state of Belgium in 1839. At first, it was officially an 'apostolic vicariate', until the reinstatement of the church hierarchy in the Netherlands in 1853. Limburg is unique in the Netherlands in that it has historically been almost exclusively Catholic: from 1809 until 1947 it hovered between 95 and 98%.[58]

The Catholic church in Limburg from the nineteenth century onwards was characterized by a strong ultramontanism (in contrast to the church in Liège for example). Within the Netherlands, Limburg was the stronghold of Catholicism, the only fully Catholic province. Limburg was a mainly agrarian society, but from 1870 onwards, industrialization and the consequent urbanization produced a new class of impoverished urban labourers. At first, the church had difficulty dealing with this new class of people. Traditionally, it saw itself as a provider of charity for the 'natural poor': old people, orphans, single women. The 'new' poor were classified as paupers, lazy and a threat to society, susceptible to Marxism. Although the papal bills 'De Rerum Novarum' (1891) and 'Graves de Communi Re' (1901) explicitly reacted to this situation by encouraging work that promoted social justice, these bills were given a primarily conservative interpretation in Dutch Limburg. It was only when socialism became a real threat, and secularization among labourers became apparent, that the church reacted by erecting organizations to promote the welfare of

---

[56] Nissen, "Confessionele Identiteit En Regionale Eigenheid"; Nissen, "Constructie En Deconstructie Van Het Katholieke Limburg"; Ubachs, *Handboek Voor De Geschiedenis Van Limburg*.

[57] Carla Wijers, "'In Een Hand De Rozenkrans, in De Andere Hand Een Glas Bier'—De Limburgse Identiteit Onder De Loep," *Studies over De Sociaal-economische Geschiedenis Van Limburg* XLV (2000): 111–134; Jo Wijnen and Theo Koopmanschap, *Hoe Katholiek Is Limburg? De Kerk En Het Bisdom Roermond* (Maasbree: De Lijster, 1981); Math Wijnands, *Op Het Dorp; Leven In De Kleine Limburgse Gemeenschappen* (Maastricht: Uitgeverij TIC, 1998).

[58] Knippenberg, *De Religieuze Kaart Van Nederland, Omvang En Geografische Spreiding Van De Godsdienstige Gezindten Vanaf De Reformatie Tot Heden*, 174.

different groups within an exclusively Catholic framework. Instrumental in the organization of Catholicism in Limburg was the priest Henri Poels.

He promoted a vision of society as a framework for these organizations based on the medieval ideal typical vision of society as consisting of estates ('standen') and professions rather than the Marxist view of society as consisting of different classes. Not the emancipation of the labourers was the goal of these organizations, but to fill in a perceived lack of moral leadership.[59] These organizations, especially for the youth, were very successful in bringing practically every domain of life within the domain and control of the church.

Thus, the fear of socialism gave rise to a strongly organized Catholic pillar, dictating the rhythm to which everybody lived: 70% of the labour force in Limburg was organized in Catholic organizations, even apart from the numerous brotherhoods with their local chapters, societies for the promotion of large families, farmers organizations, local brass bands, etc.

In the 1920s, when the financial equality between public and 'special' (i.e. religious) education became law, all public schools in Limburg where slowly brought under the control of the Catholic church. Until that time, the public schools had in practice been Catholic, because everybody in Limburg was Catholic. However, the new laws gave the church the opportunity to resist any influence from outside: it forbade teachers membership of non-Catholic organizations and also discouraged people to read too much, because they saw this as a threat to the purity of faith. This process continued until the 1950s. Many of the schools were run by congregations, and a council chaired by the local priest oversaw the schools run by lay teachers. The types of schools again mirrored the vision of society as consisting of estates: the gymnasium was for the elite, the HBS for the bourgeoisie and the MULO for the children of labourers and small entrepreneurs. For women, 'housekeeping' schools were set up.

As mentioned before, Catholics in the Netherlands were characterized as having a 'frontier mentality', they were bound by the sense that Catholics needed to unite among themselves to be able to emancipate and overtake the Protestants. In Limburg, this mentality was reinforced by the influx of 'outsiders' when the coal-mines opened in the south of Limburg around 1900. The people of Limburg were self-consciously and proudly Catholic. From the nineteenth century onwards, moreover, the bishop of Roermond had been someone 'from Limburg', confirming the identity

[59] Ubachs, *Handboek Voor De Geschiedenis Van Limburg*, 396–397.

of Limburg as separate from the rest of the Netherlands; because of its homogeneously Catholic population in a country dominated by Protestants, and because of its many distinct dialects and traditions.[60]

The percentage of 'secular priests' (as opposed to priests belonging to a congregation or monastic order) was very high in Limburg, higher than in the other provinces. This meant that the local diocese could enforce its policies very effectively on the local level. All in all, it is clear that the Catholic church had by the 1950s managed to make itself omnipresent in people's lives. Children would go to church every day before school, adults at least once a week. Through the teaching and enforcement of sexual morality, the church penetrated into the heart of the family. Leisure time was spent within contexts organized by the church. Reading materials (magazines, newspapers, even libraries) were controlled by the church. 'Religion' was the first subject mentioned on any school report. Together with the elite, it enforced an authoritarian society, where the value of 'knowing your place' was considered most important. Some historians describe Limburg as a veritable clerocracy.[61]

After the 1950s, the 'clerocracy' crumbled. Under bishop Moors, who became bishop in 1959, young critics of the church were given a chance to 'modernize' the organization of the diocese. Priests influenced by the new discourses tried to reorganize parish life in keeping with ideas of democratization and the importance of the personal conscience of people. Although many priests received these changes enthusiastically, there was also a minority (about 10% of the priests in Limburg) that organized itself to resist the modernization of the church. One of these priests was Johannes Gijsen, who was later appointed bishop.[62]

Meanwhile, in Limburg as in the rest of the Netherlands, the pillarized organizations were co-opted by the welfare state, and the influence of the priests on these organizations steadily became less, or at least different as they implemented their own democratic ideals. The number of callings dropped dramatically, and at the end of the sixties, beginning of the seventies many priests left the priesthood. On the other hand, the rise of the welfare state and the economic prosperity meant that more and more spheres of society emerged that resisted control by the church. In schools and hospitals, municipal councils and even in church affairs,

---

[60] Nissen, "Constructie En Deconstructie Van Het Katholieke Limburg," 82–83.
[61] Ibid., 86.
[62] Ibid., 93.

professionalization and the generally rising level of education meant that priests were no longer seen as the ultimate authority on every subject under the sun.

Gijsen was a surprise appointment by Rome that ripped the Dutch church apart, and broke the heart of many liberal Catholics in Limburg. Since the restoration of the hierarchy in 1853, the procedure in the Netherlands had been that the diocesan chapter would give the pope a shortlist whenever a new bishop would have to be appointed. In 1973 this shortlist had been prepared after a careful consultation of Catholics at all levels of the church. However, the pope ignored the shortlist and appointed the young and relatively inexperienced Johannes Gijsen, known for his outspoken conservative views on the role and morality of the church. Gijsen then proceeded to dismantle every form of democracy and lay participation that had become institutionalized over the years.[63]

Gijsen's agenda, and later also that of archbishop Simonis, was to push the paradigm of the church as a sacred institution, with the ordained priest as the central figure for the administration of the sacraments to lay believers. Where liberal theology had deconstructed the theology of the sacraments by situating them historically and ethically, reframing them as 'celebrations', the paradigm of Gijsen saw the sacraments as the framework for an unchanging moral order propagated by an eternal church. His attitude was 'love it or leave it', something that went directly against the conviction that had grown among progressive Catholics, expressed forcefully during the pastoral council, that 'the people are the church'. Gijsen however, referred back to the strong ultramontane tradition of Limburg: Rome is the church.

Many priests and pastoral workers in Limburg, as well as many of the orders and congregations working in the organizations left over from the pillarization, were steeped in the ideal of 'the people are the church', and had developed their ideas and pastoral practices throughout the ideological shift described in the earlier part of this chapter. This was also the way many priests and pastors had been trained at the renewed vocational pastoral and theological training school (HTP, later UTP) in Limburg. This institute trained people to become lay pastors, as well as those who would go on to become ordained priests. When Gijsen became bishop, he refused to employ non-ordained pastors, and set up his own seminary to train priests according to his paradigm.

Meanwhile, the emptying of the church pews and the out-flux of priests, as well as the professionalization of the pillarized institutions had irrevocably changed the place of the church in public life in Limburg to an extent that Gijsen proved to be powerless to change. In the eyes of many people, 'progress' meant that the church should know its place, rather than the church dictating them to know their place. The resistance to Gijsen's agenda was at times vicious, while Gijsen showed he was not afraid to use everything within his power to push his agenda.[64]

In the early nineties, Gijsen was replaced by Wiertz, who seems to promote cooperation with the more 'progressive factions' and a respectful involvement of lay believers, while at the same time adhering to a Rome dictated policy.[65] In this policy, the 'proper' administration of the sacraments and the special status of the ordained priest is again a central issue and pastoral workers are only slowly and grudgingly allowed to work for the diocese. In later chapters, this issue will be discussed as it comes up during the interviews and around death and dying. Although the pain of the polarization is lessening, it is clear that the forces of renewal have been contained within the paradigm of the hierarchical church as a sacred institution.

When Gijsen became bishop, he was sure that he could rekindle the 'fundamentally Catholic' nature of the people of Limburg. However, as historians and folklore specialists have pointed out, to the people of Limburg their Catholic identity is not so much bound up with the Catholic doctrine, but is rather a matter of adhering to certain traditions.[66] Through his policy of training volunteers and integrating parishes, at the time of my fieldwork bishop Wiertz seemed to be a little more successful in making local communities care about their church again, if only because they want to prevent their parish church from disappearing altogether. At the same time, the diocese was also developing many initiatives for Catholic

---

[64] Wijnen and Koopmanschap, *Hoe Katholiek Is Limburg? De Kerk En Het Bisdom Roermond*, 132–137, 151–152.

[65] The reasons for his Gijsen's resignation are vague (health), but generally people seem to think he had made too many enemies among the council of bishops of the Netherlands. In the background, a scandal about sexual relations between staff and students of 'his' seminary Rolduc also played a role.

[66] Nissen, "Confessionele Identiteit En Regionale Eigenheid"; Nissen, "Constructie En Deconstructie Van Het Katholieke Limburg"; Wijers, "'In Een Hand De Rozenkrans, in De Andere Hand Een Glas Bier'—De Limburgse Identiteit Onder De Loep."

youth, latching onto the enthusiasm generated by events such as Catholic World Youth day. Following up via the Internet, it seems these initiatives are successful. For these young Catholics, the polarization within the church is usually not an issue that is part of their life world.

6. CONCLUDING REMARKS

The uniquely Dutch phenomenon of pillarization meant that Catholic organizations penetrated almost every aspect of life, and was in a unique position to mold people's habitus. At the same time, this high degree of organization also meant that post-Vatican II changes were instituted relatively quickly and irreversibly: when Rome attempted to undo some of these changes, they met very strong resistance. However, as will become clear in the next chapters, the dispositions created by the pre-Vatican II Catholic discourse linger on long after the emptying of the churches.

During the immediate post-war years, the organizations of the Catholic pillar and the Catholic church itself were determined to perfect the social and spiritual mechanisms by which Catholic believers could be kept safe from modernity. In this effort, the 'mechanism of the sacraments' as a means to spiritually and socially exclude people was the cornerstone. However, during the fifties, internal criticism started to question the iron logic of this mechanism. Many Catholic intellectuals wanted the Catholic church to be more open to modernity, to political ideologies that strived for social justice, to other religions, to new developments in science. According to these intellectuals, the spiritual life of the church, although rich in display, was poor in content.

The biggest ideological shift was prepared by Catholic intellectuals influenced by psychology, psychoanalysis and the French 'nouvelle théologie' during the late fifties. This shift emerged fully and became the basis of policy within the organizations of the Catholic pillar during the sixties and seventies. The church's attempt to control and regulate sexuality became the main butt of criticism of the 'spiritual liberators'. By positioning the psychological health of the individual as something that *preceded* a morally good and spiritually healthy life, the church was convinced to relinquish its control over the individual moral life of believers to (lay) 'professionals'. The Catholic policy to ensure 'moral health' shifted from the containment and control of 'sin' via the mechanism of the sacraments, to a policy that was based on openness and sensitivity to people's psychological make-up to enable them to become more 'fully human' and inspire them to live as good Catholics. The professionals who succeeded the clergy in the many organizations of the Catholic pillar, came to see the 'mechanism of the sacraments' itself as morally wrong.

An optimistic view on human nature came to dominate Dutch Catholicism, most fully expressed in the New Cathechism (Nieuwe Katechismus). This optimistic view was also translated into a political agenda as liberation theology inspired many Catholics to become socially and politically active and feminist critiques were launched within the Catholic church as a worldwide movement. Democratization was the key word, promoting equality to realize the Kingdom of God on earth. Kennedy has described theses changes within the Catholic pillar within the context of the changes in Dutch society as a whole, remarking that these changes were facilitated by the attitude of the authorities at the time: they felt very strongly that change was inevitable, and therefore gave a lot of room to a younger generation with new ideas.[67]

With the polarization of the Dutch church into a 'progressive' camp and a strongly Rome-oriented conservative camp, the forces of renewal definitively ground to a halt halfway the eighties, and the progressive camp has been losing power and membership ever since. The optimistic, free style New Cathechism was replaced by a more traditional, hard to read Cathechism in 1995, a translation of the Cathechism published by Rome in 1992.

The Catholics that were active in the renewals of the sixties and seventies are getting older, and attracting young people with the same degree of practical commitment is proving to be a hard task. Meanwhile, bishops who are held to strict account by Rome determine the face of the 'official church'. This has resulted in a dual reality: the hierarchy maintains a conservative façade, and manages to stimulate mainly conservative seminaries, while a substantial part of priests, pastoral workers and volunteers in the church can be described as 'progressive'.[68]

The 'church as a community of believers' perspective is more and more brought within the bounds set by the 'church as a sacred institution'

---

[67] Kennedy, "Nieuw Babylon in Aanbouw."

[68] for example, they see the church more as a community of believers than as a sacred institution and see pastoral abilities as more important than being ordained Ton Bernts, *Pal Voor De Kerk. Vrijwilligerswerk in Parochies*, vol. 3 (Nijmegen: Nijmegen University Press, 1998); Tony Watling, "'Official' Doctrine and 'Unofficial' Practices: The Negotiation of Catholicism in a Netherlands Community," *Journal for the Scientific Study of Religion* 40, no. 4 (2001): 573–590.

paradigm and has thus lost its momentum to instigate further renewal and democratization. My impression during fieldwork was that the old activists simply do not find the fight worth fighting anymore, or feel defeated. To the younger generation, the message of Rome has been brought across successfully: if you do not like it, leave it. Do not try to change it. The contrast with the spirit of renewal of the sixties and early seventies could not be greater.

Although the Catholic church in the Netherlands often presented itself as a 'minority religion', it was and still is numerically the largest denomination in the Netherlands. In Limburg, Catholicism has been the majority religion for centuries, and is closely bound up with the identity of 'being a Limburger'. What this means will become clear in the next chapters.

CHAPTER THREE

NARRATIVES OF THE PAST, PROGRESS AND POLARIZATION

1. INTRODUCTION

In the literature on the changes within Dutch Catholicism and the secularization of Dutch society, the narratives of the believers who used to fill the pews of the churches do not really have a place. How did the people who were the subjects of the immense efforts that resulted in the dense network of organizations of the Catholic pillar experience all the changes? How did the place of religion in their lives change as a consequence of the crumbling of this pillar? How critical, or nostalgic, are they towards the Catholic past? Many of their narratives have been gathered in documentaries, in (auto) biographical books, and in fiction.[1] There are very few studies that systematically examine the narratives of lay believers on the changes within Dutch Catholicism to reflect on the nature of these changes and the consequences they have for the present day nature and place of religion in society.[2]

This chapter describes the 'narratives of the past' of the generation that was born before the Second World War in Welden. They came of age and had their families at the triumphant height of post-war Catholicism described in the previous chapter, and witnessed the changes that took place in Dutch Catholicism starting in the sixties. It starts with a comparison: on one side, there are the representations of 'the past' of active Catholic intellectuals who were part of the spirit of renewal unleashed after the Second Vatican Council. They emphasize that change was inevitable. This representation will be compared to the narratives of the elder generation: did they also see change as inevitable? Was their religious life really so unbearable according to themselves? (Sections 2 and 3). Section 4 will describe the 'local face' of the polarization within Dutch Catholicism,

---

[1] Kerklaan, *Zodoende Was De Vrouw Maar Een Mens Om Kinderen Te Krijgen, 300 Brieven over Het Roomse Huwelijksleven.*; Jaap de Rooij, *Waartoe Waren Wij Op Aarde* (Nijmegen: Valkhof, 1999); van Schaik, *Alfrink. Een Biografie.*

[2] For an exception see Peter van Rooden, "The Strange Death of Dutch Christendom," in *Secularisation in the Christian World*, ed. Callum G. Brown and Michael Snape (Farnham: Ashgate, 2010).

and especially the Roermond diocese already described in the previous chapter. Section 5 describes the narratives that emerged when I asked the respondents to compare the world they grew up in with the present, in terms of values and lifestyle.

The term 'narratives of the past', the title of this chapter, is intended to indicate that I take the stories that people told me not as the uncomplicated representation of attitudes and moral orientations in the past, but as the present-day result of a process of making sense of the changing historical landscape in which they lived their lives. The assumption is that the narratives expressed in the individual interviews are part of a body of *shared* narratives. Although they were at that moment created for my benefit, these narratives emerged and evolved throughout the contexts of interaction my respondents participated in: from discussions between husband and wife on how to raise their children, via conversations with a family member or close acquaintance who is a member of the clergy, to discussions among colleagues, neighbours, friends and community-members.

The interview material that formed the basis of the descriptions here resulted from 15 in-depth, open-ended interviews with respondents of the generation born before World War II, most of them living in Welden for the greater part of their life. The interviews lasted about two hours, sometimes longer. Often, I would also join them for lunch and informal conversation ensued (not recorded). Because I was mainly interested in people's own narratives about the changing religious practices and moral orientations they experienced during their lifetime, I structured my questions loosely around the personal biography of the respondent. At the start of the interview I asked people to describe to me the world they grew up in and the role of the church in their daily life. Follow-up questions focused on the role of priests and chaplains in their life, the changes in the church and local parish life, how they raised their own children, the widening gap between the doctrines of the church and general moral consensus in Dutch society, and the comparison between the past and the present.

Overcoming Hesitations, the Dynamics of Interviewing and the Burden of Secrets

For several reasons, I had some difficulty finding respondents. One reason was that some people were insecure whether they would be a good source of information for me, because they did not consider themselves very knowledgeable about 'church matters' or because they thought I was mainly interested in evaluating whether they were good believers. It took some effort on my part to reassure people that it was *their* story I was interested in, and that I was not affiliated to the church.

Another reason was that in Limburg rural communities, locals usually ignore non-locals as partners for conversation. When I started my research, the key informants I contacted warned me about this. Having grown up in Limburg, I was already aware of this difficulty. Walking down the road and greeting people in Dutch can illustrate this: many locals, especially older people, will not take the trouble to return the greeting. But greeting them with a local greeting using the proper tone and inflection usually gets a response. Generally, locals assume that no outsider is interested in them and their world and if they are interested, they will not be able to understand. Anybody who is not part of their own familiar world is therefore ignored. Furthermore, religion was a touchy and private subject for most people, both because of the polarization within the church and because of the control over the 'purity' of people's beliefs and moral life that used to be exercised by the church.

To understand these barriers it is important to understand the sentiments that go with being part of a local community in Limburg, the 'gemeinsjap', in dialect, 'gemeenschap' in Dutch. To the people of Welden and the surrounding villages, community is an irreplaceable and incomparable fact of life. Community is not only a feeling; it is a reality, a fact. Of course, this is so for many rural communities, but in Limburg it is part of an identity of 'being a Limburger' and therefore being 'different' from the rest of the Netherlands. The Limburg dialects, an important boundary marker, differ from one village to another. Only in contrasting themselves with 'de Hollanders' (the Dutch) do people from different communities in Limburg feel united.[3]

At first, the contrasts between myself and the respondents often created an almost insurmountable barrier: urban versus rural, old versus young, university educated versus an education that sometimes went no further than elementary school, someone from outside the local community versus someone from inside. In chapter 1, I introduced the concept of the 'production of locality' by Appadurai. In finding respondents, I was confronted with the strength of this sense of place: in order to be trusted as a conversation partner, people have to be allowed to enter into the

---

[3] Wijers, "'In Een Hand De Rozenkrans, in De Andere Hand Een Glas Bier'—De Limburgse Identiteit Onder De Loep."

'domain of the familiar' by those who form part of it. In my case, this was done through recognizing that I had grown up in the south of Limburg and had links with local history via my maternal family.

In the end, and through the intervention of a gate keeper (the secretary of the old people's association), I did find enough respondents. The interviews themselves often took on their own dynamic: through telling their life story, subjects were covered that people had sometimes never discussed with anyone else. I was sometimes told very personal, painful and private stories. Often, people said towards the end of the interview that they had not intended to tell this much to me, and asked me not to use them. My respondents felt that these painful stories happened only to *them*, that nobody else had had these experiences, and they did not want these stories to become public. But then, why did they tell them? And why did they sound so familiar to me, why did it seem I had heard them so many times already? Why did I immediately recognize the pain that they felt?[4]

In Kahn and Cannell, the dynamics of an open-ended interview are compared to the therapeutic interview, since in both situations it is especially the *non-judgmental context* created by the interviewer that encourages the respondent to open up, by eliminating the need to defend oneself.[5] This non-judgmental context is unusual in daily social life, and in my experience it does indeed lead people to open up and start to enjoy telling their stories. Besides, dwelling on memories and personal opinions builds up its own momentum, and creates an atmosphere of familiarity and intimacy between the interviewer and the interviewee.

Although I reassured people that I would guarantee their anonymity, I did not quite know how to handle the responsibility that came with being entrusted with these stories. Somehow, the very private nature of the grief expressed in these stories asked for a response, a connection that extended beyond the interview situation. I recognized their stories because my family from my mother's side comes from Limburg (although not from Welden). But to redress the balance was impossible: ultimately, the intimacy created in the interview situation is a false one, whatever the common ground between interviewer and interviewee may be. There is a

---

[4] I discuss this issue much more extensively in the article Knibbe, K. "Secrets, Gossip and Betrayal: Doing Fieldwork on the Role of Religion in Moral Orientation in a Dutch Catholic Province". *Fieldwork in Religion* 6, nr. 2 (2010): 151–167.

[5] Robert L. Kahn and Charles. F. Cannell, *The Dynamics of Interviewing. Theory, Technique and Cases.* (New York: Wiley, 1967).

definite power-relationship present in the interview, since it is the inter-viewer who defines the context and the purpose.[6] Besides, it was not part of my role to help them to come to terms with these stories.

In short, I felt guilty for being entrusted with these stories without being in the position to reciprocate this trust. Although one might argue that open interviews grant more space to the respondents to set the pace, context and topic (as opposed to structured or closed interviews) the sense of empowerment that comes from 'telling one's own story' can quickly turn into a sense of deflation when attention turns once more to the day-to-day life. Although I tried to end each interview with more reciprocal talk, letting them question me about my life and background, it was hard to shake off the feeling that somehow, I had tricked them into telling me details of their life they had not wanted to reveal by using my own knowledge and background.

In writing this chapter, I decided to leave out those stories that were obviously still painful to tell for my respondents. Instead, I pay more attention to some stories that were very similar, but less painful for the respondent to tell. In fact, they were part of the repertoire of stories they *wanted* to tell and it was noticeable that they were already polished and smooth, they had been told more often. The incidents around which the painful stories revolved will be summarized.

Whether they were still painful or not, they have in common that they show another, individualized, side of the coin of the shared narratives about the past: they concerned events that people had tried to forget because they were too shameful, or too painful or both, related to the mechanisms of control by the church. These stories were similar to those in the collection of letters edited by Marga Kerklaan.[7] These letters were written by Catholic women from all over the Netherlands in response to a television program discussing the question whether the church's rules on sexuality could be seen as the cause of the massive emptying of the churches starting in the sixties. So even though they seem private, shame-ful and extremely individual, they do show an important side of the domi-nance of the church: its power to keep the suffering caused out of the public domain, its power to summon mechanisms of social control to its

---

[6] Steinar Kvale, *Interviews: An Introduction to Qualitative Research Interviewing.* (London: Sage, 1996), 126.

[7] Kerklaan, *Zodoende Was De Vrouw Maar Een Mens Om Kinderen Te Krijgen, 300 Brieven over Het Roomse Huwelijksleven.*

cause. People are attuned to the mechanisms of control until this day, censoring their stories and feeling ashamed about them.

2. REPRESENTATIONS OF THE PAST

Reading the written historical representations cited in chapter 2 one could almost believe that most, if not all, Catholics were involved in the changes they describe, caught up in the climate of renewal that prevailed after Vatican II. As I mentioned in chapter 2, many of these historical accounts were written by progressive Catholics. Most of them share the view of the 'spiritual liberators' that the changes in Dutch Catholicism were an inevitable consequence of the dissatisfactions widely felt among lay Catholics in the Netherlands and in Limburg. This representation of the state of Dutch Catholicism at the end of the fifties also dominates a report commissioned in the late fifties by the diocese of Roermond.[8] This report signalled a growing dissatisfaction with the church, and especially with the authoritarian relations between the clergy and lay believers and the 'deadness' of ritual life. It mentioned the growing alienation between priests and the faithful, summed up in the expression 'the church belongs to the priest'. It concluded that beliefs were badly internalized, that there was a growing revulsion against 'moralizing', and a tendency to relativize the rules and regulations of Catholicism rather than understanding them as timeless and absolute, especially with regard to sexuality.

Significantly, this report is mostly based on interviews with local *professionals*: social workers, teachers, doctors etc. Although this report ties in with the descriptions in the previous chapter, it throws little or no light on how things were perceived at the 'grassroots' level. Of course, it is also doubtful whether one can speak of a 'detoriating' level of Catholicism: was faithfulness to the church in a better condition before? In every era, people complain about moral standards losing their timeless and absolute certainty, and there is no reason to assume that relations between the priest and his flock were better in earlier times, or sexual mores more in line with the church guidelines. In fact, it was only due to the organizational efforts developed in the twentieth century that these guidelines

---

[8] J.H. Huijts, *Geloof En Leven in De Kerk. Beschouwingen over De Godsdienstige Situatie Onder De Katholieken in Limburg, Naar Aanleiding Van Een Meningen-onderzoek*, ed. L.C. Baas, vol. 2 (Hilversum: Landelijk centrum voor katholieke actie en het Nederlands Pastoraal Instituut i.s.w. met uitgeverij Paul Brand, 1960).

came to be implemented more uniformly among all Catholics, and the clergy was able to enforce their regime consistently.

However, what *can* be concluded from reading this report is that the ideals of the growing class of professionals in the south of Limburg conflicted with the closed and tightly organized Catholic world regulated by the clergy, and that the diocese had resolved to give these dissatisfactions a place in its decision making by commissioning a social research in which not only the clergy was represented. This was a revolutionary change. Still, the world in which people in rural Limburg lived was Catholic in all its aspects and even those complaining professionals clearly wished to remain Catholic as well, they just wanted to 'let in some air'. This report was brought out before Vatican II, and if it really does accurately indicate the mood among professionals in Limburg at the time, it is not hard to understand why the changes announced by pope John XXIII were enthusiastically welcomed and developed by the Dutch Catholics.[9]

Taking these descriptions as a point of departure, one would expect the pre-war generation of Welden to have some narratives of the dissatisfaction with the church they had felt at the time when the Catholic regime was still firmly in place. That they, too, had felt that change was inevitable, that things could not continue the way they were. Alternatively, one could assume that being raised before these changes, the older generation would be critical of present day society and later generations.

Neither of these assumptions turned out to be correct. In the narratives of the older generation, it appears that in the late fifties nobody could have predicted that the closed Catholic world they knew would change so radically, nor that the church would end up taking such a marginal space in the public sphere, and often also in the private sphere of people's lives. As they remember it, it was a time when conforming to be a good Catholic was very important. Obedience, honesty, good manners and knowing your place were the prime values. 'Stubbornness', talking back and lying were severely punished.

The first part of the interviews tells the same story again and again. All school children had to go to church every morning before going to school, the children who had to come from the outlying hamlets walking miles on an empty stomach. They discussed their teachers, the friars and nuns in the boys' school and girls' school, and how strict or friendly they were. They mentioned that 'religion' was the first and most important subject

---

[9] See previous chapter and Coleman, *The Evolution of Dutch Catholicism, 1958–1974*.

on the report cards from school. They remembered the merits you could collect by going to church regularly during the week and on Sunday, and the rewards if you had collected enough merits. Some told me proudly about an uncle who was a priest (heeroom) and what he had to say about the children. They memorized going to confession every fortnight and not knowing what to confess and the trouble they would get into because of being 'wilful' or disobedient.

They remembered how important the doctor, the dentist, the mayor and the priest were, how far away and unreachable. How happy but at the same time fearful they would be when one of these important people paid attention to them. In adolescence, they remembered the courses for young adults they attended, taught by the Redemptorists; how they fired up their faith, and warned them of the sins they could commit. They joked about the bewilderment about the exact nature of these sins: "we thought you could already get pregnant by a little kiss!" The fun they used to have as girls among each other. The bewilderment some of the men had felt when they noticed that priests or friars were not as holy as they appeared to be and made sexual advances towards them. How poor people were, how hard life was, how big the families. How they used to pray in hard times, how their mother taught them to pray, and how it helped them to be able to bear those hard times, and even the war.

These stories of Catholic childhood and young adulthood are comparable to those told by the immediate post-war-generation or those born during the war. Embarrassed, some people commented that I had probably heard all those details many times before. Their stories were matter-of-fact descriptions of things that were so familiar to them that they sometimes did not know where to start describing. They did not give any opinion about it, except to apologize for not being able to explain things better, why things were as they were. When I asked how they felt about it, if they thought it was good or bad the way things were, they would shrug their shoulders and say: "that was just the way things were. The times were different then, you did things for different reasons". In their narratives there is no sense of a growing dissatisfaction naturally leading up to the changes in the sixties. Rather, as we will see later, my respondents saw these changes as appearing quite suddenly.

Inner Rebellion: You Do Not Go to Church for the Priest, You Go for God

Nevertheless, criticism of the church and the clergy was common, particularly among the lower classes. This was expressed in jokes and set expressions, such as the joke about the priest saying to the mayor: "if you keep them poor, I will keep them stupid" ('houd jij ze arm, dan houd ik ze dom'). The proximity of the mines offering employment opportunities to many men of the rural communities meant that even in Welden socialist criticisms of society made some converts.

Some respondents told how they resented the intrusion of the church into their lives. However, it rarely made a difference in the behaviour of outward compliance to the conventions dictated by the church. Nor did any narratives emerge wherein people described themselves as taking the initiative to change things. Criticism and rebellion were defensive and left the status quo intact. There was no place to go, no movement to link up with, where their criticisms could be heard. Social ostracism threatened those who openly defied the moral order of the church. The few 'reds' were seen as God-less and immoral men.

Only one man was openly critical about the efforts of the church to imprint its moral authority on peoples' lives. He attributes this critical attitude to his experience in the army, fighting in the Indies for the Dutch government against the independence movement. The men coming back from this colonial struggle (which people in the Netherlands still never refer to as a 'war', but as 'police actions') were often disillusioned, both because of what they had seen and experienced there, and because they did not come back as heroes: the Indies became the sovereign state of Indonesia, gaining independence from the Netherlands in 1949.

> When I came back from the Indies, we had a chaplain who was very fanatical. He organized all these groups, and my mother wanted me to join. I ended up at a prayer group. They were always talking about sin and confession, in a very heavy manner; it mattered a great deal to them. I thought: 'well, you talk, I will not mind'. Then the chaplain asked me: 'Hub, you just came from the Indies, how did you think about these things over there'? So I said: 'Let me tell this to you Mr. chaplain, I'm most sorry about the sins I did not commit'. The chaplain was furious! [Laughs] He also had these attendance charts, which you had to take every time you went to attend the prayer group, and they would put a stamp on it for you so you could prove your attendance. I did not like that. When they asked for my chart, I said: 'I will buy a ticket when I go to the cinema, but not when I go to church!' I had been in the East for three years, and there you learned not to agree with everything other people thought was the right thing.... Three days later, he [the chaplain] was at my mother's house when I came home from work. I looked at her face and I saw that something was wrong. I thought: what is he going to complain of now. And then it came out: 'you're so wilful, and contrary in your behaviour, and now this thing with the chart, I do not like it'. He was an authoritarian, thought that he could dictate people. 'I really

do not like it'. And I said, 'well, one thing is important Mr. chaplain, and that is whether I like it. And I do not like your pathetic little clubs, so you will not see me there anymore. But I will not interfere, and I will not go to another church' [i.e. he would continue attending the parish church rather than going to another church, which would be an open act of rebellion]....
That was something that I really did not agree with: that the priest, along with the mayor, acted like they were the conscience of the community. It's a good thing that it's not like that anymore.

This man had recourse to other frames of reference, which put the church in a different light than the other respondents—even now—, saw it. He saw the mechanisms of control clearly, and resented them: the charts, the house visits, and the 'examinations of sin'. He was an exception to the rule, and even he presented his description of the Catholic world he grew up in with the words: 'that's the way it was, we did not think of questioning it'. His rebellion was against the chaplain, not against the church or its doctrines.

He was one of the few men who said that he had had the feeling that things were going to change soon, that the church could not continue like this, that people would not accept this kind of control for much longer. Generally, there were very few stories in which people openly challenged the authority of the church, even when it was exercised in a way that was very painful or even destructive to their personal life. Consider the story of a miner's widow who got pregnant before marriage:[10]

She broke off her engagement to the son of a rich farmer when she fell in love with another boy, from a poor family. Her mother refused to give her consent to the marriage. Nevertheless, she sought employment in his village to be nearer to him. They were engaged for years, seeing each other occasionally, whenever her boss allowed it. But their parents did not allow them to save any of their salaries to be able to set up a household together. One day on their Sunday walk they could no longer 'contain themselves' and she got pregnant. Although they barely had " 'a cup and a saucer' to eat from, the only acceptable solution was marriage".

Her mother made it a point to let her daughter know how much she felt that she had disgraced the family: she ordered coffee with buns and flowers to give the marriage a more 'decent' appearance, and then sent the newly wed couple the bill, which they could not pay. She also told

---

[10] Although this is the kind of 'painful' story that would inadvertently come out, this particular narrative was obviously well worked out and had been told many times before. She clearly wanted me to hear it and retell it.

her daughter that she went to put the bridal flowers at a statue of Mary to pray for her sins. The parish chaplain too, made his disapproval clear: when the couple had found a house to rent, he decided the house should be given to a more 'worthy couple' who had been engaged for a long time (without getting indecently pregnant). The landlord went along with the suggestion of the chaplain.

Later, when her husband had found another house, he made sure a contract was signed immediately. When the chaplain again tried to prevent them from moving in, on the grounds that it was not appropriate for a miner's family to live on the posh main street, he found out he was too late.

When I asked her whether she was upset at the church for causing her so much trouble, she replied: "Yes, for some time, I refused to go to church. But my husband would always say: you do not go to the church for the priest; you go for God. And of course, he was right". During her marriage, the priest came yearly to enquire when the next child would be due. They did their best to 'live naturally' (not using periodic retention or other mechanisms of birth-control), and had ten children.

In this story, which was unique only in terms of the frankness with which it was told, we can see how the church was able to rally social pressure and disapproval. Although this woman and her husband were convinced they were justified in wanting to set up a household together in the face of so much disapproval, she did not question the general principles on which the church was acting, even in the retelling of the story to me. In fact, her personal faith, but even more that of her husband, sustained her against the social disapproval she faced and helped her conform. One reason why she was able to stand up to her mother was that she reasoned: "if God is love, that means he wouldn't want us to suffer like my mother is making me suffer by not letting us get married". Her husband told her that they were not to blame for the shameful wedding, because they had tried to live decently for years, trying to win approval, so it was 'they' (their parents, other authorities) who were to blame for the breakdown of decency.

In these narratives, it seems the church's insistence on adhering to the moral rules invoked the countermovement of a personalized, purer faith that did not care about appearances, and that turned towards prayer and the saints for strength. In these narratives, personal faith gives the power to be able to ignore or circumvent social conventions by pointing out that the 'right spirit' was lacking. However, the legitimacy of these conventions is not denied, even now.

The Mechanism of the Sacraments and the Production of Secrets

The painful stories that came out during the interviews usually had to do with the (threat of) exclusion from the sacraments wielded by chaplains and priests. Although it was not my aim to elicit stories that would rake up painful personal events, they *were* significant in the context of my research. They contrast sharply with the general efforts of the narratives of the past that people tried to impress on me: that although the past might seem 'bad' by present day standards, "it was just the way things were", a state of affairs nobody had an opinion about. The painful stories show how this state of affairs was created and maintained, and the casualties that fell by the wayside in maintaining it. Instrumental to enforcing this state of affairs was not only the cooperation between the church and the 'notables' of a community, such as the mayor, landlords and the doctor, as in the story of the miner's wife above, but also the threat of being excluded from the sacraments. The causal chain of events implied by this exclusion was instilled in people from elementary school onwards.

Exclusion from the sacraments meant that one was living in a state of sin. Living in a state of sin meant that if one should die suddenly, heaven (and the church graveyard) would be closed to you. In the same vein, children who had not had the stain of original sin removed by baptism were barred from heaven and had to be buried outside hallowed grounds. Some people remember being taught to do emergency baptisms to prevent this tragedy, especially during the war.

Some of the key-informants I interviewed (usually professionals of a younger generation whose views will be central to the next chapter) relished telling stories of women who were refused absolution ('getting the shutter', see chapter 2, section 2). After 'getting the shutter', a woman would often not dare to go into church during mass again. The key-informants who were eager to tell these stories are firmly on the side of progressive Catholicism, and they used these stories to explain their allegiance to the liberal faction, and to condemn anyone using the image of a 'punishing God' to bolster church authority.

However, the pre-war generation central to this chapter did not use these kinds of stories to argue their own position with regard to the church. They did not relish telling these stories. Rather, they had wanted to forget about them, treating them as painful personal experiences. In the interviews, I did not hear of anyone 'getting the shutter' personally, but the threat was in the background, connected to the refusal to have more children. Other incidents around which these stories revolved had to do with the burial of babies that died in childbirth: mothers often had no idea where their baby was buried, since this was done in the middle of the night while she was still exhausted from the labor.[11] As recounted earlier, getting pregnant before marriage also caused much shame and pain.

Although priests reportedly always pushed for more children, among themselves women apparently had different standards: in the interviews they sometimes commented on the inconsiderateness and lack of self-control of the husband of a woman worn out with too many children: "he should have the sense to leave her alone". "They [the clergy] made it impossible for us", is an often-heard complaint. Although couples tried to comply with the rules that the priests and chaplains instilled in them, in retrospect they all agree that in the control of sexuality and in childbearing the demands this placed on women and married life in general often surpassed the boundaries of what was bearable.

3. CHANGES

Not surprisingly, the changes with regard to birth control were welcomed as a relief. Nobody thought it a good idea to return to the days when birth control was forbidden. This change, unlike other changes was seen as inevitable in hindsight, and bishop Bekkers is fondly remembered by these people (see chapter 2). Not only did he tell people that it was their own responsibility to decide the number of children they would have, he also suggested that the church had been too harsh and insensitive in forcing parents to bury their unbaptized babies outside hallowed ground.

Other changes within the church, however, were not seen as inevitable even in hindsight. Significantly, when I asked about Vatican II in relation to the changes in the church and church life, I usually only got a blank stare as reply. When I mentioned some examples that would have had an immediate impact, such as the switch to Dutch and the priest celebrating mass facing the parish, they remembered, but not as something major: "oh, yes, we had to get used to it".

Nevertheless, there was one issue that people could get quite indignant about, even now: the loosening in the behaviour of priests. Although

---

[11] This was changed in the canon law in 1983, but even before that, babies and others who died 'in a state of sin' were allowed to be buried in hallowed ground already before that time. See http://www.geschiedenis24.nl/andere-tijden/afleveringen/2001-2002/Ongewijde-aarde.html accessed 14th of June 2012.

during the interviews they all agreed that priests were human too and should be allowed to marry, they remembered that at the time, it was quite a shock when priests started behaving more informally, and stopped presenting themselves as a-sexual, superhuman authorities on everything to do with God, heaven and hell. Perhaps because people felt that the church had placed such heavy demands on them, there is a strong sense of indignation in the narratives about clergy who 'suddenly' did not live according to their own rules anymore in the sixties and seventies. It caused people to look at the obligations and restrictions of the church with more scepticism:

> Three chaplains got out [left the clergy], two got married, and people were saying: hey, what's this, what does the church have to say about our life, why should we go to church every morning? Many people were really upset about it. So those two got married, and the priest would also go out some-times, among the people. So people would comment: look at him, he's car-rying the young girls' handbags [they would give it to him when they were invited to dance]. But for me, I would say: so what? He was a priest who was among the people, but it doesn't mean he had anything more to do with those girls!

Apparently, the authority of the priests and chaplains to enforce the rules of the church was in part based on their morally superior 'special status', apart from normal people. They inhabited a territory that could not be entered by normal human beings, and this had imbued the obligations of the church with a magical power that was suddenly lost when the cler-ics lost their special status. What is interesting here is *how* they became human in the eyes of people: because they married, because one was holding the handbags for the girls. Their moral superiority was based on their vow of celibacy, their incredible feat of sexual purity. One man told me that he advised his mother not to listen to the clergy anymore. He had been to a seminary, and saw the young priests in training go out with their girlfriends at night.

"They Cancelled Everything"

What people remember much more clearly than any of the other changes (such as the switch from Latin to Dutch) is the time their children came home and told their parents that the chaplain had said that they did not have to go to church if they did not feel like it:

> When the children were smaller, you noticed that church attendance less-ened. They came home reporting that the priest or the chaplains had said

that if they really did not want to go, they were not obliged to go. But before, you were simply not one of the decent people if you did not go. Everybody would look at you. But from that time onwards (late sixties, early seventies), people started minding less about those things.

In all the narratives, the obligation to go to church was a universally accepted fact until the priests and chaplains told people otherwise. One did not wonder whether to go or not, because everybody went. Of course, one might be bored, or reluctant, hungry because of the fasting, or like to sleep in on Sunday mornings. But *not* going was not a real option; in the way that not going to school is not really an option. When this obligation lost its 'factuality', it caused quite a surprise.

> In the sixties, many things have changed, also in the church. Suddenly, everything was allowed, everything could be done differently. If you could not go on Sundays, you could go on Saturdays, or during the week. So those changes came from 'up'. It would never have occurred to me *not* to go on Sundays. I guess they decided in those higher realms that it was nonsense for some reason, but those were the times that everything changed very fast, and everything declined.

The lady speaking here goes from the general to the specific by focusing on a seemingly irrelevant detail: from "everything could be done differently" to: "if you could not go on Sundays, you could go on Saturdays". As we can see in both quotations, the changes are perceived as something that came from above, not as something that had to do with changes in how they themselves thought about things. An expression often used in commenting about this is: "they cancelled everything" (ze hebben alles afgeschaft). Inherent in this comment is a sort of fatalism: all the efforts they had made to live up to the standards of the church were apparently null and void. When I spoke to them, they were not angry about it anymore. However, it did leave a residue of resentment against the church. And of course, this dilemma was usually resolved again through the motto: "you go to church for God, not for the priest".

The expression "they cancelled everything" also implies a criticism: the church used to give shape and a shared rhythm to community life, demanding that everybody joined in this rhythm, and even threatening those who did not with spiritual and social exclusion. And now the church has abandoned this role. The threats turned out to be empty. Some people complained: "they fooled us all those years". Furthermore, by relaxing the rules of church attendance, they upset the rhythm and the continuity of passing this rhythm and the way of life going with it from one generation to another, undermining the efforts they had made to get their children to attend church, undermining the ritual foundations of the local community. No longer was appearance in church an indicator of whether or not one belonged to the "decent people".

According to some, the emptying of the churches is "their own fault": "they" (the clergy) "gave" people their freedom too suddenly and too fast. However, according to most respondents this is not particularly tragic for religious life, because they believe that even those people who do not go to church regularly, whether of their own age or of a younger age, still "have their own faith". This is seen as legitimate enough: there is no need anymore to submit to the authority of a church and attend regularly to prove that you are a decent person.

As we saw earlier, the older generation did not wish to describe the role of the church in their childhood as bad: it was just the way things were. When things changed, it was confusing, as described above, but in some ways also a relief. None of my respondents had a problem in dealing with people who had a different background of faith. And although their opinions on abortion, euthanasia, birth control and sex before marriage were usually a bit more conservative than that of younger generations, they usually thought these things should be entrusted to people's own responsibility. Even the most 'conservative' among my respondents, followed this line of reasoning when it came to individuals, to her own children and grandchildren.

> I live like I was taught. About the youth, I say, if they want to live together [i.e. without being married, KK], should I close the door on them? No, I would never do that. I let them live their life, with my warnings.

The introduction of birth control was a good thing, whatever the opinion of the church was about the subject, but people think it should be reserved for married couples who already have a few children to prevent it from becoming an excuse to "live carelessly": in their opinion, the rules of the church and social conventions should be followed out of intrinsic motivation rather than because of external enforcement.

4. POLARIZATION

In the previous section, I described how some of my respondents blamed the changes in the church that came "from above" for the decline in community life. The church was no longer the self-evident centre of local life. However, when talking of the polarization that followed after the liberalization of church life, the liberal phase apears as a golden age for community life. It seems then, that the decline of community only really made itself felt through the introduction of a neo-conservative priest as the sucessor of the liberal priest they were used to. The polarization of the Dutch Catholic church, which started with the appointment of Gijsen, came to Welden with a delay of about ten years.

On the level of local communities, the impact of this polarization varied. Probably, in some cases it was not felt at all. But in the case of Welden, it was felt very strongly, after their parish priest suddenly died in the early eighties, and was replaced by a priest sent by Gijsen to "restore order" in Welden. The previous priest was a known opponent of Gijsen, and much loved by his parishioners. Not all local communities in Limburg were confronted by a priest sent by Gijsen. On the level of the local community, the shock of Gijsen's appointment was often not felt immediately, because local priests and chaplains continued to follow the agenda they had already developed, until Gijsen found a way to replace them. To use Berger's metaphor: Gijsen's agenda was to repair the 'sacred canopy'. He wanted people to accept the authority of the church as a self-evident fact of life again. He appointed priests that he could count on to carry out this policy, created his own seminary, banned pastoral workers from working with the diocese, and hounded the clergy who were too liberal in his eyes.[12]

"Among the People" versus "Above the People"

In Welden, the priest sent by Gijsen caused a lot of upheaval. In describing the consequences, most people tried to keep their narratives neutral, although some would still get very upset about it. Everybody agreed that the controversy over the new priest tore the local community apart, causing personal hurt to many people. To this day, it is a sensitive topic and people are careful in expressing themselves about it.

Whatever side they took, they all used the same expressions to describe the difference between the 'old' priest and the priest sent by Gijsen: the previous priest stood "among the people" while the new one wanted to be "above" the people. It was not so much theological differences that caused controversy; it was the hierarchical attitude of the new priest. The old

---

[12] Again, I refer to the sometimes emotional and adversarial descirptions in Auwerda, *De Kromstaf Als Wapen: Bisschopsbenoemingen in Nederland*; van der Baar, *Priester in Limburg Op Het Breukvlak Van De Tijd*; Nissen, "Constructie En Deconstructie Van Het Katholieke Limburg"; Wijnen and Koopmanschap, *Hoe Katholiek Is Limburg? De Kerk En Het Bisdom Roermond.*

priest encouraged people to participate actively in the church; the new one wanted to do everything "by the book". The old priest discussed, asked for their opinions, think 'with' his parishioners; the new priest wanted people to follow his orders, had no interest in the opinions of his parishioners, saw his role as thinking 'for' them. The old priest enthusiastically embraced the renewals initiated within the Dutch church, inspired by the spirit of the Second Vatican Council, the new priest tried to restore the old order, where the priest ruled his parish like a little kingdom.

The new priest took his orders from Gijsen: to re-establish the vertical dominance of the church in the community of Welden. This meant that a lot of people, especially those active in organising community life and the church, felt they were demoted from valued volunteer whose opinions and initiatives were respected to someone who was simply expected to carry out orders, clean the building or arrange the flowers. Until the late fifties, they had been accustomed to think of themselves as deferring to the authority of the church. Through the efforts of the old priest to give shape to the renewals in the church on the local level, they had learned to consider the church as belonging to the community: they had to give shape to the local religious life, as Alfrink had argued so convincingly at Vaticanum II. In contrast, the new priest made it clear that the church was his territory and that he had come to "restore order" in the community. In his view, not only the church building was his territory, but the whole parish, virtually synonymous to the whole community. To many people, this amounted to an attempt to "turn back the clock".

This affected mostly the post-war generation, while most of the respondents of the pre-war generation kept themselves out of the controversy. However, this was virtually impossible. For example, one respondent told me how the new priest undermined the leader of the local choir of the elderly, a known progressive Catholic. He told everybody that she was not a good Catholic, and not fit to lead the choir, and he forbade her choir to choose their own songs. After some hesitation, unused to openly going against the authority of the priest, the whole choir decided to support her.

One particularly vicious fight broke out when some parents decided that they did not want their children to have their Holy Communion with him. He had told everybody that the Holy Communion of the previous year was not valid because there were some parents near the altar when the host was consecrated. This made many parents angry, and they enlisted the help of a nearby monastery. To other parents, the solution of going to the monastery seemed a bad idea: they refused to 'give up' on the parish church. Not because they liked the new priest so much, but because they reasoned that it was *their* church, the symbol of *their* community, they had grown up with it, they had done their first communion there. They did not plan to let themselves be "chased away" by a difficult priest.

The parish priest condemned the role of the monastery as meddling in the affairs of his parish by providing misguided people with a way out, to escape the territorial boundaries of the parish instead of staying there and being forced to solve their disagreements with his policy. The monastery in his view encouraged disobedience to the moral authority of the Catholic church. He compared the role of the monastery in this affair with the role of monasteries in the province of Brabant in the past, where they served as a refuge for criminals sought by the secular authorities.

So these were the terms of the debate on both sides: it was not just a difference of opinion, but a drama with villains and heroes. A drama in which people were expected to take sides. Although this particular conflict involved especially the post-war generation, the whole community was affected.

In retrospect, everybody saw it as inevitable that the community did not accept the rule of the new priest, but in the more detailed accounts of the 'acts of war' between the two camps it seems that at the time, it was by no means certain whether people would cede to the priest's authority or resist it. Some people were relieved that this priest, at least, acted "proper" to his status. Everybody agrees that he does the church services "beautifully". Probably, most people avoided taking sides as long as possible.

The attitude of the new priest not only caused personal feelings of hurt and conflicting loyalties, but also caused a separation between the local village associations and institutions and the priest. The local priest was often the one with the first and the last say on the board of the village associations and the local school. With the old priest, this had developed into a network of cooperation between the associations and the church, with the priest in the role of encouraging facilitator. When the new priest came, he had a more authoritarian attitude, because he was of the opinion that the previous priest had let things slide too much. He believed in the role of the priest as the person who should enforce the moral rules of the church as conservatively as possible, and use every sanction available to him. This, according to everybody I interviewed, regardless of their personal opinion of the priest involved, had disastrous results.

The priest did not succeed in 'reconquering' the parish to be more obedient to the church; instead, the community and village societies relinquished the parish church to his authority and kept the rest to themselves.

The ties between the village associations and the local elementary school on the one hand and the parish church on the other were cut, contact was reduced to a very minimum. At the time of my research a reluctant and precarious truce had been established between the warring factions, and most people had learned to describe the conflict in neutral terms, only revealing their own sympathies as a side comment.

Those who got along with the priest, had decided to call his "above the people" attitude a lack in 'social skills', preferring a continued formal role of the church in their personal life and community life to rebellion. Many people of the older generation simply stuck to the motto that had already served them for so long: "you do not go for the priest, you go for God".

Through the process of polarization, the territory over which the priest can exercise his authority has been reduced to the church and its rituals. Community life evolves regardless of the priest. Even though his status as a priest might give some additional weight to his words, his authority outside the church is ultimately based on his credibility as a person (in other words, in other communities, a priest may still have greater authority). Except one or two respondents, none would accept it if a priest would take the attitude of the chaplain in the story of the miner's wife, or in other ways try to lay down the law outside the bounds of the physical building of the church itself. Even in the eyes of one of the more pious respondents, the status of the priest changed:

> It used to be that the priest was regarded the way we regard the pope nowadays, as someone who was far above you. Now you can just say hi to him, he has become a normal person.

Nevertheless, community life is still to a large extent dependent on the church for its rituals. As we will see in the next chapter, in this context a priest can still hold a position of power.

5. Comparison of Past and Present

Before starting fieldwork, I expected that when I would ask the older generation about the contrast of what they were told was supposed to be right and proper with the present day situation, this would elicit detailed stories about how they came to terms with these discrepancies. Usually however, this question was felt to be a challenge to explain the moral regime of the past. The past was felt to be inexplicable, at least to me: "well, that's just the way it was, we did not think of questioning it". This seems to indicate that my respondents found it hard to explain that there was only one accepted way of living, whereas now more lifestyles are possible. This answer might also implicitly admit that, with hindsight, one could argue that they *should* have questioned things: according to present-day values many things that were taken for granted then, have changed to accommodate more room for personal freedom and well-being, for equal rather than authoritarian relationships, or are delegated to the realm of personal responsibility.

However it should be interpreted, this answer made it difficult to ask more questions, because it shut off the door to comparison: it is useless to ask for opinions on things that just "were the way they were". So I also asked more explicitly how they had dealt with the ever-widening gap between the moral prescriptions of the church and the emerging consensus according to which many things that were considered sinful in the past have become accepted part of people's lifestyle, such as birth control, homosexuality, intermarriage with people of another faith, mixed schools etc. In response, people just shrugged: they said they had not experienced it as problematic. In their own life, they had lived more or less according to church doctrine and how others, including their children and grandchildren, live was up to them as long as they were not drug addicts or alcoholics and did not betray their spouse.

Progress and Loss of Community

Nevertheless, after the initial answer that led nowhere, people did mention that they worried about the decline of the local community and the increasing loneliness of many people. Of course, there is always the cliché that "in the past, everything was better". But when we take a closer look at the way these worries were framed by the lady cited below, we can see that they imply a perspective in which generally, the present is normally seen as an *improvement* on the past.

> The times were very different then. But still, I think, people have never been lonelier than they are now. They have all the modern comforts, and they know it all, but still...before, you would go to church, and you naturally formed groups to walk there together [she lived half an hour away from the parish church in a little hamlet]. And when you went back, you would go into someone's house to have some coffee, and now, you have TV, at night the curtains are closed and that's it, finished...

In this narrative it is clear that her thoughts on the subject of the decline of the role of the church in local life had already crystallized: she knows the underlying reasons for the objections other people might make, and gives us an insight into the context of meaning in which she formulated them. She starts with well-worn phrase: "the times were very different then". Often, as mentioned above, this was followed by: "we did not think of questioning it". However, she does not say this. Instead, she says: "still…" the indicator that according to the general opinion, to which she is referring to frame her own insights, not only were the times different, they were apparently different in a negative sense. We can see why in a the next sentence: "they have all the modern comforts, and they know it all, but…" So the present is an improvement on the past in terms of knowledge and in terms of material comfort. Viewed by present-day standards, which they assumed that I share, the past was indeed 'bad' because you were not supposed to question things and living standards were lower. But it was also 'good', because community life was stronger.

Sexuality

A strong exception to the understanding tolerance with which the older generation viewed the younger generation, is the way older women see the sexual behaviour of young girls. The contrast between the way that they were raised and young girls behave nowadays is something they cannot empathize with. This behaviour, which they see as indiscriminately "sleeping around", goes directly against their notions of what is right and proper. As young girls, they had been trained on how to deal with men down to the smallest details:

> The chaplains would warn us against the things that boys would try to do. Otherwise, you wouldn't know what happens to you. But nowadays, they act very differently; it is hard to understand how this came about. We wanted to go to the altar 'pure'. We were taught to be careful, and to respect the boy. Because he is not made of stone! And if you were not pure, you had to have the honesty to say: no, I will not marry in white.

Parental control and the teachings of the church were accepted as helping to prevent 'occasions for sin'. Young girls were taught specifically that it was their responsibility to check where the hands of the boy might stray. And the social exclusion that threatened when one failed to comply, was something to be feared as real and painful, as we saw earlier in this chapter. The following monologue gives more insight into the reasoning, vocabulary and emotions involved in their view of young girls now:

> If you 'had to' marry [because of pregnancy], that was really bad. Then, boys had a very different feeling for a girl. Of course, sometimes it happened,

but those were the people from the 'underside' so to speak. But now, they go with each other, and I find it really offensive that the girl is not appreciated. But of course, there are some girls who lower themselves. They invite trouble. We used to dress nicely, but nowadays they walk around half naked, what do you expect! How can a boy not go crazy? Look, if you bare yourself, a boy will think: hey, that's an opportunity. But if a girl is decent, and lets him know that she doesn't like that kind of behaviour, everything is fine. Also for the boys. Look, they are not bad really, but they are tempted. I read it somewhere in a magazine, that they said: well, if you would dress properly, we wouldn't behave like that [i.e. badly] either. And the fashion trends reinforce this. And, well, those girls just comply. And that stuff they swallow nowadays. It went wrong when they started using the pill. In itself, the pill is a good thing, but they should just give it to the women who already have a few children. But a young girl should keep her body in honour. Well, I'm just saying it the way I see it. You were always told: this is bad, that is bad, but still, we had a lot of good times. And if some boy would say: 'come, let's go into this alley', you would just say: 'are you crazy?! Why don't you go alone, what should I be doing there?' And he would know, ok, it's not possible...because that's the way we were taught, you know, with the seven healthy apples? How did it go again...if there is only one rotten, the rest is lost as well (één rotte appel in de mand is de rest tot schand). A bad girl more easily takes down seven men with her than seven men can convince one girl. They will not be able to do it. With our own children, we really had to weigh things. My husband said: you cannot leave them alone. But you should also take their own responsibility as a point of departure. But if you leave them alone at night, of course. From one thing comes another.

This monologue is very interesting not only because of the view of men it expresses (poor things!), but also in the moral outrage she feels, which was shared by most women, mingled with disgust, at the way girls 'lower' themselves, and the rhetoric with which this outrage is expressed.

Among the women of the elder generation, chastity was clearly a deeply ingrained attitude, not just a façade. The vocabulary to describe the differences in sexuality, relationships between the sexes and the body ties in with this: "honouring your body" and being "appreciated", or "lowering yourself", recognizing that he is not "made of stone" versus baring yourself and causing bad behaviour, staying "pure" and honourable versus a "fallen state" associated with "the people from the underside".

At the time when they were old enough to be courted and get married, long engagement periods were normal. 'Remaining chaste' would become more and more a challenge as affections grew. Nevertheless, none of the women who talked about this issue saw any reason for the sexual mores to become more liberal. They emphasized that the long engagement period was also a test of character for the boy, because if it turned out that he could not abstain during their engagement, how could you expect the marriage to work when she would not be available for sex because of childbirth? This is connected to the view discussed earlier that a man should be "considerate" with his wife and exercise enough self-control not to get her pregnant too often or too soon after the lastborn child.

6. Concluding Remarks

The dynamics of the interview itself revealed to what extent people are still attuned to the mechanisms of social control instilled in them in their youth, they still feel shame, although public opinion on these supposedly shameful incidents has turned around a 180 degrees. Like chastity, the mechanism of the sacraments is part of the habitus of people who grew up when the efforts to create 'good Catholics' within the Catholic pillar were at its height.

Despite the quite liberal priest that shaped the local face of Catholicism in Welden until the early eighties, there was still no shared way of recognizing the mechanisms of control and the painful secrets that these produced among the pre-war generation. This is different for the post-war generation, as we shall see in the next chapter. The fact that these narratives are still individual and felt as shameful also shows the limits of the influence of liberal Catholicism. After all, this kind of story was grist to the mill of the 'spiritual liberators' discussed in the previous chapter.

Except on the issue of birth control, my respondents presented no narratives of impending and necessary change. Their narratives of change emphasize that it was not they who changed, but the clergy. They mostly focus on the behaviour of the clergy and the breaking of the rhythm of church life. There are no narratives that explicitly describe an awareness and criticism of the 'mechanism of the sacraments' as intrinsically wrong. This is in contrast to the professionals and active community members of the younger generation who are central to the next chapter. But it does tie in with what Thurlings found: that a considerable amount of Dutch Catholics did not participate in the renewals at all, and another part were more motivated by docility and obedience to church authority, whether conservative, progressive or neo-conservative, than by a desire to change things.[13]

---

[13]   Thurlings, "Verzuiling En Beweging. Over Nut En Onnut Van Het Bewegingsmodel," 39.

This raises the question how deeply embedded this mechanism of the sacraments still is. Logically, if the elder generation still believed in the doctrine of sin, confession and absolution one would expect this generation to be very worried about the younger generation and their own children: will they go to heaven, or be damned? But they were not, far from it. Generally, the Catholic doctrine of sin the pre-war generation had been taught during their youth were not the standards by which they evaluated later generations and present-day society. In their narratives, there is no sense that the way people live now is *intrinsically* wrong and sinful, however different it is from the way they were raised, except where it concerns matters of chastity. Even in expressing their concerns about the sexuality of present-day girls, the women were not concerned about the state of the girls' souls; rather they were worried that these girls were not 'appreciated' and treated with respect. The elder generation seemed to accept that the general moral consensus had moved on and out of the bounds of the morality of the church.

On the level of institutions in Limburg, the polarization between the neo-conservative agenda of Gijsen and the movement of progressive Catholics was fought out in very acrimonious terms.[14] However, the attitude of my respondents would often be something like: "let them [the clergy, KK] discuss and decide those things among themselves". But with the appointment of conservative young priests in the local communities of Welden and some surrounding parishes, the polarization was reflected in struggles about lay participation in rituals, their influence in village associations, but also, as we shall see in the next chapter, about their influence with the curriculum of the local school, the village societies, what they told children in preparation for their first communion, etc.

In the confrontation with neo-conservative priests a diminished role of the church within the community crystallized. The general consensus seems to be that nobody seriously considered accepting the authority of the church as a given again. Although people were reluctant to condemn the pre-Vatican church as bad, attempts to 'restore' the past apparently were not appreciated either. The pre-war generation did not want to take sides for the most part, but on some occasions they explicitly chose

---

[14] Auwerda, *De Kromstaf Als Wapen: Bisschopsbenoemingen in Nederland*; van der Baar, *Priester in Limburg Op Het Breukvlak Van De Tijd*; Wijnen and Koopmanschap, *Hoe Katholiek Is Limburg? De Kerk En Het Bisdom Roermond.*

against the new priest. Nevertheless, they did not see the controversy this new priest generated as a reason not to go to church anymore.

Nevertheless, in Welden and some other local parishes in the surrounding areas, these struggles thoroughly divided communities. The gap between the parish church and community life, as well as the gap between church doctrines and generally accepted views on moral issues and hierarchical relationships, creates a field of tension that will be explored in the next chapter.

CHAPTER FOUR

RELIGIOUS AUTHORITY, RITUAL AND THE FAMILIAR

1. INTRODUCTION

The previous chapters described some important changes in the Catholic discourse on morality and religious practice that emerged from within the Catholic pillar on a national level, and the way local people reflect on these changes. From the comparison between these two chapters, the significance of 'practice' to religiosity and the reprodcution of community became clear: it was only when changes in the discourse were translated into a change in practices on the local level that the pre-war generation remembers that their own religious practices and moral orientations started shifting and the place of the church in community life and the mechanisms of social control changed irrevocably.

This chapter links the focus on the 'religious past' of the previous two chapters to the descriptions of present-day religious practices in the next two chapters. The previous two chapters described how a field of tension has emerged between local communities and the parish church, and between present day common sense notions of morality and the doctrines of the church through the dynamics of first renewal and then an attempt to "turn back the clock" within the Catholic church in the Netherlands and in Limburg in particular. Throughout this chapter I develop the argument that the nature and place of present-day religiosity is best understood as the result of an ambivalent relationship with religious authority, or even authority in general. This ambivalence has many causes that will be further explored in this chapter and other chapters. One of the major reasons is that on many occasions the Catholic rituals remain important, and 'being Catholic' remains an important identity marker for both individuals and institutions, despite the separation that has emerged between communities and the church, and the generally distant relationship people have with the Catholic church as an institution. This opens up the domain of the familiar to the interference of the church, represented by the parish priest, thus creating a potential for conflict that may not always be expressed, but is keenly felt.

Gossip and Bad Priest Stories

Parts of this chapter is based on what some people would call gossip, or
at least very partial and colored representations of reality. As with secrets,
the sharing of gossip creates a (temporary) feeling of complicity between
those telling and listening to the stories involved. By taking gossip seriously, I more or less 'betray' this complicity. Although I found this difficult, I also found that if I did not use this material, I could not really give
any insight into the relationship with the church.[1] As any anthropologist
knows, gossip is an important entrypoint to the 'backstage' reality that
they wish to get to know.

Parts of this chapter is based on stories about 'bad priests'. This was a
genre of stories that I encountered in almost every part of my research.
These stories usually centred on the young, neo-conservative priests
appointed by Gijsen or later, by Wiertz. They depicted these priests as
arrogant, insensitive and lacking normal human warmth. They often had
the function of sharing moral outrage about some misstep by one of these
priests while confirming the teller and the listeners as 'normal' people
who are capable of warm and loving relationships and thereby have an
intrinsic sense of what is right. In using these stories, I do not want to
confirm the opinions expressed in them, that is to say, I do not make
any judgement about the priests involved. Rather, I use these stories to
understand in the field of tension in which they emerge and circulate,
what insights they can give into how people relate to the church as an
institution.

I focus here on stories of bad priests that have to do with how people
perceive that they do their 'job' as a ritual specialist, especially around
death or dying. There are of course, as in any Catholic region, many stories, speculations and jokes about the sexual life and/or misbehaviour of
priests, as well as their fishy financial management. While entertaining
and unfortunately often true, and in their own way accomplishing the
creation of a shared moral universe uniting people in outrage against the
hypocrisy, abuse and corruption of priests, these stories were less important for this research. They illustrated and confirmed people's attitude to
religious authority rather than shaped it.

This chapter will first go into the rituals around death and dying. Since
it is based mostly on interviews and, as I described above, on gossip it will

---

[1] Knibbe, "Secrets, Gossip and Betrayal."

not describe the actual rituals that are the subject of these interviews and stories. Rather, it will describe the expectations different parties bring to the rituals around death and dying. These rituals then become the intersection between different discourses and practices, as we shall see. It will then describe the general changes in the rural area of Limburg under the heading 'becoming modern'; how "all the modern comforts" mentioned in the previous chapter as an important characteristic of this time changed life in the rural areas. This provides the background to exploring the relationship of the younger generation with the church and their identity as Catholics. Because this Catholic identity, like the rituals and the physical building of the church, remain important for the production of locality and the reproduction of the domain of the familiar, a need for resignification of the Catholic tradition emerges, as will be discussed in the final part of this chapter. In the conclusion, this will be linked to the findings of the previous chapters.

2. Rituals Around Death and Dying

Understanding why a funeral can become a source of conflict proved a useful way of gaining more insight into the place of religious practices and the church as an institution in present day Limburg. Several generations, secular professionals (the doctor, the nurse, the undertaker) and religious institutions are thrown together in a situation where they have to agree on a way to shape and express what it means when someone dies. To create a 'traditional' end to life, which is what many people in the village communities prefer, all these actors converge within the ritual domain of the church. The expectations of what ritual should accomplish differ widely among these actors, creating a potential for conflict. Different value-orientations, notions of the function of ritual and role definitions create tensions that have to be navigated with care.

The church has a set of rules for the 'last sacraments' as they are often called (confession, the sacrament of the sick and the viaticum), funeral mass and other services surrounding death that are clearly and conservatively stated on the diocesan level: the priest has the responsibility to protect the sacred acts of Catholic ritual from dilution. His role and the importance of the sacraments cannot be replaced because it is fundamentally different from that of lay people. In cases where the deceased has clearly died unrepentant of his or her transgressions of morality as defined by the Catholic church he should even refuse to perform the sacramental acts. However, these rules have been heavily contested in the past by the liberal Catholic faction, and are in practice often ignored or circumvented by the less strict priests.

These rules can seem very outlandish and harsh when confronted with the demands of a family that may feel that the expression of their grief supersedes any rules. Not giving in to those demands can be seen as the most cruel act a priest can commit in his entire career. In their own perception the family members have the heavy responsibility to protect the memory of the deceased and act according to his or her last wishes, e.g. to have a 'proper Catholic burial', pass away having received all the sacraments, or to have a burial service led by a priest who is a friend of the family. The parish priest is in the position to refuse to carry out these wishes: he can say that the dying person is not fit to receive the sacraments, he can refuse to hold a 'proper' mass, he can refuse to let the old family friend perform the burial service.

Finally, there are the 'professionals' surrounding death and dying: the undertakers, nurses and doctors who have to make sure that the demands of their profession to be efficient and 'cost effective' do not hurt anyone's feelings, and who have to develop their own ways for dealing with the emotional turmoil of death and dying.

All these actors agreed on what constitutes a 'good death': a process in which the person has the time to say goodbye to everybody, make his peace with God and die in his own bed having received the last sacraments. Subsequently, the family members and the community can entrust the dead person to 'the care of God' through the ritual of the funeral mass. And they all saw the same problems, even the priest I interviewed who was himself the subject of several 'bad priest' stories.

Traditionally, receiving the last sacraments and the celebration of a (eucharist) mass at a funeral are seen as part of a 'good death'. To die with unconfessed sins might mean that the soul of the deceased can not enter heaven. But nowadays, these once 'automatic' routines are dependent on the relationship of the dying person and his or her family with the parish church and with the church in general. If the relationship is not so close, people often hesitate to ask for a priest when they fall sick: they don't want to bother a stranger, who also has a certain status, to come unless someone is really on the brink of death, and then he has to come immediately. Some people might bear a personal grudge against the parish priest and wish for another priest to do the last rites for them. Often, the dying person and his or her family are also afraid that calling a priest makes things doubly final. And finally, people are afraid that the priest might simply not come, because of some 'sin' they have committed in the past (as with women who 'got the shutter', people who are separated or divorced, have a more personal 'sinful secret' or even because they never went to church often enough).

To orchestrate a 'good death' despite these ambivalences, the doctor or a close family member with connections might suggest that a priest or pastor be found who is expected to understand and address any alienation from the church and the fear of being judged that the dying person (and his or her family) might feel. Usually, this means that it will be a progressive Catholic priest or pastor, who is more liable to adapt to the specific circumstances of this death and the sensitivities of the people around it. Parish priests often resent being sidelined by a priest from elsewhere, and they might make things difficult for this strange priest in the organization of the funeral mass in 'his' parish church.

The position of the neo-conservatives is that the focus of the last rites is not the expression of grief, a celebration of life or the commemoration of the deceased, but the proper execution of certain sacred acts that will safely conduct the soul of the deceased from this world to the next. This means that there is no reason to go against the territorial organization of the Catholic church by bringing in a priest from outside. Furthermore, this means that a neo-conservative priest will try to constrain the tendency of the bereft to express their emotions and their memories of the dead or dying person during the rituals, on the prayer cards, through the choice of music and prayers. As priests remembered it, the family traditionally deferred to the authority of the priest and the undertaker to take care of these things. Now, these rituals are taken over by the family and friends to express what this person and his or her dying mean to them.

In these narratives, the arrangement of the ritual moments around death was described in terms of a series of morally charged issues for 'haggling': the bereft wanted to use the space for text on the commemorating card to remember the character and uniqueness of the deceased, while the priest thought it should have an appropriately religious prayer. The bereft wanted to speak during the funeral service, while the priest resisted intrusion into the sacred space of the mass. The priest refused their choice of music, forbade that the family friend who also happens to be a priest did the mass for the funeral, or usurped the money collected for the deceased's favourite charity during the mass on the grounds that it was collected in *his* church.

These and other stories were told to illustrate two things: first, how meaningful the dying process had been. And second, to bolster the stereotype of the anti-social, uncaring and callous neo-conservative 'young' priests. Older and neo-conservative priests sometimes complained: why is a 'normal' traditional funeral not good enough anymore? Why do people want to 'plan' their deaths? When did death become such a terrible tragedy that everybody has to show and share their grief? Nevertheless, they recognized that they had to tread very carefully in the emotional minefield surrounding death and burial.

New Expectations of Rituals

In the anthropological study of ritual, it is assumed to accomplish something. The classic cases are of course the 'rites de passage' as first formulated by van Gennep[2] and later elaborated by Turner: these rituals accomplish the passage from one state, or position in society, to another.[3] Healing rituals are also often studied in these terms: they accomplish the transition from sick to healthy, manipulating symbolic meanings.

In the stories condensed in the above, we see that especially those telling the 'bad priest' stories have particular, although implicit, expectations of ritual. It seems that in the Netherlands in general, new expectations towards ritual are emerging. The academic study of spiritual care and the role of rituals has contributed to this: rituals are assumed to help along the process of grieving, healing, to enable people to deal with trauma, etc. These notions have been popularized through different channels. Ritual is assumed to have a general psychological efficacy, rather than to accomplish something religious. The two undertakers I interviewed, both women, said that they were becoming more and more aware of the need for families to give the funeral a 'different' touch, using symbols and creating rituals that resonate with the private universe of meaning shared within the family of which the deceased used to be a part. They were diversifying their services to meet his need. They emphasized that they saw it as a part of their jobs not only to provide practical support, but also to provide emotional support, which mainly translated into 'giving space' to people's emotions and supporting their efforts to make the funeral into a meaningful event.

---

[2] Arnold Van Gennep, *Les Rites De Passage* (Paris: Picard, 1981).

[3] Victor W. Turner, *The Ritual Process: Structure and Anti-structure* (Aldine, 1995); Victor W. Turner, *The Drums of Affliction: a Study of Religious Processes Among the Ndembu of Zambia* (Oxford: Clarendon Press, 1968).

However, according to the undertakers, for the people of the local communities of Welden and the surrounding area this rarely took a form that was very far removed from the traditional Catholic format according to the undertakers. Therefore, the new expectations of rituals have to be integrated into what is perceived as the 'traditional'[4] series of rituals around death and dying.

More and more, the family and friends of the dying or deceased person want to be involved in orchestrating the rituals. As Wouters signals 'they [the bereft] take full responsibility for their performance; it is not, and certainly not unquestionably, delegated to authorities like priests'.[5] This could be related to the trends signalled by Post et al. in the Netherlands and other Western European countries: more and more, rituals are created after a disaster that has caught the public attention. In these rituals, they discern the beginnings of a civil religion, where a connection to the fate of the victims and empathy is expressed in a way that give people the feeling they are part of a larger whole.[6] It is important to note that the development to turn the last rites into something special was always sketched against a background of the indifference of society, the anonymity of modern life. During the course on wakes for example, it was clear that people wanted the rituals, but also the obituary, to express the loving care that people felt for the deceased, as well as his or her singularity as an individual.

So there seems to be a tendency to make the funeral into something personal, or more accurately, into something *familiar*: the considerations of the family and community around the dying persons take precedence over the church's protocols for the proper execution of the last rites. It is assumed that nobody outside the circle of family and friends can understand their grief, understand the importance this person had to people. Anybody who presumes to impose meanings on the event that are alien to the life world of the family and friends can count on resistance, passive or active. Paradoxically, Catholic rituals are assumed to be part of this familiar universe of meanings, whereas the person of the priest is usually

---

[4] The quotation marks indicate that what is considered to be traditional might also in fact be new. In the past, people often did not have enough money to have an elaborate funeral mass for example, yet this seems to be the implicit norm in these stories.

[5] See also Tongeren, "Individualizing Ritual: The Personal Dimension in Funeral Liturgy," *Worship* 78 (2004): 117–138; Cas Wouters, "The Quest for New Rituals in Dying and Mourning: Changes in the We-I Balance," *Body and Society* 8, no. 1 (2002): 3.

[6] Paul Post, Albertina Nugteren, and Hessel Zondag, *Rituelen Na Rampen* (Kampen: Uitgeverij Gooi en Sticht, 2002), 246.

not, except when he is a family friend. Therefore, the priest's role is that of an actor in the drama orchestrated by the family and friends, and as soon as he wants to do something that goes against the wishes of the family, he will discover that he is not the director.

Through the stories of women about how they haggled with priests over the songs to be sung, the text on the prayer card to be distributed after the funeral and who was allowed to speak when, a discourse of 'caring' is developed against a generalized 'other', which might be the alienation of 'modernity' but also against the oppressiveness of the 'traditonal' way, where everything was directed by the clergy.[7] Except for the neo-conservative priest, undertakers and priests encouraged expressions of familiarity with the deceased in the obituary, in the prayer cards, in the choice of bible-texts to be read and songs to be sung. In some narratives, the arrangements around the last rites were represented as a process that knitted networks of mutual support closer together and led to a religious re-signification of traditional ritual formats. Through these rituals, people expect that their community is created again, as Durkheim posited so long ago.[8] The community that is imagined via this ritual is caring, values the uniqueness of individual life, and values community itself. A priest who limits the expression of these values is therefore blocking the ritual re-creation of community.

The Power of Disapproval and the Mechanism of the Sacraments

Many 'bad priest' stories centred on the possibility that the sacraments might be refused, or actually were refused (i.e. the sacrament of the sick, eucharist mass, burial in hallowed ground). And even when it did not directly concern the sacraments, priests were judged more harshly and in more personal terms than for example undertakers, doctors or nurses who might also be closely involved in the emotional turmoil of death. Limiting the space for participation and expression of the family and friends during the rituals can be felt as an insult to the familiar expression of care and grief. But a priest not granting a request, not attentive and understanding enough is painted in vivid colours as a villain, a psychopath even, while

---

[7] Cf. Gerd Baumann, "Ritual Implicates Others: Rereading Durkheim in a Plural Society," in *Understanding Rituals*, ed. Daniel de Coppet, European Association of Social Anthropologists (London and New York: Routledge, 1992).

[8] Emile Durkheim, *The Elementary Forms of Religious Life* (New York: The Free Press, 1995).

an undertaker doing the same is just a grey phantom with no personality, only thinking of the bills getting paid. Why, we might wonder, is this so?

In so far as they can be assumed to be Catholics, the refusal of one of the sacraments is a disaster to people of the older generation. They were indignant and hurt if a priest delayed his visit when called to administer the 'last sacraments', or forgot to come by when he 'could have known' someone was mortally ill. In the 'traditional' frame of reference these omissions of the priests could be interpreted as judgement on them as a morally decent person. A priest is endowed with 'the power of disapproval'. In contrast, to the post-war generation the refusal of the sacraments or the omission to visit mainly reflects badly on the character of the priest: he should know to avoid giving this impression and thereby causing people pain. He should wield his 'power of disapproval' carefully.

During the course on wakes, this was discussed extensively during one of the sessions and it often returned in the other courses and in interviews.[9] One of the narratives about 'bad priests' centred around a priest who had carefully outlined, during a funeral mass for someone who had died young, the state in which one is fit to receive the sacrament of the communion. This excluded all those who were either divorced, homosexual, having sex without being married etc. This story generated a lot of indignation among the other participants of the course and led to an animated discussion.

Why, when people do not even go to church anymore and their own convictions are miles away from the formal positions of the Catholic church, why do people care so much about being excluded from the sacraments? Based on an understanding of the historical and religious context presented in the previous chapters, we might understand this in the following way:

Still within living memory, the church wielded a lot of power, and the mechanism of the sacraments was a key instrument in enforcing the social and moral order envisaged by the church. Over the past decades, the moral disapproval of the church has ceased to matter, its power has become confined to the rituals necessary for the reproduction of society: baptism, Holy Communion, marriage and death. In Welden, the church has been ceded as the territory of the priest. But at the moment of someone's death, the church is not the territory of the priest anymore but that of the family and friends of the deceased. The Catholic rituals are part of

---

[9] See chapter 6.

the familiar domain encompassing family and community. A priest has
the role of executing the familiar Catholic formats. If he does anything
that goes beyond executing these formats and does not give voice to what
the bereft feel and hope, they feel that the ritual expression of their caring and grief is highjacked as a platform for a moral agenda they do not
agree with. The last rites are considered *familiar* territory where the moral
authority of outsiders can only be validated if they are supported by the
moral emotional life of the insiders.

When a priest invokes the power of disapproval of the church in this
context, it seems that what the church disapproves of and the people
gathered in the church and even the deceased disapprove of are the same
thing, since it is 'their' funeral. But he is presuming too much, especially
when the priest outlines the guidelines of the church and concludes that
those living in contradiction to these guidelines should not take communion. This disapproval is not legitimate in the eyes of the post-war generation: it is their funeral, and they never intended that an entire generation
of young people should be excluded from the communion. Because this
would be the effect of a strict adherence to the guidelines of the church:
not only divorcees and homosexuals would be excluded, but any unmar-
ried person with some sexual experience. Which would be most friends
in the case of someone who died young.

Furthermore, the priest presumes to do this with the authority of
the pope, Jesus Christ (represented in the communion) and God behind
him. Only the staunchest atheists would be insensitive to the insult, let
alone a group of people who consider themselves (although vaguely)
Catholic. Although at other moments people might not care at all that
this particular priest thinks that certain groups of people are not fit to
receive the sacraments, during a funeral rite the women who told these
stories felt it was unacceptable. It goes against the feeling of *communi-
tas* that they wish to create at such a moment, which usually means a
de-emphasizing of hierarchy, a breaking down of the usual boundaries
between people.[10]

This puts the priest who feels he must enforce the church guidelines
in a lonely and defensive position, which is sometimes even perceived as
pathologically anti-social. In fact, as I mentioned already, furious critics

---

[10] Wouters, "The Quest for New Rituals in Dying and Mourning: Changes in the We-I
Balance."

sometimes described priests who explicitly refused the sacraments as psychopaths.

Refusing the Sacraments

Of course, this makes one curious: how often does it actually happen that a priest refuses the sacraments? There must be many occasions where, according to the church, a dying person has sinned and dies without repenting because to him (or her) there is nothing to repent. For all except the most liberal of the priests I spoke to, this was a difficult and touchy subject. It was therefore also difficult to interview them about it. The way they told it, they avoided situations where they actively had to refuse (they all saw active euthanasia as such an occasion, and to the neo-conservatives being divorced might also be a reason) as much as possible. Their solutions to avoid this kind of conflict were very creative.

The most explicitly neo-conservative priest I spoke to said that he never actually refused. According to others, he had refused on some occasions, and also asked whether the dying person was planning to commit euthanasia. But according to himself, he always avoided to know if there was euthanasia involved. He assumed that the people who called him to give the sacraments of the sick and conduct the funeral mass knew what church does and does not condone. He trusted them not to call him in cases where the dying person was not 'fit to receive the sacraments', or know what facts to hold back so that he would not be put in a position where he had to refuse.

I was puzzled by the logic of this argument; if he was being true to his faith and his calling should he not be sure he was not administering the sacraments to someone 'unworthy'? His explanation of this contradiction was that since Vatican II, Catholic doctrine specifies that a priest cannot come between an individual's conscience and God. So if the individual involved thinks he has made his peace with God and is fit to receive the sacraments, he should not question that. But if he knows of any transgressions, he is forced to implement the guidelines of the church and refuse the sacraments. That is why, in the case of a young person's funeral where a lot of young people could be expected to participate, he did not celebrate a mass, as the parents first requested, but proposed to develop another kind of service.

Another priest told me that he had once been confronted with a case of active euthanasia. He had been supporting a woman throughout her illness with pastoral care, but when she announced that she wanted to commit euthanasia he withdrew. When I asked him if she was buried in hallowed ground or not, he at first refused to answer, then said she was buried at a 'general' (algemene) cemetery, where all the ground has been hallowed.

The most liberal priest I interviewed drew the line at administering the sacraments of the sick *after* someone had died, something that the family apparently requests quite often because all the priests I spoke to mentioned it. Instead, he would propose to pray together for the soul of the deceased to be taken into God's care. In this way, he addressed the family's anxiety that their beloved could not enter heaven, because he did not receive the last sacraments.

We might conclude that even though it probably does not happen very often, the *fear* that the sacraments might be refused generates a field of tension in which 'bad priest' stories emerge and circulate to provide the contrast to the 'good and sensible' moral consensus of 'normal people' who simply want to express their grief and show that they care without presuming to exclude other grieving persons.

Despite secularization then, Catholic practices can still be quite important to people, and not only to the older generation, because they are rooted within the familiar and reproduce this domain at transitional moments. The sacraments and the rites associated with them are the most tangible aspects of Catholicism and they have remained important markers despite the out-flux from the churches of the sixties and seventies. Moreover, certain Catholic concepts associated with the mechanism of the sacraments resonate with deeply held fears and anxieties this mechanism can inspire (of being branded as sinful, denied entrance to heaven etc.), but therefore also with hopes and longing. These hopes and longings might not be articulated as clearly anymore as they used to be, when paradise and heaven were thought of as places, and a 'dirty' conscience was visualized as a soul with ugly black spots. But they are embedded within the moral emotional life and thus form part of the attitudes with which people approach religious repertoires, as will become clear in the next two chapters. Much has changed since the time when children were taught that heaven is a place where they might be denied entrance and they had to keep their souls spotless.

3. BECOMING MODERN

In chapter 3 we have seen some of the ways in which liberalization within the church, described in chapter 2, has changed the location of the church in community life and people's attitude towards the church. These were not the only changes that reshaped people's attitudes and the position of the church. The changes described in chapter 2 filtered down selectively through the pillarized organizations and through the efforts of individual priests, such as the priest who preceded the conservative priest in Welden, described in chapter 3. In this section we will take a closer look at the way general social changes reshaped community life in the south of Limburg.

After WWII, the Dutch economy recovered and prospered, and in the sixties a higher standard of living seemed within reach for everybody. The welfare state expanded and professionalized, and took over the tasks that were traditionally carried out by the pillarized organizations while the pillarized organizations themselves secularized.[11] The sharp divisions between 'standen' (estates) disappeared as the general educational level rose among the younger generations. Most people are now employed in the service sector rather than in the agrarian sector or in the mines. Mass media introduced a whole new cultural dynamic, and provided access to a wide array of opinions and lifestyles.

These societal changes had a generally 'disembedding' impact, loosening associations between employers and local communities, widening local horizons and making it possible to live in a village without participating in these local horizons.[12] People became more mobile: the roads improved, means of transport became faster, more and more people had a car. Access to a wider range of information and more leisure time led to new initiatives and organizations such as the very active cycling clubs racing around the hills of Limburg during the weekends. The general level of education improved, the son of the carpenter can now become a professor.

However, locally shared horizons did not completely disappear or fragment, on the contrary. Local communities in Limburg are characterized by a high degree of organization: the local dove-keepers association, the association for the elderly, the Rural Catholic Women's organization, the Red Cross, the choir, the brass band, the 'homeguard' association (schutterij) the association for local history, etc. These organizations were and

---

[11] W. van der Linde, *Eindelijk Religieuze Tolerantie* (Maastricht: Universitaire Pers Maatsricht, 2001); Wijnen and Koopmanschap, *Hoe Katholiek Is Limburg? De Kerk En Het Bisdom Roermond*.

[12] Wijnands, *Op Het Dorp; Leven in De Kleine Limburgse Gemeenschappen*.

to some extent still are, connected to the parish church and the (remnants of) the Catholic pillar.[13]

In Chapter 2 I described how the position of Catholic organizations moved from one where 'information' was dosed and controlled in such a way as to limit people's opportunities to deviate from the straight and narrow as defined by the church, to a position where 'information' and education was seen as a means to emancipate people by the government, school and the formerly pillarized organizations. Since the 1960s, progress and modernization became the key words of the organizations and institutions of the Catholic pillar that shaped local life. Even when Gijsen decided it was time to 'turn back the clock', for the most part he did not manage to re-establish control over the pillarized organizations to follow his agenda.[14]

This meant that new 'scientific' insights continued to be rapidly popularized and distributed through the many Catholic farmer and women's organizations and through the school curricula. Farming methods were modernized in step with changes in the rest of the Netherlands and schools, including Catholic schools, were all brought under the same national educational regime in 1968. A state university was set up in Maastricht in 1976.

The expansion of the welfare state and the general economic prosperity provided new job opportunities. New and better housing added to the old historical centres provided living space for the emancipating working class and the expanding class of white-collar workers. Whereas before, women by law had to stop working as soon as they got married, or in the agrarian sector worked alongside their husbands, they could now find work outside the domestic sphere. After the 1950s, the number of children per family dropped drastically, in Limburg more than in any other province.[15]

Not only was there an increase in the 'information' and technology becoming available, many new ideas about how life should be lived rippled from the urban centres to lap at the edges of the village communities. In the name of progress, liberation and 'de verbeelding aan de macht' (power to the imagination, the battle-cry of the flower power generation),

---

[13] Ibid.

[14] Wijnen and Koopmanschap, *Hoe Katholiek Is Limburg? De Kerk En Het Bisdom Roermond*.

[15] Knippenberg, *De Religieuze Kaart Van Nederland, Omvang En Geografische Spreiding Van De Godsdienstige Gezindten Vanaf De Reformatie Tot Heden*, 182.

the solid society that the older generation had tried to rebuild after WWII was taking harsh criticism.[16] In the urban centres, radical new ways of living were experimented with, and the traditional biography and family structures became one option among many.[17]

Although the experimenting largely bypassed rural areas, some of the results of this experimenting eventually became mainstream. Notions of equality between men and women, of equality between all peoples and nations of the world, and world peace, were translated in a less radical and experimental way via progressive Catholicism and shaped the practices of the formerly pillarized institutions such as the rural women's organizations. Insights from the social sciences and psychology became widespread via new approaches to mental health and social work, as well as in education. Fashion and popular culture inspired new ideas about sexuality, gender and the body to such an extent that most young adults nowadays would have trouble defining the word 'chastity' and the word has disappeared completely from everyday language.

As we saw in the previous chapter, new ideas regarding the status of priests and sexuality caused controversy especially when they entailed a break in established routines and relationships between people and status groups. But once new routines and formats for interaction were developed, the resistance to going back to 'the old ways', promoted by Gijsen and his priests, was strong, especially on the part of the post-war generation.

Illustrative is the way feminism entered the local community, proposing changes that were perceived as very disruptive and therefore (at first) resisted. One of my first informants told me how this came about. She used to be the chairwoman of the local chapter of the Limburg Rural Women's Association (a Catholic organization, and mainly meant for agrarian women). During the seventies, this association was given subsidies to conduct courses for female empowerment.[18] She was sceptical about these courses. For example, during the meetings they had to applaud each other when one woman reported that she did not do any household chores for one whole weekend. But, she commented drily, of course that woman had to clean up the mess herself after the weekend. She joked that they should have thought of organizing men's empowerment courses as well, so they

---

[16] Kennedy, "Building New Babylon: Cultural Change in the Netherlands During the 1960s."

[17] Ibid.; Wijnands, *Op Het Dorp; Leven in De Kleine Limburgse Gemeenschappen.*

[18] See chapter 8 in Dijk, Huijts et al. 1990 for an account of a trainer working on similar projects in the province of Brabant.

could help each other learn to organize the household. In her opinion, the teacher was too radical in encouraging women to be 'emancipated', and four marriages broke up as a result. All in all, she saw feminism as something that made women act crazily, and left men bewildered because they did not have a clue what they had done wrong. Nevertheless, as she mentioned at the outset of this conversation, she approved the fruits of feminism: women are no longer fired as soon as they marry. Although she 'never noticed' she was supposed to be subservient to her husband, she approved of these changes. While she was telling me this, her husband served us tea and pie.

The villages of rural Limburg have to some extent become the suburbs for the cities of Heerlen, Sittard and Maastricht. Urban professionals, artists, and well-off pensioners increasingly populate the formerly agrarian hamlets, villages and towns. These villages provide them with an idyllic environment, but their ties with the local community are usually not very strong. The real estate prices have gone up accordingly, which makes it difficult for the children of the locals to buy a house in the community they grew up in.[19]

The consequences of the 'tangible progress' of Dutch society in terms of values can be illustrated by looking at a study published in 1978. This study analyzes the changes in the way a popular women's weekly magazine (Margriet) with a Catholic background, replied to women's queries for advice.[20] This weekly had lower class and lower middle class Catholic women as its main reading public. During my youth, this was the magazine most often found in people's homes in the rural communities of Limburg. Although the audience of this magazine could hardly be described as being in the forefront of cultural change in the Netherlands, they were clearly not resisting it either. Magazines like this provided down to earth and practical guidance in a society that, in terms of material wealth, seemed to get better and better all the time.

Summarizing the developments in themes and moral orientation, Brinkgreve writes:

> The problems, and especially the advice given, point to a lessening of differences in power between socio-economic classes, between men and women and between parents and children. More emotions are allowed expression, and a wider range of behaviours is thought acceptable. Men are expected to be more considerate towards women, and in different ways. With regard to

---

[19] Wijnands, *Op Het Dorp; Leven in De Kleine Limburgse Gemeenschappen*, 14–26.
[20] Christien Brinkgreve and Michel Korzec, *"Margriet weet raad": gevoel, gedrag, moraal in Nederland 1938–1978*, Aula boeken (Utrecht: Spectrum, 1978), 93–94.

certain themes, Margriet changed from rejection to acceptance: voluntary childlessness, cohabitation, homosexuality, a generous standard of living. Instead of rules for behaviour, psychological advice and interpretations are offered, along with the address for the organization that one might turn to for help with a particular problem. The power to decide and responsibility to act are located within the individual. More and more often, people get the advice not to concern themselves too much with the opinion of other people: clearly, a process of individualization is going on.[21]

Although the division of tasks between men and women is not so strictly defined now, in practice there are clear gender roles: women more often take care of the children, cooking and cleaning, the sick within the extended family, and the ties within the local community. They send the Christmas cards, wrap the gifts, remember birthdays and organize parties, bake pies for fundraising for local associations and do all the necessary volunteer work in the old people's home, the local library and the local Red Cross. A good Limburg woman is a very busy person, and has her house spanking clean. Men have the fulltime job or the deserved pension, take care of finances, collect money in the parish church, dig in the garden, take care of the heavy work in the graveyard. A good Limburg man cares for his family by bringing in money and having all the repairs around the house in order. A *very* good Limburg man might also be able to cook and serve coffee to visitors, like the husband of the lady who told me her experience with feminism.

Another effect of the influx of 'imported' people is that it becomes more and more possible to remain anonymous even in small communities. This in turn means that it becomes possible that new ideas are less and less mediated 'within' the local community, but are present and accepted in the anonymous shell 'around' it. The local community ("de gemeenschap" or "de gemeinsjap" in dialect) is becoming just one segment of a population accidentally sharing the same geographical location. In combination with the rising real-estate prices, this development gives the label of Catholicism a new salience as a marker of the domain of the 'familiar' versus the 'unfamiliar'. The particularity of place is emphasized and reproduced with the help of Catholic rituals.

The Church in Community Life

Walking around Welden on a weekday you will see women washing windows, taking their children to and from school (schools close for lunch),

[21] Ibid.

an old lady with a large bag entering the church by a side door to clean, tourists sitting on an esplanade, old men sitting on a bench like over-age teenagers commenting on the passers-by, and the real teenagers hanging around the bus station loudly teasing each other and lugging book bags too big for them. Family life, the raising of children is the main business in a place like this.

In this solid, affluent life, moral guidance by the church often seems superfluous. If problems do arise (drugs, unwanted pregnancy, rebellious children) people do not turn to the priest for help and the priest does not take it upon himself to monitor these problems. Rather, they call in the help of the appropriate experts and support groups: psychologist, doctor, social worker, patient associations, groups for mourning etc.

As with the impact of feminism taken as an example above, the general, almost universally agreed on sketch of secularization should be nuanced with regard to the local horizons described here. The church did lose power, but in local community life, priests and chaplains often continued to exercise their influence even during the years that the churches emptied and afterwards. In some cases, priest and local community have been 'together' for so many years that they are quite organically entangled. This influence is becoming more and more informal, and thus dependent on the personality and social skills of the priest or chaplain involved. Even where a priest is still guaranteed a place on the board of local associations, the generally higher level of education of the lay members staffing these boards alters his authority.

Traditionally, the priest was automatically considered to be the most 'learned', perhaps next to the school principal and the doctor, but with a special aura because of his calling, the power of the institution of the church he represented, and his frightening celibacy which set him apart from 'normal' people. When this celibacy came into question, as we saw in the previous chapter, the authority of the priest and the whole church suddenly seemed to founder. Nowadays, his position is less 'exalted' and most people seem to think it would be better for the poor man to marry, not only for his personal psychological health but also to be in a better position to advise people, having more experience with the complications of family life.

As a result of the rise of the secular welfare state and in some cases—as in Welden- augmented by the polarization within the diocese of Roermond, territories were carved up between 'professionals' (health, education, etc.) and the church from the national down to the local level. The church became a bounded entity instead of all pervading. Already existing social spheres like school and the workplace became independent from the influence of the church and newly emerging spheres remained outside the scope of the parish priest's influence. Whereas before, every local organization and institution had a 'spiritual advisor' on its board, it became less and less a matter of course that the parish priest would be invited on the board, although in practice this might still be the case.

Furthermore, when church attendance was framed as something that should be internally motivated rather than externally enforced, the weekly rhythms of community life became less steady and less bound to the church; younger people go 'when they feel like it'. Even for those who had been accustomed to go to church all their lives, the rhythm changed. For example, many older people now prefer to go to church to celebrate the Eucharist on Saturday night rather than Sunday morning, since it is not obligatory to have fasted anymore.

However, the yearly rhythm of feasts and commemorations, and the celebration of the important holidays celebrated in the local associations and the local schools remain linked to the church. The various village associations all like to have their special Christmas and Easter celebrations done by the parish priest. Lately, these Easter and Christmas celebrations are under pressure because of the shortage of priests. Although the local village associations protest loudly against it, these special celebrations are now integrated with the Easter and Christmas mass celebrated for the general parish.

Aside from the Catholic rituals, the label 'Catholic' is still important to signal continuity and rootedness in the locality. This is clear in the history of the local elementary schools: when bishop Gijsen threatened to take away their 'Catholic' label because they did not comply with his standards, they protested loudly. And he did not succeed: most, if not all local elementary schools in the small rural communities of the South of Limburg are at least nominally Catholic.

They all struggle to formulate what this means nowadays: there are no more nuns and friars teaching, the content of most lessons has no connection to a traditionally Catholic worldview, and many parents are as ignorant about Catholicism as their children (and as the younger teachers). The present-day senior teachers came of age at a time when the critique of lay Catholic professionals of the 'stuffiness' of the enclosed Catholic world, the deadness of rituals, and authoritarian relations within the Catholic church were well out into the open, from the local level of the parish and diocese to the global level of the world church.

These teachers tend to emphasize the values of open-mindedness, inclusiveness and equality, summarized as 'progressiveness'. This is contrasted with the enclosed, restrictive and authoritative Catholicism dominating schools in the past, with separate education for boys and girls. They see the doctrines and practices promoted by the diocese, especially when Gijsen was still the bishop, as hopelessly and infuriatingly obsolete and irrelevant. As one teacher expressed it: "if a priest would ask me about my sex life, I would say, 'it's fine, but what about yours? Isn't that a little bit more problematic?' ". Priests should expect to be answered back, rather than obeyed without question.

Nevertheless, the local elementary schools do find it important to continue identifying themselves as Catholic. 'Belonging' to the local community and being a Catholic are still entwined, the former implying the latter. According to the elementary school teachers I met during my fieldwork, losing the label 'RK'[22] would have caused parents to look askance at them.[23] Schools without this label are seen as 'strangers', elements that don't belong naturally in the village community. 'RK' is connected to being a 'Limburger' and sending your child to a 'different' school would be equivalent to denying your roots, making a choice against the community by entrusting the education of your child to outsiders.

Being a 'Catholic' school, according to the local elementary school teachers (in Welden and other places), does not mean that they teach a certain version of how the world came into being, or how you should live. In their words, it means that they encourage children to reflect on 'the meaning of life', and to reflect on their behaviour towards others. It is a very inclusive kind of Christianity, with the emphasis on a notion of God as 'love' and the central message of Jesus as 'love thy neighbour'.[24] In classes on religion they often use a general 'Christian' teaching method, which may even have a protestant background. Some schools set up special groups to develop the celebrations for Christmas and Easter, in some cases in cooperation with the parish church, in other cases these celebrations are held separately. Another way in which they express their Catholic identity is by participating in efforts to collect money for a good cause.

---

[22] Short for Rooms Katholiek (Roman Catholic).

[23] Except of course, when the local priest is involved, like the one cited. Although the distrust towards outsiders is lessening, it is still present.

[24] In the yearly report of one local school, being part of the Catholic tradition is summarized as 'respect for every human being and every creation. Love for fellow human beings, especially those who need help, is the place where we meet God'. For their school, they take this to mean that the atmosphere should be hospitable and caring, that they have celebrations where awe and responsibility for creation are expressed, and that they participate in fundraising for charities and in the religious classes.

In this re-signified form, we might call this a thoroughly modernized and rationalized Catholicism, which has shaped itself so as not to clash with the natural sciences, the Enlightenment ideal of 'thinking for yourself', nor with other religions. The focus is on 'reflection' rather than 'content', on 'values' such as 'life is worth it to be lived' rather than specific rules. As one teacher admitted, it is hard to pinpoint the difference between a Catholic school and a protestant school, except that the first is normal and accepted in the local community, and the other is conspicuous and strange.

The Post-War Generation: "Despite..."

On an individual level, continuity with the Catholic past is also created through rituals. Choosing *not* to go through Catholic life cycle rituals was still perceived as a painful slap in the face of the community and the older generations. It amounts to a statement that what everybody considers to be the 'normal' routines and practices are not good enough for the individuals involved; that the upbringing their parents gave them is somehow lacking. For the same reason, not sending your child to the local Catholic school is a statement that creates a distance between a family and the local community. Like the local schools, the traditional Catholic life cycle rituals are part of the domain of the familiar, and derive their continued significance from this fact.

Nevertheless, it is slowly becoming more and more acceptable that parents do not have their children baptized or participate in the First Holy Communion ritual, especially in communities where the relationship between the community and the parish priest is strained, or where there are a lot of people from 'outside' ('import') who are not worried about snubbing the local ways. The justification then is that children should make their own choice what to believe when they grow older. However, the majority of parents in the south of Limburg still have their children baptized and let them do the Holy Communion, even when they are not active Catholics themselves.[25]

Local schools take care not to discriminate against non-Catholic children, especially with regard to the First Holy Communion, but parents fear that their children will be ostracized if they don't celebrate the First Holy Communion like all the other kids in their class. Social pressure is

---

[25] Theo Schepens and Leo Spruit, *De Rooms-Katholieke Kerk in Nederland, 1960–1998 Een Statistisch Trendrapport* (Nijmegen en Tilburg, 2001).

still involved, although not to the extent of formal exclusion if a child does not participate. However, social pressure is not the only reason for going through the life cycle rituals.

In the interviews with the pre-war generation they often said about their children: "they have their own faith", without discussing it further. Whatever this faith might be, it was far removed from the wholly Catholic world they themselves grew up in; and therefore did not fit into their own narratives. But they also emphasized: "still, they decided to have their child baptized", or "still, they go to church with their children every once in a while". In some cases, young parents decide to have their child baptized despite not having married in church.

According to these older people, their children explained this in variations on the following statement: "that's how we grew up, so I want to give that to my children too. Not in the way it was in my parents' time, but still, it's important to have some basis. When they [the children] grow up, they will make up their own mind". This is also what the post-war generation told me in the interviews and informal conversations.

Another often heard remark was: "I experience my faith in my own way, I don't need the priest to tell me what to believe". Implicit in these statements is the belief that everybody should be left to their own best judgements in matters of faith. However, as priests sometimes remarked bitterly, these people *do* go to the priest and the church for the life cycle rituals: baptism, Holy Communion, marriage, the last Sacraments[26] and funerary rites.

When new parents of the younger generation decided that their own children should in turn acquire the emblems of Catholicism, it seemed to signal to *their* parents the sameness of life despite all the differences between the generations. At least, that is how the older generation interpreted it: even though their children live in a time with more luxury, where "everybody has all the modern comforts and knows it all",[27] *they do not want to 'break' with the kind of life their parents lived*, they are not burning their bridges to the past. Their life remains rooted in the familiar and is governed by the predictable logic of certain life patterns, the rules and responsibilities of interpersonal relationships in this domain.

---

[26] Officially, this is the Sacrament of the Sick. But people usually refer to it as the last sacraments.

[27] See the citation of the lady commenting on the decline of community in the previous chapter.

This also became clear in the interviews and informal conversations with parents of the generation born in the late fifties and sixties: their intention was not to go against their parents, to break with them, or to have a revolutionary new lifestyle. Of course, they want to do things 'better', mainly in the freedom and sense of personal responsibility they grant their children, but this does not mean that they explicitly react against their parents. The older generation is reassured: when it comes down to the 'basics' of life, settling down and especially raising children, their children choose to reconnect with tradition, even if it is mostly 'symbolic', to pay their respects to the way their parents lived. That is why the older generation sees the younger generation as basically leading the same kind of life as they had: working hard and raising children.

The meaning of the emblems of Catholicism like baptism, Holy Communion and sending your children to a Catholic school has changed considerably. From being the signposts of a 'good Catholic life' no person can avoid passing, they have become emblems of identity, of belonging to the local community. To many people, these rituals do not have any religious significance anymore. At the same time, because of their religious roots and their significance in local life, these emblems are coveted entrance points for progressive and neo-conservative Catholics to teach their versions of Catholicism.[28] This, in turn, can lead to a process of religious re-signification or sacralization.

4. RE-SIGNIFICATION OF THE CATHOLIC TRADITION

The uncertainty about what it means to be a Catholic school provides an entry-point for re-signification by specialized religious discourses, neo-conservative and liberal Catholic. The same can be said about the life cycle rituals. Although the significance of the life cycle rituals to the younger generation seems to lie primarily in the continuity with the past and their parents' life, these rituals are also more and more actively *re-signified* in the negotiation or active cooperation of the parties involved in these rituals (school, parents, priests, doctors). This becomes necessary, because

---

[28] Gerard Lukken, "Infant Baptism in the Netherlands and Flanders," in *Christian Feast and Festival. The Dynamics of Western Liturgy and Culture*, ed. Paul Post and Gerard Rouwhorst, vol. 12, Liturgia Condenda (Leuven: Peeters, 2001), 558–564; Paul Post, "The Celebration of the First Communion. Seeking the Identity of the Christian Ritual," in *Christian Feast and Festival. The Dynamics of Western Liturgy and Culture*, ed. Paul Post and Gerard Rouwhorst, vol. 12, Liturgia Condenda (Leuven [etc.]: Peeters, 2001), 598.

despite the significance these rituals have, priests, educators and active Catholics often perceive the continued performance of the life cycle rituals as "merely going through the motions", and therefore unsatisfactory. The apparent meaninglessness of ritual provokes a search for meaning.[29]

The Catholic church (both liberal and conservative factions) is actively developing resources directed at parents and children to re-signify the traditional life cycles. This is done in the form of the books being sold in the pastoral centre nearby, and in the courses it offers (further described in chapter 6). Recently, some of these courses are offered on request by the diocese, to train parish volunteers in the region.

"Doing the traditional thing" and actively involving oneself with the parish church is becoming a conscious choice made within a larger context of perceived indifference to local community life, the church and the past. When people explain their wish to stay connected in some way to Catholicism, they often illustrate their choice by referring to the rhetorical questions other people might ask: "Why should I get married in church? Does it mean I love my wife less if we don't get married? I don't believe in heaven and hell, so why should I pray for my deceased father?" Although they grant that these can be legitimate questions, the expression of their connection to the church is a choice against the perceived indifference of modern life, affirming the value of local community united in recognition of 'something more' in life.

Another indicator that doing the rituals is becoming a conscious choice and not only a wish to conform is the choice of words in the way both the older generation and the younger generation talk about it: they often used the word "toch". This word means 'still', 'yet', 'although' or 'despite'. Despite what? This is mostly left implicit. We might fill in: despite secularization and the fact that it is easy to ignore the church, despite not going to church often, despite the difference between the life of the younger generation and the older generation, despite the fact that the church can no longer dictate how one should live.

To some, performing the rituals might be the rejection of the negative of the traditional: rejecting the notion that 'anything goes', that form is not important, that traditions are meant to be left behind in the name of progress. It can be a choice to 'stay local' and perpetuate the historical community. To others, this choice might be made in the service of

---

[29] Humphrey and Laidlaw, *The Archetypal Acts of Ritual, a Theory of Ritual Illustrated by the Jain Rite of Worship.*

'modern' ideals such as those of liberal Catholicism, but against the ano-
mie of individualization: whishing the individual in his connection to
family and community to be the ultimate meaningful unit, rather than
just 'the individual'.

5. Concluding Remarks

In this chapter, the role of religion, and specifically religious ritual, in the
production of locality has become clear. In chapter 1, I referred to insights
developed within geography that see place as the product of the intersection of processes that operate on different spatial scales. Following this
insight, we can see that village life is created through the intersection of
large scale processes of modernization, movements such as feminism,
global processes of liberalization and polarization within the Catholic
church and the always present efforts of people to create a domain of the
familiar with, in Appadurai's terms, "recognizably local subjects".

In guarding and recreating the boundaries of the safe and familiar world
of the local community, Catholic rituals and the Catholic identity play an
important part, but in a way that is very different from the role the church
used to give itself in defending its flock. Catholicism has to be kept alive,
if not the beliefs, then at least the "feeling"[30] as part of the general feeling of belonging to a particular place. At the same time, the familiar has
to be defended against intrusion by religious authorities. Acquiring the
emblems of Catholicism and the celebration of the life cycle rituals take
on new meanings: to the older generation, it signifies the continuity of
life from one generation to the other, despite the many differences. To the
younger generation, it might mean this, and many other things besides:
an expression of personal belief, conformity to tradition and community
expectations and a token of respect to the world their parents created for
them. The ritual practices associated with acquiring these emblems provide entrance points for both progressive and neo-conservative Catholic
discourses to wield power and attempt a religious re-signification.

The explicit rules and regulations issued by Catholic authorities such
as the pope, the bishop and the parish priest are usually ignored, even
deemed too irrelevant to even want to change them. There is an almost

---

[30] The slogan of the Catholic broadcasting service KRO (one of the remnants of the
Catholic pillar) is 'het gevoel blijft', meaning something like 'the feeling (or sentiment)
remains'.

magical belief in progress; most people seem to believe that the moral rules of the church are outdated and will in time be changed: "dat is toch niet meer van deze tijd!" (It's so outdated!). Professionals might wax indignant about the "outdated" morality of the church, when applied to their domain, but otherwise the conflict between these values and the general consensus embodied in the familiar world is downplayed without argument.

Rituals around death and dying are a place where the domain of the familiar and the church, having drifted apart, come together again. Having a Catholic funeral means different things to the people involved, but it is usually considered the only option apart from an anonymous, cold funeral. In the negotiations about the funeral mass, the participation of the family, the songs and prayers chosen, differing evaluations of the meaning and worth of individual life are at stake. To the family and close friends, the rituals, especially the last rites, become occasions to create and deepen the shared sense of the meaningfulness of life. Whereas the older generation was taught to believe in the 'automatic' efficacy of performing the rituals correctly and praying for the dead, the younger generation puts more emphasis on the 'psychological' importance of these rituals, to accompany the process of mourning and to share the event of someone close to them dying to reflect on ultimate meanings and affirm ties, to express that they *care* that this person has died. This creates a situation where the power of disapproval of the church might once again be felt. This power is linked to a shared bodily hexis, created through the efforts of the Catholic organizations that have now lost their power. However, this 'power of disapproval' is matched by the outrage of the post-war generation whenever a priest gives the impression of wielding this power carelessly.

The narratives about the role of priests in the last rites indicate that the role of the church is not taken for granted anymore, that the attitudes, values and beliefs of the younger generations do not tolerate authoritative pronouncements on what is supposed to be morally good and bad. It also shows that on some occasions, people feel that they cannot do without the church, even though, as the pre-war generation puts it, "they have their own beliefs". But most importantly, it shows that there is a strong sentiment among the post-war generation, especially the women, to protect the domain of the familiar against authoritarian interference. They have nothing against the church per se, as long as the attitude of the priest towards this intersubjectively shared world is respectful, does not try to subvert their expressions. A priest who sabotages or subverts the attempts of a family to express how much they cared about the deceased, or who invokes the power of disapproval of the church, can count on being painted as a "villain" and a "psychopath".

Although Catholicism and Catholic practices mark the familiar, church life and community life might go separate ways, especially in Welden. If you don't like your local church, you can go to another one without any serious consequences. Religion, for a while a structuring force in society, has become a provider of services in a pluralized religious landscape. In the region, several former monasteries and convents have reinvented themselves and offer specific services, courses and opportunities to gather around specific interests, as described in chapter 6. Specialized religious repertoires have also made their entrance, and with the popularity of New Age in the Netherlands in general, localized but fragmented and obscure traditions of spiritualism have been infused with new life. The two contexts presented in the next chapters show how people are trained, and train themselves, to find new ways of relating to religious knowledge and authority.

CHAPTER FIVE

PRACTICING SPIRITUALITY

1. INTRODUCTION

In the field of religious studies, much is known about the history and key beliefs of New Age and the assorted 'alternative spiritualities' associated with New Age. Often, these studies are based on literature, historical sources and surveys, like the ones mentioned above. Detailed ethnographic studies of the practice of what people call 'spirituality' are relatively scarce, especially in comparison to the rich ethnographies that exist on modern Paganism.[1]

On one of my first visits to Welden, I noticed a flyer on the announcement board of the community centre for flower séances held there regularly, led by the medium Maria Bemelmans.[2] When I asked some volunteers about these séances, I was told that people from all over the area came there to get a message from their deceased relatives. In an earlier research, I had already noticed that there seemed to be a strong strand of spiritualism intertwined with Catholicism in the southern regions of the Netherlands.[3] Taking a pluralist notion of religion as a point of departure, I found it important to include these phenomena within the research. In the introduction I argued that what is nowadays called 'spirituality', often

---

[1] E.g. Fedele, *Looking for Mary Magdalene. Alternative Pilgrimage and Ritual Creativity at Catholic Shrines in France*; Anna Fedele, "The Metamorphoses of Neopaganism in Traditionally Catholic Countries in Southern Europe," in *Sites and Politics of Religious Diversity in Southern Europe*, ed. Ruy Blanes and José Mapril (Leiden: Brill, forthcoming); Sarah M. Pike, *Earthly Bodies, Magical Selves: Contemporary Pagans and the Search for Community* (Berkeley: University of California Press, 2001); Sabina Magliocco, *Witching Culture: Folklore and Neo-paganism in America* (Philadelphia: University of Pennsylvania Press, 2004); Graham Harvey, *Listening People, Speaking Earth: Contemporary Paganism* (London: C. Hurst & Co. Publishers, 1997); Åsa Trulsson, *Cultivating the Sacred: Ritual Creativity and Practice Among Women in Contemporary Europe*, Lund Studies in the History of Religions 28 (Lund: Lund University, 2010); Jone Salomonsen, *Enchanted Feminism: Ritual, Gender and Divinity Among the Reclaiming Witches of San Francisco* (London: Routledge, 2002).

[2] I do not know if this is a pseudonym or not, but it is a common enough name in Limburg.

[3] Kim Knibbe and Iti Westra, "Van Ongeloof Naar 'zeker Weten': Betekenisgeving En Legitimatie in De Context Van Het Fenomeen Jomanda," *Sociale Wetenschappen* 46, no. 2 (2003): 75–93.

linked to esoteric traditions, has become one of the anchoring points for discourses and practices in relating to the category of religion in Europe. Similarly, I understand the spiritual practices of the group I describe here as experimenting with ways of relating to a kind of power and knowledge that is usually thought to be within the domain of religion. This means that, in the case of this research, Catholicism and the spiritualist practices described here have to be understood in relation to each other. I will argue that it is in particular where it concerns religious authority and the ways it is made (im)possible to relate to the supernatural that the practices described here can be understood as an answer to the problems generated by the context of Catholicism in which they take place.

Another line of argument that will be explored in this chapter is the question of the 'spiritual revolution' that is argued to take place by Heelas and Woodhead.[4] As described in chapter 1, this thesis links changes in the religious landscape to societal changes. As societies become more individualized, spirituality will become more popular. Spirituality is then interpreted as a sacralization of the self, or indeed of modernity. The material presented here will show that what goes under the name of spirituality can also embody quite different modes of practice and believing and may answer to quite different needs than those summarized in the 'spiritual revolution' thesis.

Besides the 'spiritual group' (hereafter called SG to distinguish it from other groups) I participated in, there are many other 'spiritual groups' in the villages and cities surrounding the main research area, and countless individual practitioners associated to the tradition of spiritualism, such as magnetists, mediums, and clairvoyants. According to my informants, until the late eighties these practitioners operated "in the shadows", in obscure back rooms. A favourite topic among insiders of this milieu until this day is the abuse of power that is apparently common between mediums and their followers. Nowadays, mediums operate more visibly, and public interest in their practices is growing. One medium who became particularly famous in the nineties, Jomanda, used to tour the spiritual groups in Limburg in the late seventies and in the eighties.[5]

The roots of 'Jomanda' and the networks from which she emerged go much further back in time than the relatively recent popular interest

---

[4] Heelas and Woodhead, *The Spiritual Revolution.*
[5] Knibbe and Westra, "Van Ongeloof Naar 'zeker Weten': Betekenisgeving En Legitimatie in De Context Van Het Fenomeen Jomanda."

in New Age. Although she attracted a lot of 'tourists', the main core of her visitors were middle aged men and women (predominantly women) with a lower class Catholic background and a low level of education. This public is vastly different from the public that 'New Age' attracts according to most studies done in the Netherlands and elsewhere: highly educated middle class women of the baby boom generation, with a leftist orientation,[6] young people sceptical towards science,[7] people who belong to the category of 'expressivists' in the classification of Inglehart.[8] But it is very similar to the public attracted to the SG and to the paranormal markets described towards the end of this chapter. When New Age became more main stream in the early nineties, it linked up with the spiritualist networks already existing in Limburg.

Apart from the regular séances of Maria Bemelmans in the community centre of Welden, and the presence of Jomanda in nearby Valkenburg where she had established a more permanent practice, I noticed that the meetings of a 'SG' were prominently advertized in the municipal calendar, along with other community activities such as bowling, bingo and gymnastics for the elderly. These meetings took place in another community center in one of the villages within the municipality of Welden. The announced activities for the years 2001 and 2002 ranged from séances and healings to workshops and lectures for members to develop their paranormal powers and follow up interest in spirituality. The meetings of this group, and those of others in the surroundings, were also advertized in the local free Sunday papers. New Age and alternative spiritualities, therefore, were definitely a visible phenomenon from within the local horizons of Welden and the surrounding villages.

The main ideas and practices of the networks within which the Spiritual Society is located will be introduced through a description of some of the central practices in this setting and the discussion that emerged from these practices over several meetings in the second section. The third section, on relationships and the demands of individualism describes some of the main themes of the discussions that took place: personhood and responsibility, the limits of power in personal relationships and the role

---

[6] Aupers and Van Otterloo, *New Age; Een Godsdiensthistorische En Sociologische Benadering*, 106–109.

[7] Houtman and Mascini, "Why Do Churches Become Empty While New Age Grows? Secularization and Religious Change in the Netherlands."

[8] Inglehart and Welzel, *Modernization, Cultural Change, and Democracy*; Paul Heelas, *The New Age Movement; the Celebration of the Self and the Sacralization of Modernity* (Oxford [etc.]: Blackwell, 1996), 120.

of gossip. The fourth section, on sceptical positivism, describes the practice of spirituality as a series of techniques to manipulate frequencies and train one's perception. Towards the end of the chapter I will present a perspective on the role of consumerism in relating to religious knowledge and authority and the concluding remarks.

Before moving on to the ethnographic material and its discussion outlined above, I will describe the setting of the actual fieldwork and how I moved in this context as a participant observer. In contrast to some of the other chapters, this discussion is rather long. This is necessary not only because of the context, in which participant observation may mean something quite different than in other situations in the sense that it is very difficult not to become a practitioner oneself, but also because a reflection on methodology in this case reveals a lot about the underlying characteristics and dynamics of the context.

Methodological Notes

The group where I did participant observation had both 'closed nights', when only members were welcome and 'open nights'. During closed nights, the members practiced their own paranormal powers and discussed esoteric subjects in depth. On open nights, everybody was welcome to attend the lecture, séance or healing. The persons leading the open nights were usually invited from the other spiritual groups in the area; sometimes someone from another province was invited for a lecture, healing or séance. During closed nights, members trained each other in developing skills such as aura-reading, tarot-card reading etc. I attended both kinds of evenings.

There was a group of about thirty regulars, people who attended because they were interested in developing their own paranormal or healing powers. Not all of these people attended every session: there was a core group of volunteers who came every time, led by Beth and her husband. They set up the chairs and tables, put out the leaflets, sold the entrance tickets and managed the sound system. Many members were mediums and psychics who had their own practice. They attended some meetings for their own specific reasons (e.g. to learn from a more experienced medium or get a message) or to teach during the closed nights. These practitioners usually had their own personal following of friends and relatives who turned to them for help and advice, meditated together and practiced magnetism, reiki, tarot and other esoteric practices with each other. Especially when there was a séance or a 'reading' (of aura's, objects, handprints, candle wax drawings), many new faces suddenly appeared, swelling the audience: people who had just lost somebody and hoped to get a message, people who were in a personal crisis or concerned about somebody close to them, a few who seemed to be in 'perpetual' crisis, barely hanging on to sanity. These séances and readings also drew the curious, who hoped to find the evidence they needed to believe the claims of the mediums and psychics about the existence of "the other side".

The atmosphere was always very friendly. Although there was also a lot of secretiveness on the part of some people, this was counteracted by the character of Beth, who insisted on openness and clarity in everything. She was generally recognized as the informal leader and had the last word in every discussion. Although her husband was usually very silent, he was considered an authority as well, because he was said to have written several books.[9] He led some meditation and therapy groups.

Newcomers usually felt apprehensive because of the nature of the meetings, but they were never regarded as intruders, however sceptic they were or unfamiliar with how to behave. The entrance fee for the evenings was about two euro, with a discount for members (and for me, a 'poor student'); just enough to cover the cost of hiring a space in the community centre and the posters.

I was interested in the SG because it seemed to mix 'classic' spiritualist activities such as séances and healings with more 'New Age' sounding things such as lectures on dreaming, pyramids etc. Participating in the various activities of this group also gave me the opportunity to talk to several different psychics, mediums and other practitioners informally and see how they interacted. I contacted the founder of the SG, Beth, and explained the purpose of my research to her. In our first conversation she was positive about the idea that I would do research; 'after all, we're all searchers'. But she discouraged me to visit other groups. Some groups, according to her, were prone to power games by the leading medium of that group. She had set up her own group precisely to avoid this situation; there was no one medium who played a bigger role than another, and she herself was not a medium.

In fact, I did not attend other spiritual groups, not only because of her objections but also because I did not have any means of transport from the place I was staying to the meetings of the other groups (the buses

---

[9] Which I never saw and did not find anywhere, by the way. Somehow, he discouraged questions about them.

stop running at night in that region). But I did talk to the mediums and psychics who led these societies on the paranormal markets and when they came to visit the SG. Later in this chapter, it will become clear that distrust and a critical attitude towards practitioners such as mediums and psychics are a continuous topic of discussion within these networks.

Of all the contexts described in this book, this was the easiest place to do research. Although I never managed to explain well enough what my research was about, people did not really care: I was young; I was a 'seeker' and therefore had to be protected, mothered and taken care of. Usually, I found myself with Jacky, who also gave me a ride to these meetings. She was a very down to earth person, forever despairing that she 'did not feel anything': she did not feel energies, or see aura's or receive any of the other paranormal perceptions, signs and coincidences that people keenly discussed among each other.[10] It suited me well to have a sober person like her to link with; she was a stabilizing presence in an otherwise creatively unstable and sometimes unsettling environment.

The descriptions and narratives presented here are constructed out of participant observations during the formal part of the evenings, informal conversations at the bar during breaks and after the meetings, listening to the advice to others and myself during the informal talk after the meetings. I also did some interviews with practitioners, but most practitioners did not like to be interviewed. They explained their reluctance by saying they felt that the core of their work could not be explained in words, they actually distrusted interviews as a means for gaining understanding of their practices. The whole point of the group was to develop people's *own* powers to get in touch with the 'evidence' that there is 'more' between heaven and earth than is usually accepted. Rather than discussing their worldview and teaching it as a doctrine, the practices of the Group were designed to enable people to 'see for themselves' and figure things out from their own personal experience.

Because of the difficulty I had in formally interviewing practitioners I did a private course in Tarot cards with one practitioner in Welden. During the sessions, I gathered a lot of information on the local networks in and around Welden. Besides her and Beth, whom I also interviewed formally, I found two other informants who had been involved in several

---

[10] Of course, one might wonder why she kept coming. The social dimension of this group should not be underestimated. This will be further discussed in the second part of this chapter.

spiritual groups in the eighties and since turned to the Christian Pastoral Centre, who provided me with historical background information.

Participant observation and informal conversations and interviews are standard methodologies in the social sciences. However in the context of practices connected to spirituality and New Age there is usually an exceptionally heavy emphasis on experience, altered states of consciousness. The other side is apprehended through these altered states of consciousness and through bodily experience. Participating in the practices of the SG can be daunting for researchers who do not share the beliefs of these people. To researchers who are indifferent to these beliefs, or look down at them as superstitions or the product of an overactive imagination, it could be embarrassing to follow suggestions such as 'open yourself to the divine energies'. How can you open yourself to something you don't believe in?

In my case, I went along with these suggestions and imagined myself 'opening to the divine energies' during meditations at the beginning of a meeting, leaving aside the question whether I actually believed in them or not. Although in describing this setting I confine myself to a position of methodological agnosticism, in doing participant observation I was more of a methodological 'ludist'.[11] This approach to the study of religion takes the human ability to play as its point of departure. In this way, the believer's point of view can be taken into account more fully. 'Play' in this case is defined as the human ability to handle two ways of understanding reality at the same time: 'as is' and 'as if'.

The question remains whether the boundaries between 'as if' (in this case the 'reality' of "the other side", the divine world) and 'as is' (in this case: how I as an agnostic researcher interpret the world) can be so strictly defined. In fact, part of the experience of fieldwork for most anthropologists who study religion is that these boundaries are often threatened or breached or that the difference between the two becomes a sliding scale: the researcher identifies with the people she is doing his research with to the extent that she starts sharing their outlook on life.[12]

---

[11] André Droogers, "The Third Bank of the River: Play, Methodological Ludism and the Definition of Religion," in *The Pragmatics of Defining Religion: Contexts, Concepts and Contents*, ed. J.G. Platvoet and A.L. Molendijk (Leiden: Brill, 1999), 285–313.

[12] See for an extended discussion of this issue Kim Knibbe and André Droogers, "Methodological Ludism and the Study of Religion," *Method and Theory in the Study of Religion* 23 (2011): 285–305.

During the participant observation with the SG, I defined these boundaries more strictly than I did during previous research. Although, like the
other participants, I sometimes had strange bodily experiences (like my
wriggling fingers in the narrative below) and certainly entered different
states of consciousness, I do not really attach much significance to these
things. To me, feeling dizzy, having your fingers start moving involun-
tarily, swaying in your chair and the things that you can see while under
hypnosis did not present anything of existential importance. Of course,
these phenomena did not leave me completely indifferent either. I personally considered them to be techniques of consciousness and the body
that have a particular persuasiveness to people (especially in the 'rational'
Netherlands where these phenomena are seen as exceptional and strange)
and certainly help to fix meanings memorably. But I did not normally see
these phenomena as 'signs from the other side', or as objective evidence
that my grandmother or my spirit guides wanted to tell me something.
As an anthropologist, I knew that the so-called 'paranormal perceptions'
and phenomena discussed in this context could be interpreted in many
different ways.

In knowing this, and in the distancing from what happened to my body
and my consciousness that resulted from this knowledge, I was different
from the other people participating in the context of the SG. I did not hide
this difference but it was not seen as very important in this group, where
sceptics and newcomers mingled easily with the 'true believers' and practitioners and speculation on the most outlandish ideas was regular fare
during conversations.

In the practice of fieldwork, phenomenological anthropology (not to
be confused with the phenomenology developed within the Study of Religion) proved to be an inspiration to conceptualize the problematics of
intersubjectivity and experience thrown up by this context.[13] By participating the way I did, I became aware of how the practices can make sense
on a very personal, emotional and physical level, even if I personally came
to different conclusions. Furthermore, it enabled me to see that although
the techniques of the body and consciousness encouraged and taught
here are directed at the individual, they are in fact part of collectively
shared repertoires, and connect with collectively shared dispositions; they

---

[13] Kim Knibbe and Peter Versteeg, "Assessing Phenomenology in Anthropology," *Critique of Anthropology* 28, no. 1 (March 1, 2008): 47–62.

constitute an epistemological individualism that is learned, a cultural pattern of seeing, feeling and being.[14]

2. POWER AND KNOWLEDGE

> I can see you are a magnetist. And I can see you like women. You surround yourself with women, as if you are a sort of 'Anton Heyboer'.[15] And you do not listen to other people warning you when you are going in the wrong direction. Until you crash headlong into a brick wall, you will not change your course. But in the next few months you will notice that the top of your head will start to itch. You will be getting a different kind of energy, that's why. "The other side" sees that many people in your practice are actually dependent on you. In future, when you heal them, you will get a telephone call about three days after you have treated a person, and each of them will tell you that they have gotten worse. This way, you will know who is dependent on you, and you can do something about it.

This was a message addressed to one of the men in the group whom I will call Matt. The actual message was much longer, and involved her making a drawing of his aura, describing a "ghandi-like" presence standing behind him trying to warn him, and the advice to start wearing red underwear (which prompted Matt to stand up and show that he was already wearing red underpants). It is a complicated message, in the way the message itself embodied a certain power-relationship, namely that of a trained psychic with access to special knowledge assumed to be inaccessible to others with another spiritual practitioner who should be able to apprehend these things as well, and actually reacted in a way that indicated that he was at least partially in agreement with her observations and advice by showing his red underpants. In terms of content, it is clear that the message is also about power: the psychic criticized the way Matt related to women, saying that he was making them dependent on him.

Power relationships were a much discussed topic. In theory, a medium or psychic who claims to be able to see things and transmit things from the other side is difficult to contest. However, there was also an emphasis on finding things out for oneself, findings one's own path. This has led to sociological descriptions of contemporary spirituality as 'eclectic' 'pick

---

[14] Knibbe, "An Ethnography of a Medium and Her Followers: How Learning Takes Place in the Context of Jomanda"; Knibbe and Westra, "Van Ongeloof Naar 'zeker Weten': Betekenisgeving En Legitimatie in De Context Van Het Fenomeen Jomanda."

[15] Anton Heyboer (deceased 2005) was an artist who was cared for by several women who also were his lovers. He was still alive at the time.

and mix' religion and incoherent. However, there are unifying interpretative frames that are enforced through discursive power, rather than the
direct exercise of control. In order to understand how power and knowledge are constituted in this context, we have to take a closer look at these
interpretative frames and their history, as well as at the ways that these
frames are enforced.

Interpretative Frames

The description above provides an entrance into the coherence that is
created within a creatively unstable environment, where a multiplicity
of interpretations are explored and encouraged. Everybody is supposed
to find things out by him or herself, to follow his or her 'own path', but
this evidently does not lead to moral relativism or indifference to other
people's behaviour. People were not afraid to pass judgement on each
other. Mediums and psychics can give some pretty strong advice even
when people do not agree with them. Furthermore, it is clear that there
are some core ideas drawn on in analysing, evaluating and passing judgement within these networks. Together, these ideas form a quite strong
interpretative frame.

This frame is usually not very clearly outlined, which is why many of
the practices of spiritual groups do not make sense to the casual observer.
When someone joins the meetings, they do not get a booklet with information, or an official introduction. People are left to their own devices to
figure out what is going on, helped along by explanations by mediums and
psychics during séances, exegesis during informal conversations, tips from
others on what books to read, etc. There is no official creed, and there is
no limit to the theories people can bring to the discussion or base their
practices on. Shamanism, magnetism, hypnosis, parapsychology, the existence of angels, healing with stones and the theory of the chakras were
all referred to at one time or another. As Bender has shown in a recent
ethnography, people who call themselves 'spiritual' draw on a long history
of practices, but are often not aware of this fact.[16] Rather, they emphasize
the continuously emergent character of spirituality as something that has
to be discovered through personal experience.

Despite the pluralism and 'emergent' character of the spirituality promoted by this group, the underlying logic into which these repertoires are

---

[16] Courtney Bender, *The New Metaphysicals: Spirituality and the American Religious
Imagination* (Chicago: University of Chicago Press, 2010).

fitted derives mainly from spiritualism and theosophy. This 'spiritualist-theosophical' framework is not connected to any name in particular. When someone asks for more information, the works of Blavatsky, and the Dutch medium Jozef Rulof are sometimes recommended.[17] Blavatsky was a nineteenth century medium who produced many books on her spiritual insights, calling it theosophy. Her books are heavy reading and her theories are extremely detailed and elaborate. As so many mediums still do, she reviled her competitors as charlatans, especially the spiritualists. However, in this context fragments of theosophy were peacefully lumped together with ideas from her former enemies, the spiritualists.

My impression was that only Beth, the informal leader of the group, and perhaps her taciturn husband, had actually read any of Blavatsky's works. Among each other the regulars more often referred to popular accounts of people who can remember their stay "on the other side" between this life and their previous life or who have been taken there by a 'guide', a sort of angel, to take a look. The reports of these guided tours are used to explain what happens during a séance or healing. The accounts of Rulof, brought together in numerous books, are the most famous of these.

Common denominators are a belief in reincarnation and a belief in a world (consisting of progressively higher spheres), which is usually invisible and inaccessible in this world but where people go when they die, referred to as "the other side". On "the other side" one can find universities, hospitals, and art schools, music schools etcetera, just like on earth but of course better, more spiritual, more refined. There, the soul develops spiritually, to be able to return to earth and fulfil his or her destiny better and to solve issues from a previous life. These issues are referred to as your 'karma', a concept taken from Hindu and Buddhist philosophies. In this context it is taken to mean that everything you have ever done (right or wrong), every "attachment" you have ever made, is somehow stored in energy patterns that you carry with you from one life to the next. These form the "blueprint" of the lessons you will have to learn to progress spiritually.

The spheres collectively labelled as "the other side" have a progressively higher "frequency": the more developed a soul is, the higher the frequency, and the higher the frequency of the sphere he can enter. In

---

[17] Hélène P. Blavatsky, *Isis Unveiled: a Master-key to the Mysteries of Ancient and Modern Science and Theology* (London, 1910); Jozef Rulof, *De Kosmologie Van Jozef Rulof* ('s Gravenhage: stichting wetenschappelijk genootschap "de eeuw van Christus", 1984).

some variations, a soul is considered part of a group of souls, many of whom you will also meet on earth. The aim of life on earth is to recognize the (moral) lessons you have to learn to develop spiritually, and to do your best to help others along the same path towards the "Light", the ultimate sphere where everything and everybody will be one, where everything is pure Love.

Some souls do not find the way to these spheres very easily, they get stuck in between because they do not believe they have died, or are bound to the earth by the strength of their own destructive illusions. It is these entities that are popularly called ghosts (geesten), and are the main reason why trying to communicate with the spirit world without guidance is supposed to be dangerous: these ghosts might attach themselves to you. Thoughts, events that happened a long time ago and emotions all consist of energies. The 'normal' everyday world everybody can see is simply a 'denser' version of the more refined (and therefore invisible to most people except psychics) energy patterns of the 'other side'. So in a sense, like in many New Age philosophies, people are supposed to create their own reality. However, it is considered to be an evolving reality: the more one progresses spiritually, the lighter this reality will be, the more love is able to flow freely.

Spiritism, Spiritualism and Occultism

The general ideas and the way of believing outlined here can be characterized as occultist according to the distinction Hanegraaff makes between the various modern offshoots of the age-old tradition of esotericism. He defines occultism as a transformation of this tradition in terms of causality under the influence of the rise of scientific thinking.[18] According to Hanegraaff, occultism "comprises all attempts by esotericists to come to terms with a disenchanted world or, alternatively, by people in general to make sense of esotericism form the perspective of a disenchanted secular world".[19]

Instrumental in this transformation of esotericism were the works of Emanuel Swedenborg and Franz Anton Mesmer. Swedenborg coupled a scientific causal thinking to the esoteric principle of correspondence. The natural world was viewed as subject to causal laws, rather than the laws

---

[18] Wouter Hanegraaff, "New Age Religion and Western Culture, Esotericism in the Mirror of Secular Thought" (University of Utrecht, 1995), 354–372.

[19] Ibid., 354.

of correspondence posited by traditional esotericism. In traditional esotericism it was thought that things that are alike, are somehow related
and can influence each other (e.g. as in homeopathy) because God has
created the world as an meaningful and intelligible whole; likeness, in
this thinking, indicates a link. One thing can be studied to reveal knowledge about something that is similar. In spiritualism, the normal world
is believed to be governed by the causal laws of science (dominated by a
mechanistic natural science perspective) but in the 'vertical' dimension
the law of correspondence was left intact: 'as below, so above' (and the
other way around). Heaven is like earth. This was very different from earlier esotericists, who saw nature and the whole world as an enchanted
whole of correspondences.

Mesmer too, saw it as his duty to create a 'scientific' religion where
supernatural phenomena could be proved and explained. He introduced
the notion of magnetism to explain phenomena such as hypnosis, which
inspired many entrepreneurs in his time and apparently still inspires
practices today, as we can see in the story with which this chapter opened.
Although Mesmer himself did not see his work as spiritual or religious in
any way, later occultists have integrated his theories within a spiritist/
spiritualist framework.[20]

At the time, his experiments and the phenomena displayed during
séances by Swedenborgians aroused a lot of interest among intellectuals
and scientists. Historically, Dutch spiritualism (or spiritism as it was called
here) is heir to the international movement of spiritualism,[21] which Hanegraaff characterizes as occultism in its most extreme form, most influenced by the ideals of science.

In the nineteenth century, spiritualism was first introduced to the royal
court of the Netherlands in 1858. In the 1860-ies spiritual groups were
established in Amsterdam, Rotterdam, Groningen and Maastricht. As in
the rest of Europe, the work of Swedenborg and Mesmer and the well pub-
licized events in the house of the Fox-sisters in the US inspired the curiosity of many prominent and intellectual people around the mid-eighteen
hundreds.[22] In the year 1858 the English medium Daniel Douglas Home

---

[20] Ibid., 361–366.
[21] Derk Jansen, "Op Zoek Naar Nieuwe Zekerheid. Negentiende Eeuwse Protestanten
En Het Spiritisme" (Groningen University, 1994); Jan Hendrik Sommer, *Spiritisme* (Kampen:
Kok, 2001).
[22] In the Netherlands, it is usually called spiritism, like in the rest of continental Europe.
Since around 1995, the official spiritist organization Harmonia has started calling itself

visited the royal court of the Netherlands. His séances, where it was said tables moved of their own accord, things started floating in the air, and ghosts materialized in the form of a small hand or head, were much discussed. In Amsterdam, Rotterdam and Maastricht (near my research area) spiritualist groups were initiated at the end of the 1860s and the beginning of the seventies. Among the members were doctors, high military officers, prominent Christians and some famous writers. These groups dedicated themselves to the task to determine scientifically the significance of paranormal phenomena, in order to establish certainty around the question whether life really continued after the death of the physical body. In 1888 the "brother bond" Harmonia was established, with groups all over the country. This organization, attempting to encompass the multitude of local groups, still exists today.

Until the 1950s, the magazine of Harmonia was full of critical articles written by the better-educated members discussing and explaining paranormal phenomena in a scientific manner. Nowadays, although 'scientific' jargon and methods are still part of the discourse, the interest of the members of the local groups is mainly practical, and oriented towards firsthand experience so they can 'see for themselves' whether it works or not. At the time, it was an interest of the higher classes; nowadays spiritualist practices are an accepted phenomenon among many more groups in Limburg. Spiritualist groups are usually dedicated to developing the paranormal powers of their members. Those who split off from the spiritualist groups under Harmonia sometimes confine themselves to the study of spirituality and paranormal phenomena.

In their opposition to the cold, disenchanted materialism of their time, nineteenth century spiritualists tried to prove the existence of a spiritual world in scientific ways. In this process, they came to see the spiritual world as a higher, more rarefied form of matter.

More than a century later, the people of the SG see the world and the hereafter as made of the same stuff, namely energy in different frequencies. They maintain, like the nineteenth-century spiritualists described by Hanegraaff, that this energy can be scientifically measured and proven. Much discussion on the relative frequencies of certain stones, numbers, masters (very high intelligences form the other side who can aid in spiritual development) and other therapeutic instruments is the result. When

spiritualist, linking up with the term used in England and the US and refers to itself as a member of an international spiritualist federation (www.harmonia-nl.org).

an explanation for seemingly contradictory evidence is needed, *energy* is now the concept that explains and connects everything. Even the most disparate ideas and interpretations can be translated into each other by referring to differences in frequencies of energy.[23]

The interest of 'real scientists' in paranormal phenomena has waned considerably since the nineteenth century, but the ideas and practices of spiritualism and its pretensions to be 'scientific' have been popularized. However, we should not forget what it means when Hanegraaff places spiritualism in the broader category of Romanticism. The emphasis on individuality and personal experience that characterizes all currents under this heading is part and parcel of the main ideas supported in the SG and the networks around it. This means that the framework as explicated by the 'experts' should become an embodied epistemology, second nature.

Hammer has shown for various kinds of alternative spirituality, that the epistemology posited by these theories becomes part of the way one approaches the world, identifies and solves problems.[24] However, his work is based almost exclusively on a review of emic literature. In the ethnographic descriptions in this chapter, and also in our work on Jomanda, the individual struggle to be able to see, feel, hear and experience the paranormal becomes apparent.[25] This worldview is not something one can learn from a book, as every practitioner told me. Indeed, you have to literally grow into it, train your perceptions.

The way it is described ideal-typically by the experts in the context of the SG is that a person setting out on a path of spiritual development will have strange experiences, identified loosely as "paranormal". Often, this is connected to a tragic event such as the death of one's son or spouse. The more a person learns about the "other side", the more he will be able to correctly interpret these strange experiences. It will become normal to see auras, to have premonitions, dreams predicting someone's death, to 'see' things shown by "the other side". There is a subtle hierarchy at work among

---

[23] The role of the concept of 'energy' seems to be of a later date and seems to reintroduce the principle of correspondence in a more literally causal way. It would be interesting if someone could make a historical study of the various popular magazines on paranormal phenomena to see when and how this concept developed and came to take the central place it does today.

[24] Olav Hammer, *Claiming Knowledge; Strategies of Epistemology from Theosophy to the New Age* (Leiden [etc.]: Brill, 2001).

[25] Knibbe, "An Ethnography of a Medium and Her Followers: How Learning Takes Place in the Context of Jomanda"; Knibbe and Westra, "Van Ongeloof Naar 'zeker Weten': Betekenisgeving En Legitimatie in De Context Van Het Fenomeen Jomanda."

the members of these groups: the more one treats these things as 'normal', the higher one's credibility. In this group it was Beth, who did not claim to have any kind of paranormal powers, who was most respected. Among other members, conversations about experiences classified as paranormal always had a certain strained character to them, because people were simultaneously trying to convey the extent of their paranormal powers, and trying very hard to appear nonchalant about it.

These were the basic beliefs and conventions referred to by the experts (like Beth and her husband, psychics and mediums) when discussion got tangled and things needed to be clarified.[26]

Spirit Guides do not Argue

> It's all very nice, the paranormal stuff, very spectacular, but in the end it's about spiritual development. Whether you understand what you have to learn here on this earth in order to get ahead (Beth).

Generally, there was a lot of room for eclecticism, creative appropriations and modifications of techniques and discussion. However, on some occasions it became clear that also in this context, there were boundaries that had to be enforced.

One such occasion was when a newcomer joined the discussion after a meeting. He had clearly come to find help, to get a tangible sign from the other side on what he should do.[27] However, in the telling of his story he included a detail that generated a stern lecture from Beth, supported by the other visitors: he mentioned that he had heard his guiding spirits (geleidegeesten) argue. He had been considering violent action towards his neighbour, a heroin addict who played music very loudly while his wife was dying of bone cancer. Apparently, he was convinced that his guiding spirits were undecided whether this was a good course of action. However, as Beth and the others soon made clear to him, it was impossible that these were his spirit guides, because they do not argue. He should consider his experience as a spiritual lesson, however harsh and tragic.

---

[26] In a book published by a medium of one of the other groups in the south of Limburg, she explains more or less the same basic ideas. The title also confirms the code of nonchalance described here: 'Paranormal, not so abnormal' (paranormaal, niets buitengewoons) (Schols and Verhaar 2002).

[27] This discussion is described in more detail in Knibbe, "Obscuring the Role of Power and Gender in Contemporary Spiritualities."

3. RELATIONSHIPS AND THE DEMANDS OF INDIVIDUALISM

During sessions with a medium or psychic, women were often told that they concerned themselves too much with the well-being of other people, instead of their own. One woman was even told that she was "selfish": she wanted people to be grateful to her, but she did not get the gratitude that she deserved. As I described elsewhere, this notion of individualism can therefore be disempowering to women who made their life choices during a time when self-sacrifice was explicitly valued.[28] In contrast, self-sacrfice in this context was analyzed as a kind of dependence on the approval of others that one had excise from one's way of being.

Every individual is assumed to be born with a blueprint of his destiny. This blueprint consists of the 'lessons' you still have to learn to be able to develop spiritually, and to progress along the hierarchy of spheres as you are born and return to "the other side" again and again until you can be taken up completely into the one source of Light. Everything that you meet on your "path in life" should be seen in the light of this blueprint, as a chance to learn the lessons you were born to learn.[29] In their emphasis on suffering, the interpretative framework of the SG is very different from the emphasis on well-being and happiness that characterizes some forms of New Age.[30]

Although this notion of personal responsibility is a direct consequence of the idea that everybody is born with a blueprint of his destiny, during the meetings of this group people did not seem very preoccupied with figuring what this blueprint told them to do. Perhaps the setting was too public to go too deeply into anyone's personal life. Some of the regulars consulted mediums and psychics privately, becoming part of their personal 'following' to delve more deeply into their purpose in this life and the karma of their former lives. Others had already 'figured it out' and yet others, like Jacky and Jeff, were still 'lost in translation': the interpretative framework underlying the practices of the meetings did not make sense to them yet on an experiential level. Jacky often told me that she did not know what she was supposed to do, although she had often been told

---

[28] Ibid.
[29] Cf. Knibbe, "An Ethnography of a Medium and Her Followers: How Learning Takes Place in the Context of Jomanda."
[30] For example, recently a magazine was started in the Netherland under the name 'Happinez', discussing topics to do with alternative spiritualities. See www.happinez.nl.

that it would soon become clear. She, like other regulars, was perpetually waiting for an 'experience'.

The Limits of Power in Personal Relationships

The notion of everybody's own personal 'blueprint' and karma was often referred to illustrate the limits of one person's influence over another: neither punishment nor help nor teaching can do anything to make anyone 'see the light' and mend his ways. As Beth told the stranger who heard his guiding spirits argue: "you cannot decide for him [the heroin addict] what his lesson should be, you can only learn your own lesson". This notion of personal responsibility and the limits of power of one person over another were often reinforced by the messages transmitted by the mediums, and in the lectures and workshops given by other practitioners such as psychics. The best ones could be very provocative in getting this message across.

During the evening with the medium and psychic from Rotterdam, Diane Veer, who gave such a strong warning to the magnetist, also gave some very clear marital advice to Monique, a young woman in the audience who had been coming more often recently. The room was full; as always, the promise of a message from the other side had drawn a lot of new visitors. At one point, Diane said: "I'm getting some information about a little boy. Who has a little boy here who is being labelled too quickly?" Monique and another woman stood up and said that they recognized this description.

Diane went on to describe him:

> He is very sensitive, and he has trouble concentrating. He screams for attention, but he is getting mainly negative attention. That's why he's withdrawing into his own world. Do people doubt the intelligence of this boy?

Again, both women recognized this description and answered yes. But Monique answered a lot louder than the other woman, pushing her claim that this message was intended for *her* son.

Diane went on:

> He is very afraid to be left alone. Everything is bottled up, in his stomach. He has the tendency to be more aware of what the people around him want than what he wants himself. So he has a symbiotic relationship with his surroundings. He's very much inside his head. He has difficulty communicating what he wants. Does he have to miss one of his parents?

Both women answered, one saying that the father of her child was gone, Monique saying in a louder voice: "yes, spiritually he has to miss his father". The quieter woman surrendered her claim with a shrug, and sat down.

Diane continued:

> The parents are not communicating with each other. You say: "it's the father". But in this case I strongly have the inclination to grab *both* parents by the neck and bang their heads together. Because if the parents don't communicate, the child suffers. They are busy accusing each other: "you are the one doing everything wrong!" "No, you!" That has to stop. The child is only present in the upper part of his body. His feelings are confused, because he doesn't know if he is welcome. Partly, he has no security. So the two of you have to learn how to communicate again. Learn not to point the finger at each other, because that has the guaranteed effect of making the other person get on his hind legs again. Don't attack! Maybe you could start [indicating Monique], by just staying close to your own feelings. He is a rainbow child,[31] that's why he is so sensitive. He needs a lot of physical exercise. And the two of you [husband and wife] have to draw closer again and communicate and create a safe surrounding for him.

During this speech, Monique constantly interrupted Diane: "but my husband is not open for this kind of thing, he is blind, doesn't see that this is a very special child". She practically explained her whole domestic situation, but Diane refused to confirm her view of the problem, and just talked over her interruptions. When Monique protested against the advice that they should stop fighting: "but *he won't stop!*" Diane had the last word by telling Monique: "then maybe *you* should be the first to stop".

Again, there is the notion of personal responsibility, and again this is used to point out the limitations of power and influence one individual can or should have over another. Matt was warned that he was exerting the wrong kind of power over his clients. Women are told not to expect gratitude for their self-sacrifice. On this occasion, Monique was told that she should not try to force her husband to see that his son is a rainbow child, to "open up", to join her in her spiritual practices, to stop fighting. In fact, she was told pretty bluntly that it was as much her fault as her husband's that their son was not feeling well.

---

[31] Rainbow children are considered to be a sign that the 'Age of Aquarius' is here, a fundamental shift in the spiritual life of the world that will lead to a more peaceful and spiritually advanced civilisation (the New Age). Rainbow children are said to be more sensitive and paranormally perceptive, and their aura is not dominated by one or two colours, as with most people, but by all the colours of the chakras.

In studies of contemporary spiritualities, it is often pointed out that they all revolve around the sacralization of the self: to connect to one's "higher self", to find one's authentic divine self buried underneath the conditioning of a repressive society etc.[32] Although there is a similar importance attached to the self in this context, there are a significant differences: first of all, although theoretically the self is divine, and one can train oneself to tap into divine energies, the emphasis here is more fundamentally evolutionist: everybody has to live many more lives to be able to participate in the divine sphere of Light. Furthermore, in practice the focus is not so much on finding one's own self or even on finding personal happiness but rather on reforming *relationships*: the fact that everybody has a unique blueprint is used to warn people against trying to "change" each other, "save" each other from mistakes or try to take on each other's problems.

Nevertheless, it is true that the mediums and psychics during their performances often told women to set their own priorities and not rely on other people to provide meaning to their lives. The idea behind this is that by loving yourself, and striving to develop spiritually, you will ultimately be able to 'raise' the love level around you, more than when you are over-concerned with the suffering of other people. This is echoed in the advice another medium gave a few times during a séance, also mostly to women: don't suffer along with other people when they are having a hard time, it's enough to be sympathetic (*meeleven, niet meelijden*).

The emphasis in these messages was on transforming a habitus very common among women in Limburg, instilled through the discourses described in chapter 2. However, the society that underpinned these values has since transformed itself, a woman living for others risks being cast aside as a boring housewife who has never accomplished anything in life. Many women accepted the necessity to transform themselves and work on their habitus, but as described elsewhere, this discourse also met with resistance.[33]

---

[32] E.g. Hanegraaff, "New Age Spiritualities as Secular Religion: a Historian's Perspective"; van Harskamp, *Het Nieuw-religieuze Verlangen*; Heelas, *The New Age Movement; the Celebration of the Self and the Sacralization of Modernity*; S. Sutcliffe, "The Authority of the Self in New Age Religiosity: The Example of the Findhorn Community," *Diskuswebedition* 3, no. 2 (1995): 23–42; M. Wood, "Capital Possession: a Comparative Approach to 'New Age' and Control of the Means of Possession," *Culture and Religion* 4, no. 1 (2003): 159–182; Aupers and Houtman, *Religions of Modernity*.

[33] Knibbe, "Obscuring the Role of Power and Gender in Contemporary Spiritualities."

Power, Affections and Gossip

Although people took a lot of liberty interfering in each other's private lives, this was counteracted by the freedom to ignore the strong advice and interference. Even the 'experts' such as the mediums did not have the last word because there was no way that people could be sanctioned for not following their interpretations and advice. Furthermore, although they control a rare resource (contact with the "other side", paranormal perception), their authority in spiritual matters was far from absolute. In the discussions after the main event of these meetings and the general gossip about mediums and psychics it was often affirmed that although they can "transmit" messages from a supposedly factual "other side", the content of these messages can always be dismissed as "coming from a lower sphere". Just like "the other side" consists of several spheres, each more pure than the other, people constructed hierarchies among the different mediums depending on which sphere they were supposed to be in contact with.

Because the central beliefs were nowhere clearly outlined, it was considered normal for people to take a while to assimilate them, and it might take even longer before they become rooted in their personal experience of life. Power was dispersed among practitioners. But power and the abuse of power was a very important issue, as we can see in the warnings of Diane Veer to Matt. Practitioners are often suspected of making people dependent on them and even of actually using the energy of their patients to feed their own energy. People who do this are often likened to vacuum cleaners or vampires.

The informal character of these gatherings was important also to relativize the doctrines espoused in this setting. Gossip, as an expression of informality and means of social control thrived in this group. Pronouncements by mediums and psychics tend to have an air of finality and absoluteness especially to inexperienced 'seekers'. The assumption, and their pretension, is that they transmit 'objective information' that can also be accessed by others just like a scientist assumes that his data can be confirmed by other scientists using the same research techniques.[34] But the accurateness and objectivity of the personal messages and advice

---

[34] This is contrary to the findings of Wayne Spencer, "To Absent Friends: Classical Spiritualist Mediumship and New Age Channelling Compared and Contrasted," *Journal of Contemporary Religion* 16, no. 3 (October 2001): 343–360.

transmitted is considered prejudiced by the subjectivity of the medium or psychic. Gaining experience in this scene means that one can distinguish between the different qualities of information.

Gossip is therefore a very important tool. The subject of how to separate the badly intentioned and power crazy mediums from the 'good' mediums is an all time favourite. As I described above, it was actually the first topic to come up when I contacted Beth. It was also the subject of the advice given to Matt. And when a medium, or an informed layman, wanted to describe somebody as an amateur, they accused him of contacting "malicious spirits" rather than "the other side". This was of course a very serious accusation, which I have never heard anyone make face to face with the person concerned. Usually, it was said by one medium about another practitioner.

Nobody expected anybody else to be a true 'believer'. 'Bookish' knowledge was not respected very much, rather personal experience was supposed to be the foundation of insight and spiritual growth. Gossip was indulged in freely and humourously. Confusion was openly admitted by many of the members, such as Jacky, An and Jeff. For example, Jeff was determined to remain sceptical. He did not believe any of it, because he did not 'feel' anything. He could not understand how it was possible that everybody was talking about things that he could just not perceive at all. Jacky also told me often she did not 'feel' anything, but she was a little less sceptical. She had been a member for years, like Jeff. An was non-committal and close-lipped. I had the impression that she had someone in particular that she trusted to talk things over with. Even Beth, who had the most authority, always emphasized that she was not really paranormally gifted.

These people kept coming back because they liked the atmosphere and friendship of these evenings, the thrill of perhaps suddenly gaining a life changing insight, the opportunity to talk about spiritual things with other people. Sometimes, the social aspect of getting together and sharing dominated the evening sessions more than the desire to learn anything new.

The notions of subjectivity and personal responsibility softened the objective reality of "the other side" and the advice transmitted. Each person can only perceive the 'objective reality' of the other side according to his own level of spiritual development, and there is no right and wrong, there are only lessons to learn. Nevertheless, people were very particular that these beliefs should be taken literally. The discursive power of the core beliefs could not be relativized, and whenever someone transgressed the interpretational boundaries set by the foundational beliefs, he or she was called back sharply.

4. Sceptical Positivism

In Hanegraaff's classification, the beliefs outlined here should be seen as the more extreme form of occultism. However, in present day characterizations of New Age, the impression dominates that these beliefs are becoming more and more abstract and psychological. In his inaugural lecture, Hanegraaff himself even signals the "end of the hermetic tradition".[35] Ramstedt also shows that in modern paganism, another offshoot of alternative spirituality, it is often hard to distinguish between the literal 'invocation' or the metaphorical play of symbols that characterizes fantasy, and that people often do not really care to distinguish between the two.[36]

In the descriptive parts of this chapter, it becomes clear that a *literal* interpretation of cosmologies and all the beings that are associated with these cosmologies dominates, and that people *do* care that the 'real' existence of spirits, "the other side" and paranormal phenomena in general should not be left unresolved. Rather than on basic beliefs, the emphasis was on training one's perception and on 'evidence'. People did not describe themselves as 'believers' but as "seekers" for knowledge.[37] The goal of each meeting and discussion was often to decide whether there is definitely something 'out there', outside the self that sets the standards and how to apprehend this. One could characterise the default attitude of many of the visitors as sceptical positivist.

However, most people who frequented the evenings of SG also shared a very practical attitude: a particular practice either works or it does not work, it gives you more insight or it does not, and if it does not you continue looking until you find something that works. Although among practitioners and some regulars the existence of "the other side" was an uncontroversial fact, they were still critical: does this medium really communicate with "the other side" or does he just really want to, is he overrating himself? And even if he is not making it up, is he not too subjective in his transmission? Does he know how to distinguish his own thoughts from the messages he receives? Mediums, after all, are only human.

---

[35] Wouter Hanegraaff, "Het Einde Van De Hermetische Traditie" (presented at the Inaugural lecture, Universiteit van Amsterdam, 2000).

[36] Ramstedt, "Metaphor or Invocation? The Convergence Between Modern Paganism and Fantasy Fiction."

[37] Cf. Knibbe, "An Ethnography of a Medium and Her Followers: How Learning Takes Place in the Context of Jomanda"; Knibbe and Westra, "Van Ongeloof Naar 'zeker Weten': Betekenisgeving En Legitimatie in De Context Van Het Fenomeen Jomanda."

Unlike the highly 'metaphorical' and abstract religiosity of the pastoral centre discussed in the next chapter, in the SG the existence of the other side was seen as a fact that can be proven. Practitioners took for granted that the visitors on the open nights, and their clients on the paranormal markets or in their private practice, would be sceptical. They accepted that they had something to prove and often talked among themselves about strategies for convincing sceptics.

Of course, to other believers and practitioners, and often to their clients as well, they expressed the opinion that the sceptic "in his heart" knew that what they were saying was true, and one day would be able to "open up" to this knowledge. If someone did not accept their pronouncements they speculated that this was due to a blocked chakra, cutting him off from awareness of a greater reality. It was simply a stage in their spiritual evolution. The epistemology assumed here includes embodied experience and changes in consciousness as sites for 'fact-finding', and therefore becomes a function of spiritual development. Ultimately, it was thought, this could all be measured.

So when there was talk of spirits, ghosts, guides and angels, this was intended *literally*. Even "symbols" were not symbolic in the way people usually mean the term in everyday language. For example, I once attended an informal discussion on the question whether it is allowed to "put a symbol in a room" without asking the people present for permission. Linda was the one who raised this issue. She 'saw' this symbol when she entered a room, although the others did not see it. This symbol was not visible to normal eyes but only visible psychically, because it consisted of energy. Although the other people didn't see it, if another paranormally trained person would have been there, she would also have been able to see it. The underlying assumption therefore, is that the *result* of the act of "putting a symbol in the room" can be perceived as an objective reality by someone attuned to the right frequencies of energy, even if he or she did not see the act itself happen.

5. Spiritual Consumer Culture

In recent decades, sociologists and other observers of religion in contemporary society have characterized developments in terms of the emergence of a religious or spiritual supermarket: people seem to be free to pick and mix as they want from a variety of providers. They no longer feel obliged to be loyal to their 'own' religious group, but act as consumers.[38] Underlying this characterization is the analysis that the individualization of society has fragmented and trivialized religion: from a significant social force structuring society, religion has become a shapeless amalgam exemplified by the shelf of self-help manuals in the local bookshop and weekend retreats for stressed yuppies. Following Beck's insight[39] on the effects of individualization, new spiritualities are interpreted as providing the tools to create biographical solutions to societal problems.

Some authors say that it is especially so called 'New Age' religion that is offered in this way.[40] Campbell has developed a very interesting argument that there seems to be a quite close connection between the 'Romantic ethic' (as exemplified, but not limited to, contemporary spirituality and New Age) and 'the spirit of consumerism'.[41] Indeed, one expects that religious or spiritual repertoires that cater to a strongly individualist ethos and offer a 'sacralization of the self'[42] sell best in this spiritual supermarket. Others have pointed out that it is especially in the US that religion is offered in this way, and that it has to do with the fact that religion in the US has been disestablished from the beginning, unlike in Europe, where the relationship between the state and religion has historically been quite close (and is still quite close).[43] Indeed, looking at the US it is clear that it is not only the 'sacralization of the self' type of religion that sells well, but also (sometimes quite conservative) Christianity that sells well.[44] Although characterizations of present-day religion in terms of a 'religious supermarket' can be too facile and dismissive, there is in fact

---

[38] Mara Einstein, "The Evolution of Religious Branding," *Social Compass* 58, no. 3 (2011): 331–338.

[39] Beck and Beck-Gernsheim, *Individualization*.

[40] Guy Redden, "The New Age: Towards a Market Model," *Journal of Contemporary Religion* 20, no. 2 (May 2005): 231–246.

[41] C. Campbell, *The Romantic Ethic and the Spirit of Modern Consumerism* (Oxford: Blackwell, 1987); Colin Campbell, "On Understanding Modern Consumerism and Misunderstanding the Romantic Ethic Thesis: a Reply to Boden and Williams," *Sociology* 37, no. 4 (November 1, 2003): 791–797, doi:10.1177/0038038503037401o.

[42] Heelas, *The New Age Movement; the Celebration of the Self and the Sacralization of Modernity*.

[43] Grace Davie, *Europe—the Exceptional Case: Parameters of Faith in the Modern World* (London: Darton Longman & Todd, 2002), see; Davie, *The Sociology of Religion* especially chapter 7.

[44] Mara Einstein, *Brands of Faith: Marketing Religion in a Commercial Age* (Routledge, 2007); Robert Laurence Moore, *Selling God: American Religion in the Marketplace of Culture* (Oxford University Press, 1995).

a market of spirituality, and recognizing this fact is important to understand the ways that people are able to approach spirituality and deal with religious authority.

The mode of searching for certainty described in this chapter is catered to not only through the spiritual societies, but also by paranormal market and shops specialising in spiritual and religious books and articles, associated with the rise of New Age spreading from the urban centres of the Netherlands (mainly Amsterdam).[45] There are several of these bookstores in Maastricht, Sittard, Heerlen, Geleen and Brunssum and probably there are more I do not know of. These bookstores not only cater to individual interests, but also serve as nodal points in the network connecting people with an interest in alternative spirituality because of their notice boards and the lectures and other activities they organize. Through these notice boards and the mingling of the clientele of these shops, spiritualist practitioners and New Age repertoires are increasingly connected. Thus, magnetists might become reiki-masters, and mediums might become shamans.

The psychics and mediums who circulated among the spiritual groups often offered their services for a fee at 'paranormaalbeurzen', the paranormal 'markets' that are held in big halls all over the Netherlands. These halls can usually be found just outside the city-centre and can be rented for the day, or in the case of paranormal markets, for the weekend. Practitioners can rent a table at these markets to sell their services to the people who visit. The idea is that this allows people to try these services for a relatively low fee. In most cases these practitioners and their clients are from the surrounding areas, although some practitioners travel the whole country, following these paranormal markets.

According to long term insiders of the spiritual society, the practice of paranormal markets grew out of the fairs spiritual groups organized yearly to attract new members and take away local prejudice against their practices, sometimes branded as witchcraft, backward or associated with the devil. Often, the 'services' offered at these fairs were free or for a very low price. Since the late 1990s, commercial operators started organizing them on a larger scale, attracting practitioners who wanted to make some extra money.[46] They advertise professionally along the main traffic routes of the

---

[45] Aupers and Van Otterloo, *New Age; Een Godsdiensthistorische En Sociologische Benadering* chapter 4 and 5.

[46] One example is the markets organized by Paraview. The young men organizing it also organize fairs for reptiles, jewelry, second hand PC's etc. See www.paraview.nl.

city and the surrounding villages a few weeks in advance, with cheap posters announcing the date. Nowadays, most practitioners are careful not to give away their services for free.

Interestingly, like the highbrow cultural critics who deplore the detorriation of 'real' religion into a supermarket of options, the informal leaders of the SG deplore the consumerist attitude of many of the visitors of paranormal markets and the open nights of the SG. Within networks of people interested in spirituality generally, those who emphasize the 'paranormal' are often looked down upon as profiting from the sensationalism of the general public. In fact, the paranormal is the most intriguing aspect for the visitors of these markets completely unfamiliar with spirituality. These markets are set up to thrill, pique curiosity and promise extraordinary 'knowledge' and 'evidence' of the paranormal: take a picture of your aura, measure your energy frequencies and find out if you have any blocks, contact your spirit guide, receive a message from your deceased grandmother! At the same time, every visitor is free to pass by, ridicule or ignore the promises held out by these services.

This 'consumerist' attitude then, is an important key to understand how people wish to relate to any authority that claims to be linked to, or based on, access to the supernatural. One could say that people 'buy' their freedom: by paying for services, a relationship between 'authority' and individual is created through which the individual is assumed to be in charge; he or she browses, chooses and ultimately selects or rejects a service. Furthermore, the attitude of sceptical positivism allows for the outcome that "it did not work", the claim of the product or practitioner in question is false. However, to actually understand the relationship between providers and consumers, it is necessary to develop a more subtle conceptualization of relating to religious and spiritual authority and knowledge than can be provided by the 'traditional' format of lay members of a church and religious specialists. The attitude of consumerism and the illusion of freedom in relating to religious authority and knowledge that it gives should be addressed in further research.

6. Concluding Remarks

In this chapter I have given an in-depth ethnographic description of a phenomenon that is often discussed, but often insufficiently described. As others have also pointed out, much of the literature on alternative spiritualities relies on the books and other materials written by self-proclaimed leaders.[47] Here we can see that a vibrant interpretative community is created with the help of repertoires of alternative spirituality where the leader did not want to proclaim herself as such (Beth), the books written were not published (Beth's husband), and people did not read the books they cited (Blavatsky).

This description contradicts the general (usually sociological) interpretations of contemporary spiritualities in a number of ways. Although there is a strong emphasis on individual development, this is especially linked to suffering, reincarnation and life after death, rather than a 'sacralized Self'. The visitors do not fit the usual stereotype of highly educated, left-leaning women. The mode of believing is not relativist; rather it rests on an attitude of sceptical positivism that can be developed into epistemological individualism.

The ideas and concepts described here, and especially the sceptical positivism, are common to a large part of the public that consumes products and services associated with spirituality and New Age. For people without scientific training, the emphasis on science can be very persuasive (and those people are in the majority). For those with scientific training, a relativist worldview is more attractive (including the people who study religion). More research is needed, but it indicates that differences in educational background and class are significant. This should go beyond the usual study of emic literature and interviews with practitioners to look at the actual patterns of interaction and practice. Often, practitioners and writers of emic literature have the same educational background as the scholars who study them, and they know how to glide effortlessly from a literalist explanation to a psychologized version of the same worldview, thus creating a bias in representation towards a relativist holism, rather than the literalist spiritualism characterized by sceptical positivism described here.

Participant observation also reveals that even in settings where individuals are told that their 'self' is sacred, knowledge from 'sacred sources' is solicited from *outside* the self. Rather than reflecting a 'celebration of the self', the emphasis on the self and the authority ascribed to it reflect the ambivalent nature of the relationship of individuals to institutions and institutionalized knowledge in general. In Limburg, this ambivalent

---

[47] Matthew Wood, *Possession, Power, and the New Age: Ambiguities of Authority in Neoliberal Societies* (Aldershot and Burlington: Ashgate, 2007); Matthew Wood, "W (h) Ither New Age Studies? The Uses of Ethnography in a Contested Field of Scholarship," *Religion and Society: Advances in Research* 1, no. 1 (2010): 76–88.

relationship is especially strong: the Catholic church always characterized religious knowledge as inaccessible to lay people, and created a concept of the sacred as a separate domain somewhere far away from life here on earth, guarded by special gatekeepers.

While the practices described here provide a solution to the anxieties produced by the Catholic imagery of a heaven into which one can be denied access, that can potentially withhold grace, it also reproduces the categories of this imagery: there is a 'heaven', it just looks different, and one can learn to have access to it. While priests have been proven to be not always right, nor wise, access to "the other side" is a direct result of one's spiritual development. The model of access to religious knowledge therefore seems more fair and just than that of the priesthood of the Catholic church, where a paedophile can have the right to dispense or withhold the sacraments, as long as he is a priest, but half of the population is automatically excluded because of their gender.

Authority does play a role, but is constantly tested and discussed informally. Furthermore, within spiritual consumer culture the relationship between practitioner and consumer allows people to walk away without consequences at any point in time. The advice is always that it (authority, knowledge, interference from people embodying both) should "feel right", otherwise you should just ignore it. This can be interpreted as a part of the Romantic heritage: a longing for the facts to connect to experience again. By framing embodied experience as a site for fact-finding, the disenchanting effect of science is neutralized.

Through spirituality as practice, training themselves to develop a different and experientially anchored notion of heaven and personal destiny, people are encouraged to reconstitute their relationships with others. How then, does this relate to the domain of the familiar? Do these practices entail a reconstitution of this domain? In a certain sense, they do: people are encouraged to meet everybody as a potential teacher, thus transcending the boundaries usually set between locals and non-locals. Catholicism as an identity marker is not important to these people. At the same time, many of them were involved in the preparation of the first communion of their children or grandchildren. The practice of spirituality, it seems, does not (yet) offer new rituals for the reproduction of the domain of the familiar and locality.

CHAPTER SIX

LIBERAL CATHOLICISM: THE BURDEN OF THE PAST
AND THE PROBLEM OF THE PRESENT

1. INTRODUCTION

This chapter describes a discourse that emphasizes uncertainty, in contrast to the 'skeptical positivism' that characterized the participants of the spiritual groups the goal is not to gain knowledge, but to relinquish the illusion that certainty in matters of faith is a possibility. By emphasizing uncertainty, the unknowability of God, this discourse provides a different solution to the problematic of how to relate to religious knowledge and authority. This discourse was taught in a pastoral centre located near Welden and continues the program of the 'spiritual liberators' described in chapter 2. In this chapter, I will show how this program is implemented and how it interacts both with the 'burden of the past' of a strong Catholic socialization and with 'the problem of present': the highly polarized religious landscape.

The pastoral centre is linked to a congregation: some of the pastors are members of this congregation and are ordained priests; others are hired by a separate foundation and include women pastors. When I started my fieldwork, contacting key informants in Welden, I was often referred to this centre as an example of 'modern' Catholicism that I should investigate. In the eyes of my informants, it was more relevant to my research than taking only the local parish as my subject, because this parish was dominated by one of 'Gijsen's priests'. The relationship between the pastoral centre and the parish priest of Welden had long been problematic. The pastoral centre and its staff were involved in much of the renewal within Catholicism that Gijsen and his priests abhorred. During Gijsen's reign their position was marginalized and relations between 'Gijsen's priests' and representatives of progressive Catholics such as the pastoral centre were practically non-existent.[1] At the time of my fieldwork however, the diocese was trying to break through this polarization and involved the

---

[1] Wijnen and Koopmanschap, *Hoe Katholiek Is Limburg? De Kerk En Het Bisdom Roermond*, 26–36.

pastoral centre and its staff in the process of clustering local parishes and
training parish volunteers (necessary because of the shortage of priests).
As other research has shown, the practice of local parishes is often dominated and inspired by the 'unofficical' discourse of progressive Catholicism rather than the 'official' policy and discourse of the Catholic Church
in the Netherlands.[2]

As part of my fieldwork, I participated in several courses and discussion groups, and interviewed the pastors. The courses I participated in
involved training lay volunteers from the surrounding parishes to make
family services, wake services for the bereft held the night before burial,
and to help in the pastorate for elderly people. The courses were either
commissioned by the diocese or by a cluster of parishes cooperating to
pool resources.

Some of these volunteers had no prior training at all; others were
already familiar with the discourse of liberal Catholicism dominant in
the centre. Most of the participants, especially those who had no prior
training, were primarily motivated by a desire to do something for their
local community and parish church. Their 'religious' motivation could not
be separated from this desire. In many cases the religious aspect of their
motivation was hardly articulated.

The discussion groups were mixed as well: some people had been coming to the centre for years, others joined recently. Most were from the
neighbouring parishes or even (though rarely) from the nearby cities. The
regular discussion groups centred on reading and interpreting the Bible.
Around Easter and around special issues, ad hoc groups were sometimes
created. The interest of the members of the discussion groups was usually
more purely 'religious' or spiritual. The long time members were often
quite articulate in the discourse of the pastoral centre.

This discourse is based on a historical-critical reading of the Bible
to 'extract' the message of God's love that Jesus showed in his actions
and pronouncements. The pastors all cited the influential scholar Schillebeeckx as their strongest source of inspiration.[3] In this approach, the

---

[2] Watling, " 'Official' Doctrine and 'Unofficial' Practices: The Negotiation of Catholicism
in a Netherlands Community."

[3] Schillebeeckx (1914–2009) was a Dominican priest, originally Belgian, but based in
Nijmegen, the Netherlands since 1958. He studied with the French representatives of the
'nouvelle théologie' that influenced the 'spiritual liberators' to criticize the repressiveness
of Dutch Catholicism in the 50s. Schillebeeckx was adviser to the Dutch bishops during
the Second Vatican Council. He came in conflict with Rome because (among other things)
he did not subscribe to the view that Jesus had risen 'bodily' from the grave or that he is

Old Testament is interpreted as a collection of stories of a people about the history of their relationship with God. Since all the protagonists are human, and their understanding fallible, no 'laws' and rules can be deduced from these texts. Rather, they should inspire an orientation towards certain core values that have to be reinterpreted anew in every time and place. What they show is people trying to make sense of their situation and their life in light of their understanding and experience of what God wants. The emphasis is on the moments of 'grace' in these stories, such as when miracles convey God's love for his people. These miracles are interpreted symbolically, as an indication of the impact a certain configuration had on the relationship between the people involved and their God.

In terms of the classification of present-day religiosity developed by Heelas and Woodhead,[4] the discourse of the center falls squarely into the category of 'religions of humanity', whereas 'traditional Catholicism' enforced by the clerocracy of Limburg would fall into the opposing category of 'religions of difference'. The worldview endorsed at the centre and the contrast with pillarization and neoconservative Catholicism matches their description point by point:

> Whereas religions of difference exalt the divine over the human, religions of humanity shift the locus of authority from transcendent to human. Whilst the human is not as closely identified with the divine as it is in spiritualities of life, God and humanity are nevertheless brought into closer ontological and epistemological relationship with one another than in religions of difference. Rather than being viewed as awesome, fearful, and set-apart, the deity is seen as much more approachable, tolerant, compassionate. The human is like the divine, an image of the divine, it can even participate in the divine. Indeed, many religions of humanity insist that it is *only* by starting with the human and human experience that one can come to know something of God.[5]

Like other strands of Catholicism, the liberal Christianity taught at the centre was linked transnationally in many ways: through missionaries working in other parts of the world, through their affinity with the liberation theology developed in Latin America, and simply through the fame of the Dutch experiments in creating a more democratic church, transforming it into a movement of 'God's people under way' as described in chapter 2

'bodily' present in the Eucharist Erik Borgman, *Edward Schillebeeckx: A Theologian in His History. A Catholic Theology of Culture (1914–1965)* (Continuum International Publishing Group, 2004).

[4] Woodhead and Heelas, *Religion in Modern Times*.

[5] Ibid., 70.

and in enthusiastic descriptions in the media and books such as that of the Jesuit Coleman.[6] Nevertheless, as in the rest of the book, the emphasis here is on how this transnational, global discourse is embedded into the local context and entwined with the ongoing production of locality. As we saw in chapter 4, people often felt that they did not know what it meant to be a Catholic: they had distanced themselves from the church and from what they perceived as the 'traditional' Catholicism of the generation preceding them. At the same time, the rituals, the building of the church and the identity of being a Catholic and a Limburger remain important for the production of locality. Thus, a space is opened up for the kind of resignification offered by the discourse of the centre. Through this discourse, lay Catholics were exhorted to work on their relationship to religious authority and knowledge, sometimes against their own wishes and expectations.

In section 2 of this chapter, I show how the discourse of the pastoral centre was conveyed during one of the courses, training women from several different parishes to make family-services. In a subsection, I also show how this discourse works in the confrontation with someone who identifies himself as a 'casualty' of the radical changes in the religious landscape in Limburg. The third and fourth sections situate the discourse of the centre in the local religious landscape, highlighting in more detail 'the burden of the past' and the 'problem of the present' (polarization), how these were brought up by the participants and how this was dealt with by the pastors. Section 5 discusses some of the most important values of the discourse of the centre and how they connected to the attitudes and expectations of the participants. In the last part of the chapter, I focus on the contrast between the taboo on moralizing within the carefully non-judgmental atmosphere enforced by the pastors, and the moralizing embedded within informal interaction such as gossiping and stereotyping.

Methodological Notes

Although I had access to most of the courses and discussion groups for observation, it was hard to really do 'participant' observation. In most cases, my role was confined to taking notes during the discussion, which I elaborated into full descriptions immediately afterwards. In rare cases, I joined the discussion. Participation was made more difficult because

---

[6] Coleman, *The Evolution of Dutch Catholicism, 1958–1974.*

of the formalized character of the meetings and the fact that everything centred on talking (which meant, of course, that I wanted to write it all down). Everybody knew I was a researcher and why I was taking notes. They did not really expect me to join their discussion, because my motivation to be there was considered to be completely different from theirs. In the context of the courses and discussion groups the fact that I was young, not involved in parish life, and had a different background and an 'urban smell' automatically put me outside the group on the informal level. This was in stark contrast to the Spiritual Group, where I was easily included as a 'searcher' (rather than as a researcher).

In the informal interactions with volunteers and supporting staff, I also remained an outsider. Although everybody was friendly, they knew each other for a long time and spoke in dialect among each other, which automatically excluded me. Although I could understand it, I could not speak it and this put me in the domain of the unfamiliar, the people from 'above the river'. Here also, a difference in background and experience, and of course age, played a role. Furthermore, as I explained in chapter 1, I felt uncomfortable because I was not a Catholic and I did not want to be a Catholic, although the worldview and moral orientations elaborated here came very close to my own.

Another difficulty was the fact that anonymity was very important. Although relations with the diocese were improving, the bishop should be kept 'officially unaware' of some of the things that take place at the pastoral centre and some of the discussions, just like the neo-conservative priest said that he did not want to know if someone had died of euthanasia. That is the reason why I do not refer to the pastors individually. Although there were significant differences in personal style among the pastors, they all represented more or less the same discourse and they had more or less the same teaching techniques and ways of handling group processes. As far as the descriptions of events in the discussion groups and courses go, there is no great loss in 'homogenising' the voice of the pastors.

2. The Sacralization of Uncertainty

The discourse of the centre emphasized uncertainty, to the point that one could say that God was equated with uncertainty. Uncertainty was sacralized in the sense that it was considered taboo to try to probe this uncertainty. It was considered intrinsic to faith that one should face uncertainty, the intangibility of faith and one's personal responsibility to keep it alive and act on it. Faith means the admittance that one does not know everything, or understand the reason of suffering, and *still* puts one's trust in God.

As one woman told her fellow participants once:

> When I lost my baby, I cursed God, I hated him. I had prayed and prayed to him to let my baby live and he had not answered my prayers. But then I got pregnant again, and I had twins! Then I started to understand the words: "not my will, but thy will be done".

This emphasis on uncertainty went against the disposition instilled into people that faith was supposed to be about certainty. In the following description I want to show how the search for certainties and answers was turned around. The meeting I will describe centred on the interpretation the resurrection of Christ, and as a participant, I found it a particularly succesful meeting in the sense that both the participants, the pastor and I (as silent observer) were completely involved in the process of reading, interpreting and discovering the meaning of a certain bible text. In this case, I was convinced that the message the centre tried to convey was received loud and clear. However, as we shall see later on in this chapter, this also created new problems for people.

Interpretations of the Bible were never presented as 'strict' or exclusive, and always relied on the input of the participants. Nevertheless, the pastors were meticulous in guiding the participants how to interpret the stories of the Bible line by line, discussing the role and psychology of each character in the story in depth, giving historical backgrounds and reformulating the 'common sense' interpretations of the participants in more abstract religious terms.

In this case, the meeting was a follow-up of a course to train lay believers to prepare family-services, all women, most with young children and some teachers. These women did not consider themselves to be especially pious Catholics; rather they were active community members and mothers, and involved in the church as a consequence.[7] They had expected to learn how to make the proper decorations for family-services and how to choose the right songs. They were quite surprised that they were supposed to learn how to read the Bible, interpret the stories and distil the basic theme from a story to use it as a guideline in preparing family-services.

---

[7] As I explained in chapter 4, the local community and the parish are not necessarily the same thing. If the parish priest is very active and accessible, they can be congruent. But usually, they are not.

Although they were happy to learn this, they were also insecure whether they would be able to implement the insights they had gained during the course. That is why they had requested to have follow-up meetings.

In his introduction, the pastor reiterated what he had taught during the course itself:

> Don't read the Bible as if it is a newspaper or an encyclopaedia. The gospel of Mathew was written 40 years after Christ died. Mark was written ten years before that, and the gospels of Luke and John after it. They are stories of faith. They are stories of people's experience, and the faith that grew out of these experiences. Their experience was that Jesus did not remain dead, but lives on among the people. Of course this is hard to express. It's just like when I ask a couple before they get married: "why this person". They can only stammer in response.

The participants discussed this point. One participant remarked (almost complaining) that if experience precedes faith, it is hard to have faith without experience. She was referring to the miraculous experiences of the stories in the Bible, which they considered to be very far from their own mundane experience. The pastor replied:

> In those cases you have the tradition of faith, how people believed. We may be very far from that experience. However, in some moments our faith may be deepened. Although in every-day life, things may seem dull, dead, chaotic and destructive, you can compare this to autumn: things die, but every spring new life comes forth and it is always different from what you expect.

Another participant asked: "so how do you get to this experience, if the 'facts' are so unreliable?"

> Through imagery and symbolism one might get close. Or through experiencing nature. Even in science, reasoning through cause and effect reaches a point where it can get no further. Scientists have to admit that they cannot know more. Or when you are confronted by illness: a doctor might tell you what's wrong with you biologically, but he cannot tell you why this is happening to *you*. So it is up to you to make sense of your illness.

He continued explaining how one should see the Bible, and especially the stories around the resurrection of Christ.

> They are an elaboration of the declaration of faith; they try to tell about things that cannot be put into words. Just like people cannot explain why they want to marry this person and not another one. The Bible is a love letter. You need the key to be able to understand it.

The women compared this to having children: you cannot know how wonderful it is until it happens.

The discussion turned to the practical side of using symbolism in services to bring the experience that Jesus lives closer to people's heart. The participants agreed that it is not enough to rely on the routine of the rituals they were used to, such as the Eucharist or marriage. These are only the outer acts, and one should focus on the meaning that underlies these acts. As with the Bible, these rituals should not be considered to be a 'formula', a recipe for how to do things. However, to convey this meaning it is also important that people are open to what you are saying or they will not see it. Or as the pastor put it: "one should work with the grace you receive. Faith is a grace of God that makes you see the world differently".

After the coffee break, the pastor asked one of the participants to read Mark chapter 16, verses 1 to 8.[8] He started interpreting the story: "everything that is described here is in fact a function of the central message: you are looking for Jesus in a place where he is no longer. And this is told by someone who is an outsider". At first, the participants started comparing the events described in this story with the version of events they knew from the other gospels and the Catholic tradition of the stations of the cross, pointing out similarities and differences, arguing over who was present and who was not and therefore which version of events of which gospel must have been closest to what actually happened.

However, the pastor wanted them to focus on the main message of the text:

> The central sentence here is: "Jesus from Nazareth, who was crucified, has risen from death". It is about life, which always wins. That does not mean

---

[8] 1 When the sabbath was over, Mary Magdalene, Mary, the mother of James, and Salome bought spices so that they might go and anoint him.
2 Very early when the sun had risen, on the first day of the week, they came to the tomb.
3 They were saying to one another, "Who will roll back the stone for us from the entrance to the tomb?"
4 When they looked up, they saw that the stone had been rolled back; it was very large.
5 On entering the tomb they saw a young man sitting on the right side, clothed in a white robe, and they were utterly amazed.
6 He said to them, "Do not be amazed! You seek Jesus of Nazareth, the crucified. He has been raised; he is not here. Behold the place where they laid him.
7 But go and tell his disciples and Peter, 'He is going before you to Galilee; there you will see him, as he told you.'"
8 Then they went out and fled from the tomb, seized with trembling and bewilderment. They said nothing to anyone, for they were afraid. (Mark Chapter 16, 1–8)

that there is no death, it just means life always continues. The 'stranger' sends them away to tell this to people. The fact that it is a total outsider who tells them what happened, indicates that these people could not have come up with this insight by themselves. Sometimes, this figure is called an angel; nowadays we would say he was an ambassador. The response of these women is that they get frightened.

One of the participants asked: "so if we interpret this story symbolically, that means that literally, there was no resurrection? [i.e. he did not physically rise from the dead]" Rather cryptically, the pastor responded: "in this story it is told that the things that faith will make happen are more important than the faith itself [i.e. what you believe in exactly, whether he really physically rose from the dead or not]". He referred to Ghandhi and Martin Luther King: "These were people who stood up and told of their dream. And because they did, because they stood up as defenceless humans, they changed history".

Then one of the women delivered the insight that drove the message home to all the participants:

> Perhaps the fact that they could not find a body made these women anxious. Maybe they got frightened: because the body of Jesus was gone, that what he stood for was also gone. That now, it is up to themselves. Of course, every time you read the story it is different, but perhaps this is one interpretation.

Coming from one of the women, this was a very bold interpretation and much more sophisticated than anything that had been said in the discussion preceding it. Everybody was surprised, and a bit scared at the daring of this lady. It was a statement that also summarized their own role as believers: scared and anxious of the responsibility. Instead of commenting on her statement, the pastor allowed a tense and expectant silence to stretch.

Then he stated: "the most important thing is to *live it.* When you realize that, you get frightened [i.e. just like the women in the story]". Relieved and happy, the women started breathing again. Then the pastor told about the night before he was made a priest, that he was so scared he wanted to cancel everything. Someone else told him: "calm down, everybody has that feeling". The women laughed at his story, and commented in dialect: "it's the same when you get married".

This affirmation by the pastor broke the tension of the previous moment, and evolved into a humorous and comfortable sharing of experiences of pre-wedding nerves that was cut short by the pastor who brought everybody around to consider the main message of the story:

I'm telling you this to show: sometimes you walk away from it. And nowadays, faith has been changed into tradition. So the meaning has changed.
But what is important to us is how you could make a family service based
on the stories of the resurrection.

While discussing this question, the participants confronted another problem: how to make symbolical language understood to people in the way
that you want it to be understood. Some said that perhaps you should
not even try: the people who go to church already know what everything
means. Or they go because they always went. "They are not looking for the
things we are looking for in our faith". But another participant countered
this: "you cannot presume to know how other people experience things.
Whatever your reason, they are all good to go to church, to occupy your
mind with religious things".

The participants of this course were pleasantly surprised and even
moved by what they learned in the centre, although they were uncertain
of their own capacity to challenge other people to see things the way they
were learning to see them. The contrast with 'traditional Catholicism' was
too great, according to them. To these women, this mainly raised 'political'
problems in their relationship with their parish priest who might not agree
with their interpretation. In section 3 I go into the 'political' problems in
more detail.

The Backwardness of Looking for Certainty

Most newcomers to the centre were not experienced in reading the Bible,
or if they were, they would read it "like a newspaper", as the pastor put
it. This is understandable if one realises that in traditional Catholicism,
the reading of the Bible was not encouraged. Although the stations of
the cross, the nativity plays at Christmas and other Catholic traditions
re-enact stories in the Bible, most Catholics only know snippets of Bible-
texts, conveniently quoted by their parish priest to underscore some argument or chanted by their mother to ward off some evil (like the first verses
of the gospel of John to ward of lightning). The readings during church
services are often hardly understood.

In the session described above, we can see that the pastor took considerable time to explain that the stories in the Bible should not be taken literally. Apparently, he found this necessary even though he had explained
all this many times before during the course. Even though the participants
accepted this view, they still found it difficult to tear themselves away
from questions such as who was there during the resurrection and who

was not because they wanted to determine "what really happened". In short, their attitude towards the text was a positivist one. In this case, the pastor was successful in leading them away from these pre-occupations, and they were delighted by what they learned. This pattern was repeated every time a group I attended read a bible text together.

During the meetings of one discussion group I attended, one of the participants was less easily deterred from a positivist line of questioning.[9] In this discussion group, texts from the Bible that told of specific events around Moses, Isaac, Joseph and Jesus were compared to texts in the Koran that more or less tell the same story. One of the participants was very concerned about clearing up the literal details of a story, despite the teaching that one should not read the bible like a newspaper. He could not distance himself from the past, when he had to take these stories literally and even had exams on them. To the other participants, it was clear that taking a story literally was a foolish idea. As one participant expressed it: "if we took these stories literally, we would still be taking 'an eye for an eye' "! They expected the man to get past the literal stage, and see those priests and Catholics who are, in their eyes, not able to get past that stage as occupying another stage of spiritual and psychological development.

The more experienced participants and active Catholics who had witnessed this evolution from religious certainty to religious uncertainty in their own lifetime often saw this as an inevitable outcome of modernization and progress. This was also projected onto Islam: although the pastor explained that the Koran is considered to be a revealed text dictated to Mohammed, the participants assumed that Islam would also enter a development whereby religious certainties would be reassuringly turned into uncertainties and thus promote tolerance and respect between religions. However, to temper this optimistic view someone added: "we also have Rome" (considered to be "still" too literal minded as well).

3. THE BURDEN OF THE PAST

The interviews with the older generation discussed in chapter 3 might lead us to believe that the changes taking place within Catholicism were

---

[9] I describe and analyzed this incident in an article on certainty and uncertainty, this is a summary of the argument in that article: Knibbe, "The Role of Religious Certainty and Uncertainty in Moral Reasoning in a Catholic Province in the Netherlands".

mainly confusing to people on the level of changing practical routines, such as the lifting of the obligation to attend church regularly, upsetting the continuity of community and family-life. However, the confrontation between the participant cited above and the discourse of the pastoral centre shows how the past attempts of the Catholic Church to provide certainty and security and the emphasis on uncertainty of the pastoral centre can also create existential dilemmas. How is one to know what is fate, God's will, absolute and unchangeable truth and what is not, if those who are 'supposed to know' keep changing their minds? When certainties suddenly change into uncertainties and bad things become good things and the other way around? When other religions are discussed not to determine what is right and wrong about them but just for the sake of discussing? To some, the past is a significant obstacle to accepting the discourse of the centre. 'The past', in this case, refers to embodied dispositions instilled by a Catholic upbringing that were usually not reflected on until they were brought into consciousness through a confrontation with the discourse of the centre. This can be compared with the process through which even people who are far removed from an active religious life can become upset about the ways the last rites are conducted, as described in chapter 4: in everyday life, these dispositions do not play a role, but when the necessity for ritual forces people to negotiate with religious authorities, suddenly the mechanism of the sacraments and the power of disapproval come into play again. So what were the dispositions that were activated here?

As we saw, taking the theology and emphasis on rules and dogma of pre-Vatican II Catholicism as a point of departure, which many newcomers implicitly did, it can be difficult to explain that the Christianity preached in the centre is also Catholicism. In the Koran/Bible study group, the past evidently threw its shadow. Bert, the man asking all those inappropriate questions, had been trained to expect certain answers, and found only uncertainties instead. If everything they used to tell him turned out to be untrue, what are the answers to the ultimate questions? Should we pretend that it doesn't matter whether God exists or not? It cannot be denied that whenever a worldview and the values it implies involves deities or supernatural entities there are a few very simple questions that will not be laid to rest: *does God really exist?* And if so, *how are we supposed to live?* To which he added: *if they are not true, what is their value?*

The discourse of the centre was entirely different in style, content and values from the Catholicism that the participants knew. Most had simply drifted away from a practicing Catholic lifestyle, and had only vague notions of the beliefs that used to underlie the Catholicism of their youth.

Even for those people who were not thrown into a state of existential confusion, the contrast between the dispositions embedded through a Catholic upbringing and the discourse of the centre raised questions. For Bert, the contradiction was problematic. On the other hand, the younger participants who were sent by their parishes to be trained at the centre were often delighted once they learned to consider the Bible as a text they could read by themselves. They were surprised to find that it could be interpreted in ways that were consistent with their own outlook on life, and moreover an inspiration.

Their personal history with the church was often characterized by a resignation that they, as women, lay people, simple folk, would never fully understand the mysteries of religion and theology but that being a Catholic is an inalienable part of being a Limburger. They saw the church as an important part of community life and traditions, and were therefore willing to put up with its being old-fashioned. They were willing to lend a hand in these services to perpetuate community life, traditions, to give to their children what they themselves grew up with and out of a general feeling that God, after all, represents the highest moral values, even if the rules and rituals of his church are a bit outdated and boring. It was natural for them to ignore any disagreement between their personal outlook on life and what they assumed to be the teachings of the church, which anyway they would not be able to challenge, since they did not consider themselves to be as "learned" as the priest.

This aim to instill the notion of the fundamental uncertainty of faith into newcomers clashed with the expectations of these newcomers. They usually expected to be told some timeless truths about the nature of God, Jesus, and the way you are supposed to live. To most Limburgers, that is what they understand religion to be. And even experienced participants fell silent in amazement when the role and authority of the priest was relativized by giving the historical background of how this role developed out of necessity, and could in fact be criticized using the passages of the gospel where Jesus gives the Pharisees a piece of his mind. Although most participants were happy to deconstruct the authority of priests in this way, they were not accustomed to hearing it from 'religious experts' (who were sometimes also ordained priests) themselves. All this was clarified by describing Catholicism (or rather, Christianity in general) as a faith that is continuously evolving, along with people's imperfect understanding of God and the message of the gospels.

Central to adressing the burden of the past was the construction of a clear opposition between the pre-Vatican church and the post-Vatican church. The "old church" was often described as hierarchical, insensitive in enforcing its rules, petty in detailing the kinds of sins and their penances, stifling real faith by imposing a heavy burden of duty, discriminating against women, distrustful of human nature, fear inspiring, denying people's individuality, in short: not a happy message. Using people's personal memories as illustration, this kind of Catholicism was placed firmly in the past, something that you need not dwell on too much: since Vatican II, the church recognizes the importance of personal conscience, is more sensitive to the role of women, less hierarchical, less dogmatic.

Nevertheless, it was also recognized that this past could still play a role that needs to be addressed, especially in the course on lay pastorate for the elderly. An important topic during this course, also used as a case during the actual training in pastoral conversation, was how to cope with the negative feelings that people might have about the church, because they might project those feelings onto the lay parish volunteer visiting them. The volunteers in training had no trouble imagining that this was still an issue, especially for older people who might feel as if they have been deceived: what happened to the all-powerful church of their youth that used to have all the answers?

The strategy proposed by the pastors was that the volunteers should try to separate the identification between church and God by asking questions. To simply halt at the conclusion that the church has failed does not provide any comfort. The important thing in these cases, they were taught, was to find ways to bring the subject around to God again and to suggest ways that the person in question could start thinking of God as benign and loving, rather than punishing and cold.

So although the pre-Vatican II church might be responsible for some painful personal memories and in general for an image of a "punishing" God that should be dispelled, the discourse of the centre carefully constructed the stereotype of pre-Vatican II Catholicism as only one, relatively short, chapter in the long history of people trying to figure out the best way to live according to the message of Jesus. Putting it this way, the burden of the past was lightened.

When the participants indeed came to accept this past as harmless and unthreatening to their present outlook on life, the impression of a status quo, a consensus was created where the idea of a punishing God and its attendant dispositions of fear and tension could be left behind, although it was also recognized that this required much 'inner work'. It became possible to see the church as a human construct, rather than as a divinely ordained hierarchy in which the assigned role of lay people and especially women was to be that of silent figurants.

Interestingly, this opposition between the pre-Vatican II church and present-day Christianity was most often reiterated by those participants that had been coming to the centre for a long time. It seems that this particular image of the Catholic past was necessary to accomplish the inner work that had to be done to change not only one's image of God, but also one's relationship to religious knowledge and authority. This was complicated by the fact that the hierarchical church promoting a version of Catholicism that rests on the mechanism of the sacraments, and thereby (the threat of) exclusion, is definitely *not* something of the past. While newcomers sometimes hesitated to point this out, regulars were quite explicit about this. For the centre, however, it was politically difficult to admit to this explicitly.

4. THE PROBLEM OF THE PRESENT

As we have seen in the previous chapters, the diocesan neo-conservative program of restoration represents one side of an extremely polarized Catholic Church, especially in Limburg, of which the discourse of the pastoral centre can be taken to represent the other side. The beliefs, values and mechanisms of exclusion that course participants are encouraged to leave behind, are very much part of the 'present' created by the Roman policy of appointing conservative bishops. This creates problems both for the pastors and for the participants of the courses.

The pastoral centre does not explicitly present itself as 'progressive' to the course participants, and usually does not admit to being at odds with the Catholicism of the diocese. Rather, as we saw, they present themselves as the 'next stage', where 'people are the church'; using much the same rhetoric as was used during the pastoral council in Noordwijkerhout described in chapter 2. However, Noordwijkerhout also led to the drastic measures of Rome and the appointment of neo-conservative bishops to 'put things right' again in the Dutch church province as described in chapters 2 and 3. Since the appointment of Gijsen, neo-conservative Catholicism belied the 'inevitable' progress predicted by progressive Catholics and became politically more powerful in the diocese of Roermond. In terms of church-politics, progressive Catholicism, and therefore also the discourse of the centre have been marginalized during the years of Gijsen's reign and afterwards, although in terms of values it is much closer to Dutch mainstream moral consensus than the policy of the diocese.

This created dilemmas for the pastoral centre that were only rarely addressed openly. For example, following the official line of the diocese might mean excluding people from the sacraments if they do not live in accordance with the moral rules of the church. This is at odds with the ideals of the pastoral centre: *not* to exclude, *not* to prescribe what is right and wrong, *not* to emphasize certainty and the authority of the church in religious matters.

Politically, the pastors of the centre were involved in a balancing act between being true to their own interpretation of the gospels, and the policy of the diocese. There were the 'standard' moral issues concerning (homo) sexuality, marriage, and divorce. These were mostly solved on a case-to-case basis away from the eyes of the bishop. During the courses and in their publications, the pastors avoided discussing particular 'rules' explicitly and the topics of sexuality and birth control were avoided altogether. This avoidance came not only from a desire not to stir up animosity with the diocese, but also because the issue of what is and what is not allowed by the church was completely irrelevant within the discourse of the centre. What is relevant is whether behaviour is respectful of other people, puts into practice the values of 'loving thy neighbour as thyself' and protects the weak. Whenever behaviour was discussed that was unquestionably 'bad' in the sense that it was destructive towards other people or towards one's own person (e.g. alcoholism or criminality) the efforts were directed towards understanding why people would 'turn away from God', the unhappiness and hurt this implied, and looking for ways to promote harmony, forgiveness and love. Because the policy of both Wiertz and the pastoral centre was to avoid confrontation, the rules for the application of the sacraments were not really an issue.

Most visitors of the centre were in some way aware of the neo-conservative 'hard line' of the diocese: Gijsen's reign lasted for more than twenty years, and the many conflicts he had are embedded in collective memory somewhere. Almost all of the course participants agreed that the positions of the hard line should be considered outdated. To the people of Limburg being a Catholic, being active in the church has almost nothing to do with the question whether you would agree with everything the pope in Rome proclaims. Neither is it necessary to have any knowledge of what is in the Bible. As long as you are baptized and celebrated first communion, you are a Catholic and part of the local community. Being born in Limburg still almost automatically ensures that you will go through these rituals. In everyday life the discrepancy between this common sense understanding of 'being Catholic' and the 'official' church doctrine is not very problematic. Yet, as I described in chapter 4, what 'being a Catholic' meant was often very unclear to people themselves, thereby providing an opening for resignification that was used very well by the pastoral centre. Below, I will show how a discussion of baptism was turned into an opportunity to discuss the concept of sin and the value of inclusiveness promoted by the centre in relation to the mechanism of the sacraments. Crucial to the process of resignification is the turn from 'moralizing' to 'psychologizing' described in chapter 2.

The Deconstruction of the Concept of Sin and the Mechanism of the Sacraments

The influence of psychology was evident in many ways in the discourse of the centre, e.g. in the way the Bible was interpreted from the perspective of the psychologies of each of the actors in a story and then related to contemporary issues. The psychological turn was especially evident in the way the 'old fashioned' concept of sin was re-interpreted: sin was primarily seen as the result of psychological ineptness, fear and mistrust, a turning away and closing off from God. Putting one's trust in God, as Jesus did, and keeping faith in his fundamentally loving and inclusive nature can remedy this.

The contrast between the 'old' and the 'new' way of understanding sin were addressed explicitly when stories were discussed where Jesus or one of the prophets from the Old Testament makes a negative statement about someone or some group of people in the vein of: those who will not recognize the truth will be damned. This reminds of the old 'mechanism of the sacraments' that was at the root of the painful stories that would sometimes come out during the interviews with the older generation described in chapter 3: those who do not adhere to the rules of the Church will be excluded.

In the centre, these stories were turned around, by focusing on the promise held out to those willing to listen, rather than on the punishment of those *not* willing to listen. The punishments for those who were unwilling to listen would also be interpreted psychologically: by not listening to God's messenger, people condemned *themselves* to stay in a state of psychological and spiritual darkness and confusion. Rather than a mechanism of exclusion, the sacraments were interpreted as a ritual celebration of key religious and psychological moments, linking these moments to the religious symbols of the Catholic tradition.

One example was the way the wish for baptism was represented in one of the discussion groups. The subject was the story describing how John baptized Jesus. This was interpreted as a spiritual rebirth for Jesus. One member used this to criticize traditional Catholic baptism: babies are not aware, so they cannot be reborn spiritually. Her criticism was even more vehement on the subject of the way baptism was used as a 'marker': if a baby was not baptized, it was buried outside the cemetery because the stain of original sin was not washed away yet. If you are not baptized, you do not belong, you are an outsider, you are still marked by original sin. According to her, this was "sick". Other participants however, said that nevertheless, parents often want to have their children baptized even when they themselves are not married in church. Then the pastor explained how he approached this phenomenon:

> Often, parents want to have their baby baptized despite not being active believers, for example they were not married before the church. Some priests would say: it's useless to baptize the child, because you will never see it again. But to me [the pastor], this situation indicates that they see marriage as something between the two of them, whereas when they have a baby, they feel the responsibility for a new life and they want to give it something. They want to have the child baptized because they realize it's not something that belongs to them alone. The point is to give the child the baggage for his life, of the life as Jesus of Nazareth lived it. So perhaps baptism could be seen more and more as the sacrament of the parents.

This example shows how 'old meanings' (those parents are careless and inconsistent Catholics) are removed and new meanings are discovered through a process of imagining the feelings and thoughts of the people involved. This process is remarkably similar to the way biblical texts are read in terms of 'imagining' the historical context and the psychology of each of the actors in order to arrive at the central revelation depicted in the text. The way this pastor interpreted the apparently inconsistent behaviour of parents was greeted with thoughtful approval.[10]

Whenever disapproval was voiced during the discussion groups and courses, relativizing remarks were quickly added, or rules were established by which people were admonished to "keep their pronouncements on a personal level": no one could get away with generalizing from their personal experience to make judgments on others. The taboo on moralizing is perhaps the only absolute in the discourse of the centre.

Although the 'classic' Catholic moral topics were not much discussed in the courses, there were also the issues of lay participation in religious services, and the degree of openness towards other religions. On both, the

---

[10] Note that although it is similar to the way people described their motivations for having their children baptized (see chapter 4), it has a much more explicitly religious slant.

diocese has strict guidelines, although local priests had widely different practices. This impacted directly on the ability of volunteers to contribute to parish life. Therefore, it is interesting to take a closer look at how the contradictions between 'traditional' and 'neo-conservative' Catholicism and the discourse of the pastoral centre were perceived by the participants of the courses.

The pastoral centre actively promoted openness to other religions and ecumenism, and saw lay participation as the present-day translation of what Jesus was preaching against the 'rule minded' Pharisees. To any participant who listened closely, the message was clear: it is not the rules that matter, it is the spirit of God's love shown in the life of Jesus that has to be discovered and promoted in daily life.

Often, it took some time before new participants were motivated and had the courage to really participate in interpreting the gospels. But mostly, it was an exciting experience for them. For example, during the second meeting of a course, one woman commented: "I have been thinking and thinking things over this week, my mind was whirling". Some people even reported to have dreamt about what they had learned.

The shift in attitude that the pastoral centre tried to provoke was for people to start taking their own thoughts and evaluations as a point of departure, to start trusting and developing them as legitimate. The aim was to replace the residual attitudes of unflinching acceptance of the authority of the priest over religious 'facts' and ritual acts. The shift in attitude from being 'born' Catholic to actively reflecting on it usually created enthusiasm, but also revealed confusion, uncertainties and tensions, as we saw in the description of the meeting on interpreting the stories of resurrection.

Confusion; because some of the participants found it hard to learn how to think "metaphorically" to extract the main message from a story or a ritual act. Uncertainty; because the participants did not trust that they would be able to reflect like this on their own, outside the context of the course. And tension; because they were especially uncertain whether they would be able, even if they had managed to interpret a Bible text according to their own insights, to defend their conclusions to their local priest and fellow parishioners.

The tensions this confusion and uncertainty generated were usually just below the surface. In the course on creating a family service, this tension was addressed during the same meeting discussing the resurrection described in section 1. This description picks up where I stopped in the first section, with the pastor passionately explaining his views of the gospels,

and finding an attentive audience who had just experienced a moving
insight of their own responsibility in 'living' the message of Jesus:

> Every time again, you are confronted by the question: will I let my life just
> go on quietly as it is, or do I try to go through barriers, get to the essence
> of things. Comparing what you learn here with what used to be taught as
> Catholicism before is not the important issue [this refers to earlier discus-
> sion about the past]. The gospels were written to tell people who did not
> know Jesus about his life. Nowadays, you see that caring for other people
> is often a problem. So the message of Jesus is still relevant. And then, you
> get frightened sometimes. However, don't expect to get any ready-made
> answers from the Bible.

Everybody agreed to this, but then, one woman burst out: "this is not what
the parish priests are preaching in our church! Now you find things out
for yourself. But you have to come up with the courage to shut down the
voice of the priest [in reading the Bible]". At first, the pastor awkwardly
sidestepped this comment on his colleagues: "if people are touched in
their hearts and minds, it's fine. If they get irritated, they're also touched,
but in a negative way". Another participant took up this issue: "but sup-
pose you would protest? Those priests wouldn't care at all. They will just
shut the door. We think we are right, but they also think they are right".
The pastor asked: "like the old priest in A?". But the participants dismissed
him as a problem: "he's not so bad, at least he's open to discussion, and
too old to change anyway. It's the young priests that are the worst! They
are not open to change. They don't care about our views at all".

They were referring to those priests who follow the diocesan policy
very strictly, who had been trained at Rolduc or another conservative
seminary, and explicitly discourage people from participating in the communion if they are not living in accordance with the moral rules of the
church. Obviously, this goes directly against what the participants had
been taught during the course at the centre, and they were trying to get
a pronouncement from the pastor confirming that this was unacceptably
callous behaviour. Still sidestepping, the pastor said: "well, but he will also
have to account for his life before God when he dies".

With the subject out in the open, the group was gathering steam in
sharing stories expressing their indignation about 'bad priests'. The pastor allowed them the space to tell their stories without commenting.
Finally, one woman could not contain herself any longer, broke through
the taboo on expecting certainties and ready-made answers, and explicitly
asked for the final verdict of the pastor: "are they allowed to deny people
communion?" Amused, the pastor winked to me, sharing his enthusiasm

about the astuteness of these women who were putting him on the spot. He answered: "that was the question between Jesus and the Pharisees. I would never refuse the communion. Of course, I know the rules of the church. But how can I judge if someone is sinful or not?" Pushing the point home even more explicitly, another participant said: "But even if you could judge, the gospels say Jesus was there exactly for those people, for the sinners, wasn't he?" To which the pastor answered: "the point is, that *you* decide. Don't think too much of the priest, because he sends you home empty handed".

As we can see here, the problem of the past was manageable in terms of the discourse of the centre, the problem of the present much less so. A straightforward confrontation (we think we are right, but they also think they are right) raised difficult issues that cannot really be resolved on the level of the official discourse. The pastors never dismissed anybody as 'wrong' or 'bad' during the courses and discussion groups. Not only was it politically inadvisable, it also would go directly against the restraint in moralizing that they promoted.

Usually, it was only when course participants pointed out that it was especially the *young*, newly trained priests who were taking the hard line (rather than the *old*, who could be explained as relics of the past), that the reality of polarization within the church was admitted into the discussion.[11] However, it was precisely on these issues that people were most vocal, and hardest to restrain by the pastors in expressing their indignation. Some people claimed that in their reaction against cultural change and modernization, "they" (the neo-conservative priests and Gijsen) "chased people out of the church". Older people who had been active Catholics during the time the forces of renewal were dominant in Limburg complained that they could not recognize themselves anymore in the present day Catholic Church: "I'm a religious refugee".[12]

---

[11] In the discussion groups where people knew each other for a longer time this was an accepted topic.

[12] Another 'problem of the present' is the prevalence of non-believers and people who are estranged from the church. However, this was addressed straightforwardly during the courses, and adequate strategies had been worked out to deal with it. In fact, according to those who referred me to the center in the first place it is one of the strengths of the center to establish communication about religious subjects no matter what the background of the person they were talking to. In all their courses, the pastors taught the participants to be flexible, to tune into the level of understanding, vocabularies, objections and negative perceptions their target group might have against religion, without compromising the religious message.

5. Gossip and Stereotyping

The stereotyping of 'bad priests' has an important function in validating the discourse of the centre. Interestingly, this validation can only take place through the genre of gossip. Generally, gossip was discouraged during the meetings: there were strict rules for the kinds of pronouncements one was allowed to make. For example, one was not allowed to say anything about any person without qualifying this as a personal opinion or impression, thus leaving room for other interpretations. Due to this rule for discussion, one might expect there to be very little space for gossip in and around the courses and discussion groups. However, *not* to gossip is impossible between people who share a significant amount of time and acquaintances with each other. Among the supporting staff and volunteers of the centre, gossip was shared during coffee breaks, but the topic was often changed quickly when a pastor came in. With me, pastors only shared gossip in personal conversations. However, as it turned out, this genre was crucial in resolving the 'problem of the present' described earlier in this chapter. Again, it was the stereotype of the 'bad priest' that was the subject of much of the gossip. This stereotype proved to be crucial to liberal Christians in proving themselves right without claiming access to an absolute truth.

In anthropology, gossip is seen as a genre of conversation through which people share their views on the moral ordering of the community and indirectly enforce social control and bonding.[13] Anthropological and sociological studies have paid attention to these genres, although not as much as might be expected, as giving important insights into 'what really matters' to people, but also into how groups function, and how moral orientations are reinforced. Sharing gossip is one way that people indicate that they feel comfortable with each other: sharing horror, outrage and disgust, loyally sympathizing with each other, creates a warm 'we-feeling'. And of course, this 'we-feeling' is crucial to bonds of trust and reciprocity and delineates the familiar from the unfamiliar.

The moralizing in gossip is based on personal feeling, it can be explicitly disapproving, and it is based on stereotypes and prejudices. Moreover, the disapproval and judgments passed are based on personal loyalties

---

[13] Alex Straating, "Roddelen En De Verbale Constructie Van De Gemeenschap," *Etnofoor* XI, no. 2 (1998): 25–41; Pamela J. Stewart and Andrew Strathern, *Witchcraft, Sorcery. Rumors and Gossip* (Cambridge: Cambridge University Press, 2004).

rather than on systematic consideration. The 'we-feeling' created in this way is thus premised on 'othering' and stereotyping. In all these characteristics, it goes against the discourse of the centre, which emphasizes inclusiveness, loving relations, a reserved attitude towards judging others and careful consideration of the psychology of anyone being discussed. After all, no one human being can claim 'true knowledge' and certainty. Furthermore, there was an undercurrent of awareness that the scars of the exclusivist moralizing of the past made it absolutely taboo to pastors to be nonchalantly disapproving in making pronouncements on other people. So the language used in the centre was almost always politically correct, avoiding all 'othering'.

This politically correct language and the values that underpin it are in stark contrast with the stereotypes of the young diocesan priests often referred to in informal interactions and gossip. These stereotypes were already discussed in chapter 4, and they also came to the surface during the session when the participants of the family-service course put the pastor on the spot by demanding that he condemn these priests in section 4 of this chapter.

In practically everything, the stereotype of these priests is the 'negative' of the positive promoted by the discourse of the centre. Not only are they thought to be exclusivist and arrogant in passing judgment on others according to 'outdated' moral standards, they are also reputed to be very insensitive in personal interactions, casually and, in the eyes of the participants and volunteers of the centre, cruelly, making ironic remarks to their parishioners.

For example, one priest was reported to have said to a widow visiting her husband's grave: "well, how can you be sure your husband entered heaven hmm?" When a remark such as this was discussed among the participants, most attention was given to the effect this had on the widow. The theological niceties of discussing whether heaven is really a 'place' into which one can be 'denied entrance', or a metaphor for a more elusive truth, might be pointed out by a pastor or a more experienced participant, but in informal discussion it would not be brought up. Everybody would simply side with the person who was hurt, condemning the priest.

Apparently, the only 'others' in the pastoral centre were the neo-conservative priests trained by Gijsen and his personal allies such as the priest of Welden, although this was only admitted on the level of informal interaction. The exchange of stories about these priests, especially in formal settings of the courses and discussion groups, was usually limited

before this exchange could heat up emotions to the point of creating that
warm 'we-feeling' of moral righteousness among the participants.

However, judgment of these priests in particular, and anyone espousing a 'literal' and exclusive worldview in general, was underpinned by
the evolution from certainty to uncertainty projected onto Christianity,
Catholicism and social organization as well as people's personal spiritual
and psychological development. This 'inevitable evolution' was supported
on the level of official discourse as I showed in section 2. Thus, the more
experienced participants could set aside these priests as psychologically
immature people that one did not have to take too seriously, as people
who wanted to "turn back the clock", an attempt inherently doomed to
fail. Although the stereotyping was not part of the formal discourse, the
pastors did not contradict this view, nor could they offer any other view
that would make these priests more 'human' and less stereotypical in the
eyes of those who judged them.

The question of 'who is right', which was sidestepped on the level of
formal discourse, could only be resolved on the informal level: they (the
people espousing progressive Catholic values) were right, because their
stereotypical archenemies were immature young priests, oblivious to the
hurt they caused people. This created a tension that was perhaps unprob-
lematic to the 'insiders' of the discourse of the centre, who knew better
than to ask such questions, but was keenly felt by new participants and
sometimes came to the surface in indignant outbursts.

Interestingly, the older priests who invoked the mechanism of the sacraments and their prerogative as a priest were not similarly judged. Usually, they were viewed with a mixture of compassion and acceptance: they
are too old to change now, and anyway, "imagine if we did not have our
old priest, we would have no priest at all and that is even worse!"

6. Concluding Remarks

Strikingly, some values central to the discourse at this centre are based
on the explicit acknowledgment of *uncertainties* rather than certainties. It
emphasizes what we, as humans, do *not* know, can*not* control. To pretend
to know, to pretend to be able to control is seen as 'bad'. Rather than positing an ontology of the world and deducing prescriptions for living from
it, it takes the 'mainstream' modern understanding of the world as a point
of departure and sees the Christian tradition as a chequered attempt to

understand the 'radical message of love' that can be read in the life and actions of Jesus. This is in direct contrast with the practices of the spiritual group described in the previous chapter, where there is an emphasis on certainties gained through an indvidualist epistemology.

Generally, the participants were receptive to the discourse of the centre. However, the understanding of Catholicism among new participants was shaped by the "dogmatic" Catholicism the pre-war generation and the immediate post-war generations in Limburg grew up with and traditional Catholic customs. Usually, the pastors were quite skilful in clearing up this barrier.

Nevertheless, the tendency to interpret stories literally and ask how things "really are" or what "really happened" was strong. Why is this? One might speculate that this is an attempt to probe and question the moral reasoning of pre-Vatican II Catholicism enshrined in collective memory in fragments mainly connected to things not allowed and reasons to exclude people from the sacraments. The power of disapproval vested in anything or anyone connected to the church is still great, as well as the need for 'definite' answers to ward of this threat of disapproval.

Combining the themes that emerged in this context with an insight into the larger religious landscape of which the pastoral centre is a part, we can conclude that it is both the 'burden of the past' and the 'problematic present' that are shaped through this discourse and adressed. It is both 'the burden of the past' and the 'problematic present' that make the discourse of the centre relevant, especially to those Limburg Catholics who are prepared to give a more specifically 'religious' (as opposed to 'merely' traditional) content to their Catholic identity. The discourse of the centre easily negotiates the distrust towards religious authority described in previous chapters, and explicitly puts itself 'at the service' of the domain of the familiar. At the same time, the interaction between context, past and present, created dilemmas that could not be solved on the formal level of discourse.

Through stereotyping conveyed in gossip and through the construction of a stereotypical image of the Catholic past, a particular way of believing was cast as backwards, psychologically regressive and un-modern. To some participants this indeed helped them to liberate themselves from dispositions that they experienced as limiting. To others, this emphasis on uncertainty was too cerebral and created more problems than they were prepared to face in their relationship with the local priest and other parish volunteers.

CHAPTER SEVEN

CONCLUSIONS

Sociological theories on religious change often posit a more or less direct link between societal change and religious change. This is most clearly the case for secularization theories, that saw the industrialisation and modernization of society as causes for the decline of religion, but it is also the case for theories that see a new salience of religion emerging. Some of these theories see the rationalization of society that ultimately exhausts itself as a trigger, others point at the individualization of society that throws us all back onto ourselves as leading to a subjectivized religiosity, still others link the current 'resurgence' of religion to processes of globalization, triggering a turn to religion as a defence mechanism.

The religious change remembered here, and the current location of religion and spirituality in local life however, do not seem to have much to do with either industrialization, individualization or rationalization, or even globalization very directly. Secularization, in the sense of de-churching, is remembered as a process that was initiated 'from above', first through liberalization, which reformatted religion as a personal choice, and then through the polarization within the Catholic Church. When people had gotten used to the notion of religion as a personal choice and started to take seriously the opportunities for participant democracy this offered, the reverse movement was again initiated from above: suddenly, the rules were again important. However, these rules were no longer plausible to people, and most rejected them as an attempt to "turn back the clock". The belief in progress had become firmly established even in the local life of Welden.

Rather than positing an a-priori relationship between social structural change and 'religion', it seems that the popularization of sociological notions of modernization, secularization and progress have to be included in the study of the cultural and historical processes by which religion is constituted, understood and related to. This means an integration of a cultural perspective focusing on practice and discourse with theories of social change. On the level of local life, the positioning of people vis a vis religion can be best understood through tracing the cultural changes that have taken place in society in general and within the Catholic pillar in particular, leading to different social structures. When we look at those cultural changes in turn, we can see that they are inspired by different notions of 'where things are going' among cultural elites. In the fifties, liberalization was initiated by an elite inspired by psychology that believed that the Catholicism of that time was 'not healthy'. Vatican II wanted to bring the church 'up to date', which involved notions of modernity and progress, as well as openness, equality and democracy. Social change, most notably democratization, was deemed inevitable by those in power in the pillarized institutions and politics in the Netherlands then, as Kennedy has shown. Many of these notions of societal change were developed within sociology. Therefore, sociology played a crucial role in the changes it describes.

This book has focused on one particular place to discuss a wide range of developments regarding religion. In the process, the cross-cutting and entanglement of different social and cultural processes have come to light from quite different angles. Each of the chapters complicate the assumed link between social structural change and religious change in several ways: religion did not decline *as a result* of social change, but was transformed *in anticipation* of social change. Religion did not disappear, but remains intrinsic to the production of locality. Contemporary religion and spirituality do not primarily address the stresses of modern life, but provide different answers to problems created by the understanding of religion based on a particular remembering of the role of religious authority in the 'old church' and the confrontation with the present day church. Both the pastoral centre and the Spiritual Group provide the means to experiment and learn new ways of relating to religious knowledge and authority.

Presently, the religious landscape of Limburg is self-consciously pluralistic: where previously, the Catholic Church was able to create a plausible facade of unity, monopolizing knowledge and religious authority, nowadays it is possible to explore the options freely, and people view themselves as autonomous actors vis à vis religion. In the eyes of many people the 'official' church only pays lip service to this 'freedom of consciousness'. 'Spirituality' on the other hand, is quite well attuned to the situation of pluralism. It has become a catch-word for the networks, meetings and sites that facilitate a new attitude towards religious authority. Both the spiritual group and the pastoral centre were characterized by discourses that emphasized that each individual should think (and feel, experience) for her or himself. Nevertheless, in both settings, it is clear that the boundaries of the interpretative frameworks are enforced discursively and informally. Clearly, an emphasis on individualism does not mean that 'anything goes'. Furthermore, the emphasis on individualism can take quite different cultural forms.

In one respect, it seems 'spirituality' cannot perform the same tasks as 'religion': the Catholic rituals remain important for the perpetuation of the domain of the familiar and the production of locality. Ritual creativity is relatively low in the rural areas of Limburg, in contrast to the more urban areas. The need for ritual to reproduce the domain of the familiar opens up the domain of the familiar to the interference of an authoritarian church. The rituals become the site of contestation between the church and the friends and family of the deceased. The church is usually not explicitly rejected, but it becomes clear, especially in rituals to do with death and dying, that the authority of the priest as a representative of the church and God is no longer accepted. Rather, he is expected to hallow the central values held dear by the relatives and friends of the deceased, to help them express that they cared and loved the person now dead.

Although the rites and routines of the Catholic Church are still crucial to constituting this domain, the representatives of the church are often considered to be external to it. Sharing stories about 'bad priests' has become a way of affirming shared values in opposition to the negative examples these priests provide. The complicity generated by sharing these stories set the boundaries of the domain of the familiar. Within the pastoral centre, bad priest stories moreover resolved contradictions and problems that could not be resolved on the level of the formal discourse.

One of the puzzles that sparked off this research was the discrepancy between sociological accounts of social change that often inform new attempts to theorize religion and the social context that I knew as a child. In this context, religion as a set of beliefs seemed absent, but it could suddenly reappear at unexpected moments that seemed to have nothing to do with religion, in determining who belongs and who does not, who is familiar and who is not. Looking back it seems that an important factor in explaining the different nature and pace of social change in these kinds of non-urban communities is the proximity of the generations: the people who do not leave the area in which they grow up feel a greater responsibility to negotiate, explain and make intelligible any innovations in lifestyle to their parents and neighbours. Sociological theory of social change, on the other hand, is often focused on developments in urban areas, on novelty. What this book makes clear, I hope, is that the non-urban areas cannot be assumed to follow in the footsteps of the novel lifestyles of the urban areas, but that change takes place in different ways. Sometimes people cast themselves as victims of changes initiated from above, or outside ("they changed everything", "it never occurred to us to do things differently"), yet the agenda of restoration was resisted more vigourously than the changes.

An important question for future research is whether the Catholic rituals will remain important to reproduce the connection to place and the domain of the familiar. We could speculate that over time, the distinctive role of these rituals can be substituted by other rituals, as the pre-war generation steeped in Catholicism is dying now, and the post-war generations increasingly see themselves as part of a pluralistic religious landscape, including the option of no religion or 'spirituality' rather than religion.

It is interesting to observe that the *dispositions* enforced by the mechanism of the sacraments, instilled into several generations of Catholics with enormous efforts, have survived less well across the generations than some of the *rituals* associated with them (notably baptism, Holy Communion, marriage and the last rites). These rituals have come to represent continuity with the past and connection with place. The moral order they uphold in people's eyes is not the one envisioned by conservative Catholicism, but that of the local community that has "gone with the times" and is modern, yet connected to the past and 'tradition'. As observed in chapter 3, the word 'chastity', so important to people's education, has disappeared from everyday language.

To return to the subject of grand theories: not only would a new grand theory need to integrate sociological and humanities perspectives on social change in relation to religion, it also needs to look more closely at the role of locality and what I have called the domain of the familiar: not necessarily community, nor necessarily ethnicity, but the field generated by the subtle everyday ways in which people recognize each other as fellow inhabitants of the same life worlds, rather than as strangers.

BIBLIOGRAPHY

Akkerman, Tjitske, and Siep Stuurman. *De Zondige Riviera Van Het Katholicisme. Een Lokale Studie over Feminisme En Ontzuiling 1950–1975.* Amsterdam: SUA, 1985.

Appadurai, Arjun. *Modernity at Large: Cultural Dimensions of Globalization.* Minneapolis: U of Minnesota Press, 1996.

Asad, Talal. "The Construction of Religion as an Anthropological Category." In *A Reader in the Anthropology of Religion*, edited by Michael Lambek, 114–132. Blackwell Anthologies in Social and Cultural Anthropology. Malden [etc.]: Blackwell Publishing, 2002.

Aupers, Stef, and Dick Houtman. *Religions of Modernity: Relocating the Sacred to the Self and the Digital.* Leiden and Boston: Brill, 2010.

Aupers, Stef, and Anneke van Otterloo. *New Age; Een Godsdiensthistorische En Sociologische Benadering.* Kampen: Kok, 2000.

Auwerda, Richard. *De Kromstaf Als Wapen: Bisschopsbenoemingen in Nederland.* Baarn: Arbor, 1988.

Van der Baar, P.A. *Priester in Limburg Op Het Breukvlak Van De Tijd.* Beek: Stichting Vrienden van Frans Hennissen, 1995.

Bartley, Brendan, Phil Hubbard, and Rob Kitchin. *Thinking Geographically.* Continuum International Publishing Group, 2004.

Bauman, Zygmunt. "Consuming Life." *Journal of Consumer Culture* 1, no. 1 (2001): 9–29.

——. "Morality in the Age of Contingency." In *Detraditionalization*, edited by Paul Heelas, Scott Lash, and Paul Morris. Oxford: Blackwell, 1996.

——. "Postmodern Religion." In *Religion, Modernity and Postmodernity*, edited by Paul Heelas, David Martin, and Paul Alfred Morris. Oxford: Blackwell, 1998.

——. *Postmodernity and Its Discontents.* Cambridge: Polity Press, 1997.

Baumann, Gerd. "Ritual Implicates Others: Rereading Durkheim in a Plural Society." In *Understanding Rituals*, edited by Daniel de Coppet. European Association of Social Anthropologists. London and New York: Routledge, 1992.

Beck, Ulrich, and Elisabeth Beck-Gernsheim. *Individualization: Institutionalized Individualism and Its Social and Political Consequences.* London and New York: Sage Publications Ltd, 2002.

Becker, J.W., Joep de Hart, and J. Mens. *Secularisatie En Alternatieve Zingeving in Nederland.* Vol. 24. Rijswijk: Sociaal en Cultureel Planbureau, 1997.

Becker, J.W., and J.S.J. de Wit. *Secularisatie in De Jaren Negentig. Kerklidmaatschap, Veranderingen in Opvattingen En Een Prognose.* Den Haag: Sociaal en Cultureel planbureau, 2000.

Bender, Courtney. *The New Metaphysicals: Spirituality and the American Religious Imagination.* Chicago: University of Chicago Press, 2010.

Berger, Peter. *The Sacred Canopy.* Garden City: Doubleday & Company, Inc, 1967.

Berger, Peter, Brigitte Berger, and Hansfried Kellner. *The Homeless Mind.* Middlesex [etc.]: Penguin Books, 1977.

Bernts, Ton. *Pal Voor De Kerk. Vrijwilligerswerk in Parochies.* Vol. 3. Nijmegen: Nijmegen University Press, 1998.

Bernts, Ton, Gerard Dekker, and Joep de Hart. *God in Nederland, 1996–2006.* Ten Have, 2007.

Beyer, Peter, and Lori G. Beaman. *Religion, Globalization and Culture.* Leiden and Boston: Brill, 2007.

Blavatsky, Hélène P. *Isis Unveiled: a Master-key to the Mysteries of Ancient and Modern Science and Theology.* London, 1910.

Borgman, Erik. Edward Schillebeeckx: *A Theologian in His History. A Catholic Theology of Culture (1914–1965)*. Continuum International Publishing Group, 2004.

Borgman, Erik, Bert van Dijk, Theo Salemink, Bert van Dijk, and Theo Salemink. *Katholieken in De Moderne Tijd: Een Onderzoek Door De Acht Mei Beweging*. Zoetermeer: De Horstink, 1995.

Bourdieu, Pierre. *Distinction: A Social Critique of the Judgement of Taste*. Cambridge: Harvard University Press, 1984.

——. "Habitus." In *A Sense of Place*, edited by Jean Hillier and Emma Rooksby. second edition. Aldershot: Ashgate, 2005.

——. *Outline of a Theory of Practice*. (Esquisse D'une Théorie De La Pratique). Transl. by Richard Nice. (Repr.). Cambridge: Cambridge University Press, 2003.

Brinkgreve, Christien, and Michel Korzec. *"Margriet weet raad": gevoel, gedrag, moraal in Nederland 1938–1978*. Aula boeken. Utrecht: Spectrum, 1978.

Brown, Callum G. *The Death of Christian Britain: Understanding Secularisation, 1800–2000*. Taylor & Francis, 2009.

Bruce, Steve. *God Is Dead: Secularization in the West*. Oxford: Wiley-Blackwell, 2002.

Campbell, Colin. *The Romantic Ethic and the Spirit of Modern Consumerism*. Oxford: Blackwell, 1987.

——. "On Understanding Modern Consumerism and Misunderstanding the Romantic Ethic Thesis: a Reply to Boden and Williams." *Sociology* 37, no. 4 (November 1, 2003): 791–797. doi:10.1177/00380385030374010.

Casanova, José. *Public Religions in the Modern World*. University of Chicago Press, 1994.

——. "Public Religions Revisited." In *Religion: Beyond the Concept*, 101–119. Fordham: Fordham University Press, 2008.

——. "Religion, European Secular Identities, and European Integration." *Religion in an Expanding Europe* (2006): 65–92.

Coleman, John. *The Evolution of Dutch Catholicism, 1958–1974. Berkeley and Los Angeles: University of California Press*, 1978.

Coleman, Simon. *The Globalisation of Charismatic Christianity: Spreading the Gospel of Prosperity*. Cambridge studies in ideology and religion 12. New York: Cambridge University Press, 2000.

Coleman, Simon, and Peter Jeffrey Collins. *Locating the Field: Space, Place and Context in Anthropology*. Oxford: Berg Publishers, 2006.

Coleman, Simon, and John Eade. *Reframing Pilgrimage: Cultures in Motion*. Routledge, 2004.

Davie, Grace. *Europe—the Exceptional Case: Parameters of Faith in the Modern World*. London: Darton Longman & Todd, 2002.

——. "Europe: The Exception That Proves the Rule?" In *The Desecularization of the World. Resurgent Religion and World Politics*, edited by Peter Berger, 65–83. Washington D.C.: Ethics and Public Policy Center, 1996.

——. "Praying Alone? Church-Going in Britain and Social Capital. A Reply to Steve Bruce." *Journal of Contemporary Religion* 17, no. 3 (2002): 329–334.

——. *Religion in Britain Since 1945. Believing Without Belonging*. Oxford: Blackwell, 1994.

——. *Religion in Modern Europe: a Memory Mutates*. Oxford University Press, 2000.

——. "The Persistence of Institutional Religion in Modern Europe." In *Peter Berger and the Study of Religion*, edited by Linda Woodhead, Paul Heelas, and David Martin. London [etc.]: Routledge, 2001.

——. *The Sociology of Religion*. London, New Delhi and Singapore: SAGE, 2007.

Davie, Grace, Paul Heelas, and Linda Woodhead. *Predicting Religion. Christian, Secular and Alternative Futures*. Aldershot: Ashgate, 2003.

Dekker, Gerard. *God in Nederland, 1966–1996*. Amsterdam: Anthos, 1997.

Denzin, Norman K., and Yvonna S. Lincoln. *The SAGE Handbook of Qualitative Research*. SAGE, 2005.

Van Dijk, Bert van, Liesbeth Huijts, and Trees Verstegen. *Katholieke Vrouwen En Het Feminisme: Een Onderzoek Door De Acht Mei Beweging*. Amersfoort: De Horstink, 1990.

Dobbelaere, Karel, and Liliane Voyé. "From Pillar to Postmodernity: The Changing Situation of Religion in Belgium." *Sociological Analysis* 51, no. S (1990): S1–S13.

Droogers, André. "The Third Bank of the River: Play, Methodological Ludism and the Definition of Religion." In *The Pragmatics of Defining Religion: Contexts, Concepts and Contents*, edited by J.G. Platvoet and A.L. Molendijk, 285–313. Leiden: Brill, 1999.

Dubisch, Jill. *In a Different Place: Pilgrimage, Gender, and Politics at a Greek Island Shrine.* Princeton: Princeton University Press, 1995.

Durkheim, Emile. *The Elementary Forms of Religious Life.* New York: The Free Press, 1995.

——. "Durkheim's 'Individualism and the Intellectuals'." Edited by Steven Lukes. *Political Studies* 17, no. 1 (1969): 14–30.

Einstein, Mara. *Brands of Faith: Marketing Religion in a Commercial Age.* Routledge, 2007.

——. "The Evolution of Religious Branding." *Social Compass* 58, no. 3 (2011): 331–338.

Fedele, Anna. *Looking for Mary Magdalene. Alternative Pilgrimage and Ritual Creativity at Catholic Shrines in France.* Oxford and New York: Oxford University Press, 2012.

——. "The Metamorphoses of Neopaganism in Traditionally Catholic Countries in Southern Europe." In *Sites and Politics of Religious Diversity in Southern Europe*, edited by Ruy Blanes and José Mapril. Leiden: Brill, forthcoming.

Fedele, Anna, and Kim Knibbe, eds. *Gender and Power in Contemporary Spirituality: Ethnographic Approaches.* London and New York: Routledge, 2013.

Foucault, Michel. *Archaeology of Knowledge.* Routledge, 2002.

Gemzöe, Lena. "The Feminization of Healing in Pilgrimage to Fátima." In *Pilgrimage And Healing*, edited by Jill Dubisch and Michael Winkelman. University of Arizona Press, 2005.

Van Gennep, Arnold. *Les Rites De Passage.* Paris: Picard, 1981.

Giddens, Anthony. *The Consequences of Modernity.* Cambridge, UK: Polity Press, 1990.

Goddijn, Walter. *De Beheerste Kerk : Uitgestelde Revolutie in Rooms-Katholiek Nederland.* Amsterdam: Elsevier, 1973.

Goddijn, Walter, Jan Jacobs, and Gérard van Tillo. *Tot Vrijheid Geroepen: Katholieken in Nederland: 1946–2000.* Baarn: Ten Have, 1999.

Goddijn, Walter, Hans Wewerinke, and Fons Mommers. *Pastoraal Concilie (1965–1970): Een Experiment in Kerkelijk Leiderschap.* Baarn: Nelissen, 1986.

Grootenhuis, Manfred te, and Peer Schepers. "Churches in Dutch: Causes of Religious Disaffiliation in The Netherlands 1937–1995." *Journal for the Scientific Study of Religion* 40, no. 4 (2001): 591–606.

Haenen, Henri, and Hugo Verweij. *De Verscheurde Katholieken.* Weesp: De Haan, 1985.

Halman, Loek, Felix Heunks, Ruud de Moor, Harry Zanders, Felix Heunks, Ruud de Moor, and Harry Zanders. *Traditie, Secularisatie En Individualisering.* Tilburg: Tilburg University Press, 1987.

Hammer, Olav. *Claiming Knowledge; Strategies of Epistemology from Theosophy to the New Age.* Leiden [etc.]: Brill, 2001.

Hanegraaff, Wouter. "Het Einde Van De Hermetische Traditie." *Inaugural Lecture.* Universiteit van Amsterdam, 2000.

——. "New Age Religion and Western Culture, Esotericism in the Mirror of Secular Thought." *PhD-thesis* University of Utrecht, 1995.

——. "New Age Spiritualities as Secular Religion: a Historian's Perspective." *Social Compass* 46, no. 2 (1999): 145–160.

Hanegraaff, Wouter J. *New Age Religion and Western Culture: Esotericism in the Mirror of Secular Thought.* Leiden and Boston: Brill, 1996.

Van Harskamp, Anton. *Het Nieuw-religieuze Verlangen.* Kampen: Kok, 2000.

De Hart, Joep. *Zwevende Gelovigen. Oude Religie En Nieuwe Spiritualiteit.* Amsterdam: Bert Bakker, 2011.

Harvey, Graham. *Listening People, Speaking Earth: Contemporary Paganism.* London: C. Hurst & Co. Publishers, 1997.

Heelas, Paul. *The New Age Movement; the Celebration of the Self and the Sacralization of Modernity.* Oxford [etc.]: Blackwell, 1996.

——. "The Spiritual Revolution: From 'Religion' to 'Spirituality'." In *Religions in the Modern World: Traditions and Transformations*, edited by Linda Woodhead, Paul Fletcher, Hiroko Kawanami, and David Smith, pp. 357–377. London New York: Routledge, 2002.

Heelas, Paul, and Linda Woodhead. "Homeless Minds Today?" In *Peter Berger and the Study of Religion*, edited by Linda Woodhead, Paul Heelas, and David Martin. London [etc.]: Routledge, 2001.

——. *The Spiritual Revolution: Why Religion Is Giving Way to Spirituality*. Oxford etc.: Wiley-Blackwell, 2005.

Hellemans, Staf. "Verzuiling En Ontzuiling Van De Katholieken in Belgie En Nederland, Een Historisch Sociologische Vergelijking." *Sociologische Gids* 35, no. 1 (1988): 43–57.

Hermkens, Anna-Karina, Willy Jansen, and Catrien Notermans. *Moved by Mary. The Power of Pilgrimage in the Modern World*. Aldershot: Ashgate, 2009.

Hervieu-Léger, Danièle. "Present-Day Emotional Renewals. The End of Secularization or the End of Religion?" In *A Future for Religion? New Paradigms for Social Analysis*, edited by William H. Swatos. Newbury Park etc.: Sage, 1993.

——. *Religion as a Chain of Memory*. Oxford and Cambridge: Polity Press, 2000.

——. "The Twofold Limit of the Notion of Secularization." In *Peter Berger and the Study of Religion*, edited by Linda Woodhead, Paul Heelas, and David Martin. London New York: Routledge, 2001.

Houtman, Dick, and Peter Mascini. "Why Do Churches Become Empty While New Age Grows? Secularization and Religious Change in the Netherlands." *Journal for the Scientific Study of Religion* 41, no. 3 (2002): 455–473.

Huijts, J.H. *Geloof En Leven in De Kerk. Beschouwingen over De Godsdienstige Situatie Onder De Katholieken in Limburg, Naar Aanleiding Van Een Meningen-onderzoek*. Edited by L.C. Baas. Vol. 2. Hilversum: Landelijk centrum voor katholieke actie en het Nederlands Pastoraal Instituut i.s.w. met uitgeverij Paul Brand, 1960.

Humphrey, Caroline, and James Laidlaw. *The Archetypal Acts of Ritual, a Theory of Ritual Illustrated by the Jain Rite of Worship*. Oxford: Clarendon Press, 1995.

Inglehart, Ronald, and Christian Welzel. *Modernization, Cultural Change, and Democracy: The Human Development Sequence*. Cambridge University Press, 2005.

Jackson, Michael. *Minima Ethnographica: Intersubjectivity and the Anthropological Project*. Chicago: University of Chicago Press, 1998.

Jansen, Derk. "Op Zoek Naar Nieuwe Zekerheid. Negentiende Eeuwse Protestanten En Het Spiritisme." *PhD thesis*. Groningen University, 1994.

Jong, J.d., B.J. Alfrink, J.H. Lemmens, J.P. Huibers, W.P.A.M. Mutsaerts, J.W.M. Baeten, and J.M.J.A. Hanssen. "De Katholiek in Het Openbare Leven Van Deze Tijd: Bisschoppelijk Mandement 1954," 1954.

Kahn, Robert L., and Charles. F. Cannell. *The Dynamics of Interviewing. Theory, Technique and Cases*. New York: Wiley, 1967.

Kennedy, James. *Nieuw Babylon in Aanbouw. Nederland in De Jaren Zestig*. Amsterdam and Meppel: Boom, 1995.

Kennedy, James C. "Building New Babylon: Cultural Change in the Netherlands During the 1960s." University Microfilm International, 1995.

Kerklaan, Marga, ed. *Zodoende Was De Vrouw Maar Een Mens Om Kinderen Te Krijgen, 300 Brieven over Het Roomse Huwelijksleven*. Baarn: Ambo, 1987.

Knibbe, Kim. "An Ethnography of a Medium and Her Followers: How Learning Takes Place in the Context of Jomanda." In *Meister Und Schüler in Geschichte Und Gegenwart: Von Religionen Der Antike Bis Zur Modernen Esoterik*, edited by Almut Barbara Renger, 383–398. Göttingen: V&R unipress, 2012.

——. "Obscuring the Role of Power and Gender in Contemporary Spiritualities." In *Gender and Power in Contemporary Spirituality: Ethnographic Approaches*, edited by Anna Fedele and Kim Knibbe. Routledge, 2013.

——. "Secrets, Gossip and Betrayal: Doing Fieldwork on the Role of Religion in Moral Orientation in a Dutch Catholic Province." *Fieldwork in Religion* 6, no. 2 (2011): 151–167.

——. "The Role of Religious Certainty and Uncertainty in Moral Reasoning in a Catholic Province in the Netherlands." *Social Compass* 55, no. 1 (2008): 20–31.

Knibbe, Kim, and André Droogers. "Methodological Ludism and the Study of Religion." Method and Theory in the Study of Religion 23 (2011): 285–305.

Knibbe, Kim, and Peter Versteeg. "Assessing Phenomenology in Anthropology." *Critique of Anthropology* 28, no. 1 (March 1, 2008): 47–62.

Knibbe, Kim, and Iti Westra. "Van Ongeloof Naar 'zeker Weten': Betekenisgeving En Legitimatie in De Context Van Het Fenomeen Jomanda." *Sociale Wetenschappen* 46, no. 2 (2003): 75–93.

Knippenberg, Hans. *De Religieuze Kaart Van Nederland, Omvang En Geografische Spreiding Van De Godsdienstige Gezindten Vanaf De Reformatie Tot Heden.* Assen/Maastricht: Van Gorcum, 1992.

Knoblauch, Hubert, Grace Davie, Kim Knibbe, Manuel A. Vasquez, and José Casanova. "I. Portrait: Jose Casanova." *Religion and Society: Advances in Research* 2, no. 1 (2011): 5–36.

Kvale, Steinar. *Interviews: An Introduction to Qualitative Research Interviewing.* London: Sage, 1996.

Lambert, Yves. "A Turning Point in Religious Evolution in Europe." *Journal of Contemporary Religion* 19, no. 1 (2004): 29–44.

Van der Linde, W. *Eindelijk Religieuze Tolerantie.* Maastricht: Universitaire Pers Maastricht, 2001.

Lukken, Gerard. "Infant Baptism in the Netherlands and Flanders." In *Christian Feast and Festival. The Dynamics of Western Liturgy and Culture*, edited by Paul Post and Gerard Rouwhorst, 12:551–581. Liturgia Condenda. Leuven: Peeters, 2001.

Luykx, Paul. *Andere Katholieken. Opstellen over Nederlandse Katholieken in De Twintigste Eeuw.* Nijmegen: SUN, 2000.

Lynch, Gordon. *The Sacred in the Modern World.* Oxford University Press, 2012.

Magliocco, Sabina. *Witching Culture: Folklore and Neo-paganism in America.* Philadelphia: University of Pennsylvania Press, 2004.

Mahmood, Saba. "Rehearsed Spontaneity and the Conventionality of Ritual: Disciplines of Ṣalat." *American Ethnologist* 28, no. 4 (2001): 827–853. doi:10.1525/ae.2001.28.4.827.

Massey, Doreen B. *Space, Place, and Gender.* University of Minnesota Press, 1994.

Moore, Robert Laurence. *Selling God: American Religion in the Marketplace of Culture.* Oxford University Press, 1995.

Nissen, Peter. "Confessionele Identiteit En Regionale Eigenheid." In *Constructie Van Het Eigene. Culturele Vormen Van Regionale Identiteit in Nederland*, edited by Carlo Van der Borgt. Vol. 25. Amsterdam: P.J. Meertens-instituut, 1996.

——. "Constructie En Deconstructie Van Het Katholieke Limburg." *Studies over De Sociaal-economische Geschiedenis Van Limburg* XLV (2000): 79–97.

Ortner, Sherry B. *Anthropology and Social Theory: Culture, Power, and the Acting Subject.* Durham: Duke University Press, 2006.

Van Osselaer, Tine, and Thomas Buerman. "Feminization Thesis: A Survey of International Historiography and a Probing of Belgian Grounds." *Revue d'Histoire Ecclésiastique* 103, no. 2 (June 1, 2008): 497–544. doi:10.1484/J.RHE.3.180.

Paul VI. "Humanae Vitae. Encyclical of Pope Paul VI on the Regulation of Birth," 1968.

Pike, Sarah M. *Earthly Bodies, Magical Selves: Contemporary Pagans and the Search for Community.* Berkeley: University of California Press, 2001.

Pius XI. "Casti Connubii," 1932.

Post, Paul. "The Celebration of the First Communion. Seeking the Identity of the Christian Ritual." In *Christian Feast and Festival. The Dynamics of Western Liturgy and Culture*, edited by Paul Post and Gerard Rouwhorst, 12:581–599. Liturgia Condenda. Leuven [etc.]: Peeters, 2001.

Post, Paul, Albertina Nugteren, and Hessel Zondag. *Rituelen Na Rampen.* Kampen: Uitgeverij Gooi en Sticht, 2002.

Post, Paulus Gijsbertus Johannes, Paul Post, Jos Pieper, and Marinus van Uden. *The Modern Pilgrim: Multidisciplinary Explorations of Christian Pilgrimage*. Peeters Publishers, 1998.

Ramstedt, Martin. "Metaphor or Invocation? The Convergence Between Modern Paganism and Fantasy Fiction." *Journal of Ritual Studies* 26, no. 1 (2007): 1–15.

Redden, Guy. "The New Age: Towards a Market Model." *Journal of Contemporary Religion* 20, no. 2 (May 2005): 231–246.

Reynolds, David S. "The Feminization Controversy: Sexual Stereotypes and the Paradoxes of Piety in Nineteenth-Century America." The New England Quarterly 53, no. 1 (March 1, 1980): 96–106.

Robertson, Roland. *Globalization: Social Theory and Global Culture*. SAGE, 1992.

Robertson, Roland, and JoAnn Chirico. "Humanity, Globalization, and Worldwide Religious Resurgence: A Theoretical Exploration." *Sociology of Religion* 46, no. 3 (September 21, 1985): 219–242.

Van Rooden, Peter. "The Strange Death of Dutch Christendom." In *Secularisation in the Christian World*, edited by Callum G. Brown and Michael Snape. Farnham: Ashgate, 2010.

——. "Long-term Religious Developments in the Netherlands, 1750–2000." In *The Decline of Christendom in Western Europe*, edited by McLeod, Hugh and Ustorf, Werner, 113–29. Cambridge University Press, 2002.

De Rooij, Jaap. *Waartoe Waren Wij Op Aarde*. Nijmegen: Valkhof, 1999.

Rulof, Jozef. *De Kosmologie Van Jozef Rulof*. 's Gravenhage: stichting wetenschappelijk genootschap "de eeuw van Christus", 1984.

Salomonsen, Jone. *Enchanted Feminism: Ritual, Gender and Divinity Among the Reclaiming Witches of San Francisco*. London: Routledge, 2002.

Van Schaik, Ton.H.M. *Alfrink. Een Biografie*. Amsterdam: Anthos, 1997.

Schepens, Theo, and Leo Spruit. *De Rooms-Katholieke Kerk in Nederland, 1960–1998 Een Statistisch Trendrapport*. Nijmegen en Tilburg: Kaski, 2001.

Schiller, Nina Glick, Ayşe Çaglar, and Thaddeus C. Guldbrandsen. "Beyond the Ethnic Lens: Locality, Globality, and Born Again Incorporation." *American Ethnologist* 33, no. 4 (2006): 612–633.

Schoonheim, Monique. *Mixing Ovaries and Rosaries. Catholic Religion and Reproduction in the Netherlands 1870–1970*. Amsterdam: Aksant, 2005.

Simons, Ed, and Lodewijk Winkeler. *Het Verraad Der Clercken: Intellectuelen En Hun Rol in De Ontwikkelingen Van Het Nederlandse Katholicisme Na 1945*. Baarn: Arbor, 1987.

Sointu, Eeva, and Linda Woodhead. "Spirituality, Gender, and Expressive Selfhood." *Journal for the Scientific Study of Religion* 47, no. 2 (2008): 259–276.

Sommer, Jan Hendrik. *Spiritisme*. Kampen: Kok, 2001.

Spencer, Wayne. "To Absent Friends: Classical Spiritualist Mediumship and New Age Channelling Compared and Contrasted." *Journal of Contemporary Religion* 16, no. 3 (October 2001): 343–360.

Stewart, Pamela J., and Andrew Strathern. *Witchcraft, Sorcery. Rumors and Gossip*. Cambridge: Cambridge University Press, 2004.

Straating, Alex. "Roddelen En De Verbale Constructie Van De Gemeenschap." *Etnofoor* XI, no. 2 (1998): 25–41.

Von Stuckrad, Kocku. *Western Esotericism: A Brief History of Secret Knowledge* (translation of Was ist Esoterik? Kleine Geschichte des geheimen Wissens). London: Equinox, 2005.

Sutcliffe, S. "The Authority of the Self in New Age Religiosity: The Example of the Findhorn Community." *Diskuswebedition* 3, no. 2 (1995): 23–42.

Taylor, Charles. *Sources of the Self; the Making of the Modern Identity*. Cambridge, Mass.: Harvard University Press, 1992.

Thurlings, Jan. "Verzuiling En Beweging. Over Nut En Onnut Van Het Bewegingsmodel." *Trajecta. Tijdschrift Voor De Geschiedenis Van Het Katholiek Leven in De Nederlanden* 13 (2004): 18–39.

Tongeren. "Individualizing Ritual: The Personal Dimension in Funeral Liturgy." *Worship* 78 (2004): 117–138.

Trulsson, Åsa. *Cultivating the Sacred: Ritual Creativity and Practice Among Women in Contemporary Europe.* Lund Studies in the History of Religions 28. Lund: Lund University, 2010.

Turner, Victor W. *The Drums of Affliction: a Study of Religious Processes Among the Ndembu of Zambia.* Oxford: Clarendon Press, 1968.

——. *The Ritual Process: Structure and Anti-structure.* Aldine, 1995.

Ubachs, P.J.H. *Handboek Voor De Geschiedenis Van Limburg.* Hilversum: Verloren, 2000.

Veer, Peter van der. *Conversion to Modernities: The Globalization of Christianity.* 1st ed. Routledge, 1996.

Van der Veer, Peter. "Spirituality in Modern Society." *Social Research: An International Quarterly* 76, no. 4 (2009): 1097–1120.

Watling, Tony. "'Official' Doctrine and 'Unofficial' Practices: The Negotiation of Catholicism in a Netherlands Community." *Journal for the Scientific Study of Religion* 40, no. 4 (2001): 573–590.

Weibel, Deana. "Of Consciousness Changes and Fortified Faith: Creativist and Catholic Pilgrimage at French Catholic Shrines." In *Pilgrimage and Healing*, edited by Jill Dubisch and Michael Winkelman, 111–134. Tucson, 2005.

Westhoff, Hanneke. *Geestelijke Bevrijders. Nederlandse Katholieken En Hun Beweging Voor Geestelijke Volksgezondheid in De Twintigste Eeuw.* Nijmegen: Valkhof, 1996.

Wetherell, Margaret. *Discourse Theory and Practice: A Reader.* Edited by Simeon Yates and Stephanie Taylor. SAGE, 2001.

Wijers, Carla. "'In Een Hand De Rozenkrans, in De Andere Hand Een Glas Bier'—De Limburgse Identiteit Onder De Loep." *Studies over De Sociaal-economische Geschiedenis Van Limburg* XLV (2000): 111–134.

Wijnands, Math. *Op Het Dorp; Leven in De Kleine Limburgse Gemeenschappen.* Maastricht: Uitgeverij TIC, 1998.

Wijnen, Jo, and Theo Koopmanschap. *Hoe Katholiek Is Limburg? De Kerk En Het Bisdom Roermond.* Maasbree: De Lijster, 1981.

Wilson, Bryan. "Secularization: The Inherited Model." In *The Sacred in a Secular Age: Towards a Revision in the Scientific Study of Religion*, edited by Philip E. Hammond. Berkeley [etc.]: University of California Press, 1985.

Wood, Matthew. "Capital Possession: a Comparative Approach to 'New Age' and Control of the Means of Possession." *Culture and Religion* 4, no. 1 (2003): 159–182.

——. *Possession, Power, and the New Age: Ambiguities of Authority in Neoliberal Societies.* Aldershot and Burlington: Ashgate, 2007.

——. "W (h) Ither New Age Studies? The Uses of Ethnography in a Contested Field of Scholarship." *Religion and Society: Advances in Research* 1, no. 1 (2010): 76–88.

Woodhead, Linda. "Gendering Secularization Theory." *Social Compass* 55, no. 2 (June 1, 2008): 187–193.

Woodhead, Linda, and Paul Heelas. *Religion in Modern Times: An Interpretive Anthology.* Oxford etc.: Wiley-Blackwell, 2000.

Woodhead, Linda, Paul Heelas, and David Martin, eds. *Peter Berger and the Study of Religion.* London and New York: Routledge, 2001.

Wouters, Cas. "The Quest for New Rituals in Dying and Mourning: Changes in the We-I Balance." *Body and Society* 8, no. 1 (2002): 1–27.

INDEX OF MODERN AUTHORS

INDEX OF SUBJECTS AND PERSONS

Printed in the United States
By Bookmasters